No Labels

Lynn Devine

Copyright © 2024

All rights reserved.

All rights reserved. No part of this publication may be reproduced, distributed, or transmitted in any form or by any means, including photocopying, recording, or other electronic or mechanical methods, without the author's prior written permission, except in the case of brief quotations embodied in critical reviews and certain other non-commercial uses permitted by copyright law. For permission requests, please get in touch with the author.

Contents

Dedication i
About the Author ii
Chapter 1 1
Chapter 2 17
Chapter 3 25
Chapter 4 29
Chapter 5 42
Chapter 6 50
Chapter 7 57
Chapter 8 68
Chapter 9 75
Chapter 10 83
Chapter 11 87
Chapter 12 92
Chapter 13 104
Chapter 14 110
Chapter 15 128
Chapter 16 138
Chapter 17 147
Chapter 18 155
Chapter 19 169
Chapter 20 177
Chapter 21 182
Chapter 22 190
Chapter 23 194
Chapter 24 205

Chapter 25	211
Chapter 26	226
Chapter 27	235
Chapter 28	248
Chapter 29	259
Chapter 30	275
Chapter 31	278
Chapter 32	301
Chapter 33	323
Chapter 34	332
Chapter 35	345
Chapter 36	357
Chapter 37	376
Chapter 38	385

Dedication

To my son Steven for his invaluable advice on how not to offend or alienate a young person struggling with their sexuality….And for the design of the front cover.

To my son David for his scuba diving stories.

To my husband for his unwavering support

About the Author

Lynn is a recently retired Dental Practice Manager. She is married with two adult sons.

As the mother of a married gay son with an adopted child and trans friends, Lynn experienced what many other people are struggling with just now: unlearning some deeply imbedded ideas about gender and sexuality. She hopes this novel might provide some understanding of the struggles faced by people who just want to Love, not Label.

Chapter 1

'Four pints of Fosters please mate.' Lorenzo Murphy peered in his mirror, practising his deep, confident voice and wondering if he should ditch the mate. A bit too cocky, he thought. He smiled in the mirror, leaning nonchalantly on the bathroom sink, and tilted his head to gain the imaginary bar staff's attention.

'Ah yeah, can I get four pints of Fosters, please?'

Finally, happy with his opening line, he rummaged through his wardrobe, tempted by his new black shirt but not wanting to look as though he'd tried too hard. Finding his favourite T-shirt, he pulled it on, flexing his biceps so he could see them beneath the tight sleeves. A last-minute sniff of his armpits had him whipping off the T, dropping it in the corner before grabbing the black shirt.

Checking his phone for last-minute messages, he popped his head into his younger sister's room. A bought of coughing and sneezing had her spluttering into her handkerchief as she lay sprawled in bed.

'You off then?' A croaky voice asked from under the duvet.

'Yeah…going to the pub.' Lorenzo said proudly as he hovered by her door, unwilling to risk life and limb in Alice's virus-ridden room.

'I s'pose Sam will be there?' She shuffled up a bit and peered over the duvet, clutching her hanky.

'Yeah, course. He's my best mate; I wouldn't go out for my first pint without Sam, would I?' Lorenzo smiled to himself; he knew how his sister felt about Sam.

Alice pouted and held her arms out, pleading for a hug, before she saw the look of horror on her brother's face.

'Oh, come on, Rez, I'm stuck in here, and you get to go out; it's not fair.' She folded her arms crossly.

Feeling sorry for his little sister, Lorenzo relented and stepped gingerly into the danger zone, keeping as far away from the epicentre as possible. Approaching Alice's bed, he lifted his hands, dramatically covering his mouth. Alice giggled at the antics of her beloved big brother as he managed to plant a kiss on the top of her head before dashing downstairs.

'See you later.' He called to his parents, who were sitting zombie-like in front of the TV.

'Have a nice time, love, stay safe,' his mother smiled at him.

'Make sure you're home by 11 pm, or that front door gets locked,' barked his father, eyes still glued to the TV screen.

He left the house, wondering if his parents ever got any pleasure out of life at all.

***

Sam was waiting for him at King Alfred's statue, hands in his pockets and bouncing up on his toes, as he did when he was nervous.

'Hey, mate.' Lorenzo greeted him with a grin.

'The others aren't there yet.' Sam looked up from his phone, fingers tapping as he spoke, 'I said we'd meet them at the pub.'

'Did you go out with that girl, you know, the dark-haired one?' Sam asked, brushing a lock of black hair off his face as they walked through Winchester.

'Yeah, she's nice; we didn't do much, just walked around town…got a burger 'n stuff.' Lorenzo shrugged, wishing he was older so he could take Tessa on a proper date. As they passed a young couple kissing, Sam asked: 'D'you think she'll, you know?'

'Bloody hell, man, I've only been out with her twice; give us a chance.'

Lorenzo didn't like probing questions about his dates, and Sam always seemed to want to know all the details. The boys cut through the cathedral grounds, dodging the annoying tourists who happily blocked the path to get the perfect selfie. Arriving at the pub, Lorenzo nervously cleared his throat, wiping sweaty palms on the backs of his jeans.

'Are you sure about this, Sam? I mean, what if—' Sam cut him off, almost pushing him through the door. 'You've got this, Rez,' he said assuredly.

The Bishop's Tavern was over three hundred years old, and the roof was low with dark wooden beams, causing Lorenzo to duck his head as they went in. It was dark inside due to the small leaded windows, which suited the boys as they could sneak into a side nook and not be seen by the bar staff. Sitting back and puffing out their chests manfully, they assumed the position of seasoned drinkers.

'I still don't see why it has to be me.' Lorenzo grumbled, beginning to lose his nerve.

'Oh come on Rez, we've been through all this…you're the tallest, they won't ask for ID…it has to be you, mate,' Josh said irritably.

Lorenzo glanced at Sam, looking for an ally, but Sam just grinned as he tapped his phone.

'Moneys in your account mate.'

Conceding defeat, Lorenzo strolled nonchalantly up to the bar, ducking his head as he passed under a particularly low wooden beam. Taking his place at the bar he leaned nonchalantly on his elbows, clutching his card whilst praying it wouldn't be declined due to lack of funds.

'What can I get you?' He could feel the sweat pooling on his top lip, his tongue glued to the roof of his mouth.

'Do you want a drink or not?' The barmaid sighed and looked at her watch.

'Erm…can I get four pints of Fosters, please?' Lorenzo was relieved when his tongue decided to co-operate at last. He handed his card over whilst keeping his eyes firmly on the barmaid's face lest they drift down to her low-cut top.

'If you want another round, you'd better make it quick, coz my shift is ending soon, and Dave will ask you for ID…alright, love?' Placing the precious beer on a tray, she smiled and handed it to him. Grinning back at her with relief, he managed to negotiate his way back to the table without spilling too much.

'Nice one, mate.' Sam eyed his pint appreciatively before taking several glugs whilst trying masterfully to control a grimace.

'Mmm, I needed that.' Lorenzo wiped his lip, hiding a shudder as the bitter liquid slid down his throat.

'Maybe I'll go up next time.' Josh's eyes lingered on the barmaid's ample bosom as she walked past.

'Nah mate…she'd never serve you…little squirt.' Lorenzo laughed and shook his head.

The banter continued for a while as the boys described in detail what they would do with the busty barmaid, assuming, of course, that she would deign to look twice at any of them.

'Hey Emma…over here,' Josh called to a group of girls from their college who had just come bustling in. Lorenzo grinned as the girls sashayed over, pulling up chairs to join them.

'Hi Sam, how did your English exam go?' Emma Jones sat down beside Sam, flicking her long dark hair over her shoulder.

'Erm… yeah, it was ok, I s'pose.' Sam shrugged, totally indifferent to Emma's charms as she leaned across him, talking to her friend.

Lorenzo watched enviously as Emma's breast brushed against Sam's arm. The look of horror on his face was almost comical, recoiling from Emma as if someone had tossed a venomous snake into his lap.

You lucky bastard, if that was me, I'd be there like a shot. Shaking his head in bewilderment, Lorenzo frowned as Sam tried to squirm away from Emma's clutches. What's up with you, man? She's the hottest girl in college; any guy in his right mind would be all over her.

Having decided their college boys were too boring, the girls flounced out to go to a club. The boys' eyes all followed the retreating girls, Alex commenting on Emma's assets in tight jeans. Lorenzo agreed wholeheartedly and glanced at Sam for his opinion on the matter. Sam wasn't looking at Emma in her tight jeans; he was watching a young guy in tight jeans standing at the bar. Puzzled, Lorenzo continued to watch over the rim of his glass as the guy smiled at Sam. Flicking his eyes casually over to Sam, Lorenzo was shocked to see him shyly return the smile. The realisation suddenly hit him.

Why have I never noticed this before? It's so obvious…Sam is gay.

Trying to ignore the band that was tightening around his heart, he stared into his glass, convinced that when he looked up at Sam, he would realise he was wrong. Slowly raising his eyes, Lorenzo reluctantly accepted he'd been right as Sam continued to silently flirt with the guy at the bar. He wondered what he should do; should he bring it up and offer his support? Or would it be best to wait until Sam decided to tell him? He fleetingly felt a jolt of disappointment flicker down his spine.

Why hasn't he told me? Doesn't he trust me? What does he think I'm going to say?

'Come on mate, drink up. What's wrong with you tonight anyway?' Alex impatiently waved his empty glass at Lorenzo.

'Ha-ha, he's mooning over wasshername, didn't she put out then, Rezza?' Josh made a crude gesture as he drained his glass.

Sam stood up quietly, mumbling about needing the toilet. Lorenzo briefly considered following him but realised he didn't have a clue what to say. A memory suddenly surfaced; he and Sam at their karate club a couple of weeks ago. Lorenzo remembered a good-looking guy who'd gently caressed Sam's hair; he'd thought it a strangely intimate gesture but brushed it off when Sam didn't seem perturbed by it.

After getting served once more before the bar shift changed, Lorenzo grinned at the barmaid, feeling more confident now.

'Better down those quickly lads.' She looked at her watch and winked at him. Lorenzo grinned back, feeling like a million dollars, but the revelation about Sam hovered at the back of his mind, overshadowing all else.

***

'What a great night, wasn't it, Rez?' Sam slapped Lorenzo on the back as they walked home from the pub.

'Hmm…yeah, I 's'pose.'

'What's up with you, man? It was amazing.' Sam play-punched his friend on the arm, frowning in confusion at his glum mood.

'Did you know that guy at the bar, Sam?' Lorenzo demanded, giving vent to his frustration.

'Erm…what guy?

'You know damn well what guy Sam, the one you were smiling at all night.' Lorenzo snapped irritably as they dodged a group of hen party girls out on the town.

'I can smile at whoever I want, Rez. What the hell is wrong with you tonight anyway?' Sam stopped walking and turned to face his friend before adding: 'You know what? I don't answer to you, Rez. I'm off.' Turning back the way they'd come, Sam stomped off into the night.

Winchester Cathedral loomed menacingly over Lorenzo, reflecting his black mood as he sat down on an old tombstone. He was glad, in a way, that Sam had stormed off; they needed some time apart to cool down. Convinced he was right about Sam, he tried to analyse his feelings; why was he so distraught? He'd known some guys at college who were gay, but he'd never had an issue with them; it was no big deal…but they weren't his best friend, his Sam. What about their future friendship? Could they still go out to pubs and clubs together? Gay clubs? Lorenzo had never even considered entering a gay pub or club before. His thoughts turned to the good-looking guy in the pub earlier, the way he smiled at Sam, and how enraged he'd felt when Sam smiled back. The worst feeling was that of betrayal, all the years they'd been friends, knowing each other's darkest secrets—or not, so it seemed.

Arriving home, Lorenzo slumped up to his room, berating himself for having handled the situation so badly. His phone pinged—Sam.

Hey Rez…erm, can we meet up tomorrow morning? I dunno what's up, but we need to talk.

Yeah, mate, I'm sorry for being a dick; see you at the water meadows…with the dog no doubt?

Haha…yeah, course.

Feeling somewhat relieved that Sam was still talking to him, Lorenzo tried but failed to sleep. Various scenarios of what tomorrow would bring were swirling around in his head. Was this the end of their long friendship? Was Sam going to go off and find a gay scene…new friends that didn't include him? Glancing at his clock, it was 3 am, tomorrow had arrived, just a few more hours and he'd know.

***

The river Itchen twinkled in the bright sunshine as it wound its way through the water meadows. Lorenzo spotted Sam's large German Shepherd long before he came in to view along the narrow path. The dog recognised him immediately and bounded up with great enthusiasm, almost knocking him to the ground.

'Hey, boy.' Lorenzo ruffled the dog's huge ears and glanced nervously at Sam.

'Emergency supplies.' Sam grinned as he held his backpack aloft. Lorenzo heard the beers rattling within as he smiled at Sam with relief…nothing had changed.

'Nice one mate, where'd you get those then?' Lorenzo was impressed.

'My dick-head brother had a party; I found these in the fridge…shame to let them go to waste.'

They sat down on the soft grass and watched as the dog threw himself into the river with glee. Lorenzo cracked open a tin. It was a bit warm from the sun, but they glugged down a good few mouthfuls.

'How come you're on dog duty?' Lorenzo asked, just as the dog in question bounded back and shook himself dry, showering them with cold water. The boys both screeched with laughter, and Lorenzo threw a ball, the soggy dog dashing off as if his life depended on it.

'My parents are away, me and Dan are taking in turns to take Rez out. He was meant to be on duty today, but he's hungover. I left him throwing up in the toilet.' Sam grimaced as he remembered the sight of his odious brother bent over the toilet.

Lorenzo frowned and shook his head. 'I'm still not sure whether I'm flattered or insulted that you named your bloody dog after me.'

'Well, he looks a bit like you, don't you think?' Sam tilted his head, comparing his two best mates as Lorenzo flung his empty can at him.

'I mean, he's German, isn't he? You should have given him a German name.' Lorenzo looked critically at the dog whilst fishing his phone out to check a message.

'Humph…well you're not Italian, are you Looorenzo?' Sam knew his friend was touchy about his name and immediately regretted his comment.

'Who was that?' Sam peered over Lorenzo's shoulder, trying to see his messages.

'Bloody Tessa again.' Stuffing the phone back in his pocket in irritation, Lorenzo took another swig from his tin.

'Oh man, this is so bad.' He grimaced as the warm lager trickled down his throat.

Sam chuckled. 'Beggars can't be choosers, me old mate.' He patted Lorenzo on the back.

'What's up with Tessa then? I thought you two were alright?' Sam asked nonchalantly.

'I dunno mate…she seems to think she owns me.'

'Yeah, well, that's girls for you. Dunno what you see in her anyway.' Sam shook his head.

'No…I don't suppose you do, do you, Sam?' Lorenzo looked pointedly at his friend with a tell me, or I'll kill you look on his face. His heart pounded as he waited for Sam's reaction. *What if I'm wrong? What if he never speaks to me again?* Having waited for the right moment, now that it was here, he was terrified. Sam stared wide-eyed at his best friend; his mouth opened, but no words came. Taking a long swig of beer, he stared up at the sky for a long moment before seeming to come to a conclusion.

'I…ok. The thing is—' He shuffled his feet, glancing up at Lorenzo from under a long strand of black hair.

Unable to stand it any longer, Lorenzo interrupted.

'You're gay, Sam.' He shrugged, holding his hands up. 'It's no big deal; I've been waiting for you to tell me.'

It actually was an extremely big deal for Lorenzo, but he realised he had to be supportive and gain Sam's trust, which had seemingly been missing from their relationship.

'I…well, yeah, I 'spose I am.' Sam gazed at the river, then at his dog. Anywhere but at his friend.

'So are you gonna' 'come out'? Like, officially?' Lorenzo leaned back on his elbows, pleased with himself for his pragmatic approach.

'Erm…I don't think so, not just yet. I mean, it's not as if I'm going to start chatting up guys at college, is it?'

'Well, I don't see why not. I mean, sooner or later, you're going to want to…erm…you know.' Suddenly embarrassed at what he was trying to say, Lorenzo stumbled over his words.

'One step at a time, eh? Just let me get used to you knowing for a while first…but thanks, Rez, I was a bit worried about telling you, you know?' Sam opened another can, taking a long slurp.

'Oh right, well, thanks for the vote of confidence, mate. What did you think I'd say?' Lorenzo allowed his annoyance to show.

'I dunno. Sorry Rez, it's all been so bloody hard, you know? Wondering what was wrong with me, realising I was gay—then accepting it, then trying to figure out when and how to tell people…if I needed to tell them at all. It was all going round and round in my head.' Sam lay down on the grass, shielding his eyes from the sun.

'Have you told your parents yet?'

'What? You're kidding, right? There's no way I'm telling them anything. Not 'til after I'm away at uni anyway.' Sam looked around for his dog, calling him over to clip his lead on as they walked back along the towpath.

'Have you decided about uni yet, Rez?'

'Yup, I'm not going, Sam; there's no point in me getting into all that debt for a degree I don't need, is there? It's different for you; you can't do Dentistry without going to uni, can you?' Lorenzo shrugged as they walked along in silence for a while.

'So…you're ok? I mean, you're cool with me knowing?' Lorenzo asked tentatively.

'Yeah, I'm glad. It might make it harder, though, you thinking I'm eyeing up every guy that talks to me from now on.' Sam chuckled, dropping their empty tins in the bin.

'What, like that guy in the pub last night?' Fighting to keep the sneer out of his voice, Lorenzo forced a grin.

'Oh…so that's what you were pissed off about, was it?'

'I was pissed off, Sam, coz you bloody knew you were gay, and you never told me; you've only told me now coz I've forced it out of you. How do you think that makes me feel? We're supposed to be mates.' Lorenzo struggled once again to keep his emotions under control; he didn't understand why he felt so betrayed, and Sam's attitude wasn't helping.

'This isn't about you though, is it Rez? I'm the one going through all this.' Sam said quietly but with an edge to his voice. 'I was hoping for your support, mate. I didn't expect to get a hard time coz I hadn't deigned to tell you.' Sam had a few pissed-off feelings of his own, which he gave vent to.

'Okay, okay, I'm sorry, Sam. It's just that I didn't expect this to happen. I thought we'd be out on the town, pulling girls, but—' Not at all sure what he was trying to say, Lorenzo just shrugged a shoulder and found a convenient stone to kick around.

Realising with horror that his eyes had filled with tears, Lorenzo sniffed deeply and feigned a sneeze, hoping Sam would think it was hay-fever.

'We'll be fine, Rez—nothing's gonna change between you and me.' The boys moved towards each other, each needing the comfort of a hug but settling for a mutual slap on the back… man-style.

Keen to move on from the awkward moment, Lorenzo glanced at his watch, saying he had to get to work, so they headed off through the fields, closely followed by a curious herd of cows. Sam let the dog off his lead as they approached the gate, and he bounded over it, eager to get away from the circling herd.

'Erm…cows are veggies, aren't they?' Lorenzo asked nervously as the cows inched closer, snorting and chewing with big, soft lips.

'Idiot! Course they are…they have been known to squash people to death, though.' Sam was highly amused at the look of terror on his friend's face. Lorenzo bolted for the gate, leaping over it to join the grinning dog on the other side. Sam strolled confidently through the gate, giving his best friends a very superior look.

Chapter 2

The boys both found summer jobs working in an Italian restaurant in the town. For the first time in his life, Lorenzo knew how it felt to have some money; sometimes, the tips from generous tourists would double his take-home pay for the week. Tonight was his night off. He'd been hoping to go out with Sam, but it seemed their boss at the restaurant had put them on opposite shifts, a tactic they both knew was designed to keep them apart to stop them larking around at work. Disappointed that Sam wasn't available, he'd texted his girlfriend Tessa, and after enduring the usual *'you only text me when you have no-one else'* protest, she agreed to meet at King Alfred's statue.

'Where d' you wanna go? D'you fancy a pizza?' Tessa flicked her hair and batted her extra-long false eyelashes. Lorenzo stared in fascination at the flapping lashes, expecting them to take flight at any moment.

'Ah…hmm…I think I've seen enough pizza to last me a lifetime, Tess.'

They decided on a Kebab take-away and strolled along to join the queue. Tessa frowned in confusion when Lorenzo bought three Donners.

'Erm…d'you know how much fat there is in one of those Rez? Think about your arteries.'

'It's not for me Tess; come on, you'll see.' Lorenzo chuckled before leading her towards a narrow passage.

'Where the hell are you taking me, Rez?' Tessa pulled back in alarm as they left the busy high street.

Rez continued to a dark doorway tucked in a corner. Bending down to ground level, he gently shook the sleeping vagrant awake.

'Sid…it's me, Rezza.'

A bleary-eyed man peered over the top of his sleeping bag, a gap-toothed smile spreading over his face as Lorenzo gave him the kebab.

'Thas right nice of you lad, I 'prethiate your kindneth,' he whistled through his remaining teeth.

Tessa hovered uncertainly as she watched Lorenzo chatting amiably with the vagrant.

'Where'th your friend today?' The man asked through mouthfuls of juicy kebab.

'He's working tonight; he'll probably be along with some pizza later.' Lorenzo smiled, resisting the temptation to recoil as the body odour assailed his senses.

'Rez, can we go now, please?' Tessa pleaded as a noisy group of revellers entered the alley.

'I think your girl wanths you.' The man nodded towards the pretty girl, who looked at him with such disgust. 'I hath a girl like that--- onth,' he mumbled, confusion setting in once more.

'What on earth—' Tessa muttered as they left the putrid alley, returning to the safety of the high street.

'Me and Sam have sort of adopted Sid, we always give him some food or a hot drink when we're in the town.' Lorenzo explained, amused by her flustered attitude.

'Well, you're not with bloody Sam now, are you? I can't believe you made me do that, Rez.' She pouted.

'Make *you* do what?' Lorenzo sighed in exasperation.

'Erm…well, I wasn't expecting it, that's all.' Tessa shuffled her feet and shrugged before adding, 'that was a lovely thing you did, though, Rez.' She pulled him down and kissed him on the cheek.

The sun was beginning to go down over the cathedral, sending golden shadows rippling over the park as they sat down to eat their food. The silence lay heavy between them as they processed the events in the alley.

Tessa wiped her mouth with her napkin. 'D'you think Sam likes Emma?' she mumbled, catching a drip of kebab in her napkin.

Lorenzo was caught off guard.

Why are girls so obsessed with who fancies whom?

'Dunno' he shrugged, stuffing more food in.

'Well, he's your mate; surely he's said something?' Tessa persisted.

'Bloody hell, Tess, what does it matter who Sam likes or doesn't like?' Lorenzo wished she'd shut up about Sam.

Walking over to the bin, Tessa dumped the remains of her dinner. Lorenzo hoped that was the end of this particular conversation…but he was wrong.

'I mean…he's gorgeous, with those big blue eyes, all the girls fancy him…but not my type at all,' she continued as she sat down again, inching her skirt up a bit. Lorenzo was watching a small child running away from its mother. He wished he could run away from Tessa and her endless probing questions.

She took his hand and batted her eyelashes again. 'You're more my type; I like my men tall and muscly.'

My men?

Lorenzo cringed at the term and wondered how many *men* she'd been through. He resolved at that moment to end the relationship—such as it was tonight.

By the time they caught the bus home, it was dark; they were alone on the top deck at the back. Tessa leaned in for a kiss, pushing her breasts up against Lorenzo's chest.

'Do you want me, Rez?' she mumbled through wet kisses.

'Mmm…yeah, course I do.' His hand groped for her breast, all thoughts of ending it gone in a heartbeat. Far too soon, the bus arrived at their stop; Lorenzo managed to hobble off, desperately trying to hide his embarrassment from the passengers on the lower deck. As they struggled to walk along the road, their need for each other growing ever more desperate, Lorenzo spied a field with a conveniently open gate.

'Let's go in here.' He was desperate now; it had to happen soon.

'What? If you think I'm gonna lie down in a filthy field, you've got another thing coming, Rez.' Straightening her skirt, Tessa stomped off down the road, stopping at a huge car dealer's. An enormous sign proudly proclaimed Murphy's Cars. Tessa looked up, 'This is your dad's place, isn't it?'

'Erm yeah, but I—' Lorenzo suddenly realised they could easily gain entry to his father's offices as he knew the passwords for the alarms and doors. Grabbing Tessa's hand, he pulled her round to the back door and punched in the numbers, hiding his face from the CCTV camera, which he knew was trained in the back yard. The door clicked open, and they fell in, giggling and kissing each-other.

'Wait…wait…the alarm.' Lorenzo dived over to the control panel as the incessant beeping got faster and faster. He knew they only had a matter of seconds before the beeping turned into a full-on siren. He quickly tapped in the four -digit number, which happened to be his date of birth, and the beeping stopped. Tessa looked at him and grinned.

'So...all alone at last,' she drawled, movie star fashion. Lorenzo switched on the torch on his phone as he led her through a long back corridor, past his father's office and into the vast car show room.

'I've never been inside one of these places before.' Tessa looked around in wonder at the luxury cars on display, their back- tail gates lifted up for display.

'C'mon.' Lorenzo grabbed her hand and opened the back door of a particularly large Range Rover, its soft white leather seats gleaming in the torchlight.

'Your carriage awaits, madame,' he chuckled as he clambered in behind her. Tessa lay back, peeling off her T-shirt. 'Have you got condoms?' she whispered whilst arranging her legs.

'Yeah...course I have.' Delving around in his back pocket wasn't easy in the cramped space, but at last, he produced the small packet triumphantly. Tessa watched in fascination as Lorenzo wrestled with the slippery rubber sheath.

'Do you remember those sex ed lessons in school, with the cucumbers?' she giggled.

'Oh god, not now, Tess,' he moaned, desperately trying to get the thing to stay on.

Tessa wriggled around helpfully as the would-be lovers finally got themselves into position. Propping himself up on his elbows, he looked down at her, suddenly feeling very grown up as he remembered the consent issue.

'Right then, you're sure about this?' He didn't have a plan in mind if she said 'No', but he hoped and prayed she wouldn't.

'Yes, Rez, I'm sure,' she said dramatically as she reached up and pulled his head down, kissing him deeply. It was all over pretty quickly, but after the second and third time, Lorenzo laughed, 'I think I'm getting the hang of it now.'

It was 2 am when they finally emerged tired and disheveled from the back seat of the Range Rover. Lorenzo re-set the alarm as they crept out of the building, feeling like a couple of burglars. On the walk home, Lorenzo poured over every detail of his momentous first time in the back of the car. It wasn't at all like he'd imagined—the first time, anyway. Tessa had seemed very quiet; in the porn videos, the girls all made appreciative noises, shouting and groaning at the end. Terrified he'd done something wrong but desperate to find out, he plucked up courage.

'So…was it ok…in the car, I mean?' he asked, hesitantly.

'Why…what happened in the car?' Tessa giggled but took pity on him. 'Yeah…it was nice Rez.'

Lorenzo was gutted, *nice?* Surely, she could do better than that; he was looking for 'Amazing, Fantastic...' the sort of thing he'd heard in the videos.

'Erm, Rez...'

Ok, here it comes, it was rubbish...I was rubbish; as he waited for the verdict, his imagination conjured up all sorts of terrifying images; his mates laughing at him, Tessa's friends nudging each-other as he walked past.

'I'm sorry I was such a bitch earlier...about your homeless guy, it's just that...um...I've never really thought about them much, you know?' She shrugged, embarrassed now.

'But that's the thing, Tess, he's not that much older than us; he told us his story once; he was in care, booted out at eighteen, tried to find a job...the usual story. I think he's probably about twenty-one or so.'

'That's so sad, isn't it...we don't realize how lucky we are, do we, Rez?' Tessa smiled sadly.

'Ooh, I do...I got very lucky tonight, Tess,' Lorenzo chuckled.

'Me too, Rez...it was really great.'

Lorenzo floated home in an ecstatic haze, Tessa's last words echoing in his head...maybe it wasn't over just yet.

Chapter 3

Sam could hear the raised voices as he shut the front door. He listened for a while before quietly tiptoeing upstairs, avoiding the creaky stair. His brother Dan and his father were arguing again, his mother sobbing, begging them to stop.

As the battle raged downstairs, Sam put his headphones on and turned up the volume, but not before he heard Dan decree that he would not be ordered around like a small child, whilst his father countered that it was his house and his rules.

Lying on his bed, laptop propped up on his knees, Sam tried to concentrate on his studies, scribbling notes on the anatomy of the jaw, when he heard footsteps stomping up the stairs. *Please don't knock on my door* he prayed…just as the knock came on the door.

'Sam…I need to talk to you, mate.' Dan strutted in, still bristling with rage and sat down heavily on Sam's bed, scattering his pile of anatomy notes. Sam sighed and shut his laptop.

'I can't stand it anymore…I've had it, I'm getting out.' Dan leaned forward, head in his hands.

'Where will you go?' Sam didn't see any point in pretending he cared.

'I'll move in with some of the guys, they're planning to get a place.'

'Yeah, well, I s'pose that's the best thing to do.' Sam started to gather up his precious notes.

Dan turned his head, glancing at the notes with a sneer.

'What is this anyway?' Grabbing a handful of papers, Dan began to read out loud. '*Pulpitis and its causes*…what the hell's Pulp— oh fuck it, who cares.' Dan threw the notes down dismissively and began pacing around the room, commenting on various items of Sam's stuff. His eyes rested on letters from various universities, offers of another life away from here, increasing his resentment.

'Think you could take me on, little brother?' Dan had found Sam's karate black belt, fingering it thoughtfully; he turned to look over his shoulder.

'Yeah, easily, *big brother*…wanna try?' Sam looked up menacingly through his lashes.

'Haha…nah, you're alright. Wouldn't want to upset the parents now, would we.' Dan continued his prowling, but the venom in his brothers' words had clearly un- nerved him. He changed tack.

'You're lucky, mate…being able to get away, I never got that chance.'

'It's not luck Dan; I'm working my balls off to get a place.' The brothers had had this conversation over and over. Sam was sick of having to justify himself once again.

'You were always Dad's favourite…little goody-two-shoes, he never shouts and screams at you when you come in late.' Dan continued to pace, agitation building once more.

'Oh yes, he bloody does. The difference is that I don't stand there arguing with him.' Sam jumped off the bed and faced his brother. Dan was a much bigger guy and prone to using his fists. He'd never tried it on with Sam though; he'd never live it down if his little brother floored him with a karate move, and they both knew it.

But Sam had had enough. He didn't care anymore; he was done tiptoeing around his brother's fragile ego.

'You know your trouble, Dan? You think the world owes you something. You could have stayed at school, got your A levels, you're a clever guy…but no, you chose to go out with your so-called mates getting wasted, so don't accuse me of having an easy time of it…you don't know anything about my life, so just get off my back and get out of my bloody room.' Sam felt the adrenaline rushing through his body. He braced himself, fists clenching as he glared at his older brother. Dan stared open-mouthed and laughed nervously.

'Well, well, little brother, I never thought you had it in you…maybe there's hope for you after all.' Slapping Sam on the back, Dan strolled out of the room with as much dignity as he could muster.

Replacing his earphones, Sam lay back on his bed, waiting for his raging temper to cool. Mulling over the row, he wondered if he really could have hit his brother. He chuckled as he remembered the look on Dan's face. He could hear angry voices again downstairs and then footsteps coming up the stairs. Lifting his head, he watched as his door slowly opened, and a soft brown muzzle pocked through. The German Shepherd lopped over to his bed and waited, tail wagging with expectation.

'Come on then.' Patting his bed by way of invitation, Sam scooted over to the side as the huge dog jumped up beside him and stretched out, burying his soft head in Sam's armpit. Sam wrapped his arm around his beloved pet, and they both fell asleep, snoring quietly.

Chapter 4

Jim Murphy was seated behind his large mahogany desk, staring intensely at the CCTV recording, rewinding it over and over. His office manager, Harry, stared at him, both men shaking their heads in disbelief.

'It's that new cleaner, I'm sure of it…Thallo…Thalis, something or other.'

Harry leaned in closer, prodding the screen with a stubby finger. 'Where's he from again?' he muttered.

'Doesn't bloody matter where he's from Harry. He left three feckin' used condoms in one of my prize motors, the bastard.' Jim's profanities reverted to his native Galway when severely provoked.

'You sure it's him? That little tart with him looks far too young.'

Jim stopped pacing and peered again at the grainy image on the screen.

'Yeah, must be him; he's the only one who knows the code.'

Harry stared down the corridor, frowning at the offending doorway as if it were the culprit.

'You have to admit, boss, it's bloody funny.' Pulling at his nose, hand over his mouth to try and hide a large grin, he glanced over at his boss.

'Oh, funny, is it? Well, you can get out there and feckin' clean it. I'll not have my cars smelling like a feckin' brothel.' Trying to suppress the amused twitch at the corner of his mouth, Jim turned away, staring out the window.

***

'I'm telling you, Angie, the customer's wife climbed into the back seat and screamed in horror, she almost fell out the door.' Jim was recounting the *condoms in the car* story as he and his wife were having breakfast in the kitchen. Angie had sat, open-mouthed as she listened to the telling of the story for the third time, each version slightly more comical than its predecessor. Her husband enjoyed a good story, but trying to decipher the facts was not always easy when Jim was on a roll.

'So...the condoms were on the back seat?' Angie handed her husband another slice of toast and marmalade as she tried to picture the scene.

'Well, of course, they'd be on the back seat love. You wouldn't go for a fu— I mean...you wouldn't erm...in the front, now would you?' Jim always tried to curtail his language in front of his wife, unless, of course, the situation warranted it, which on this occasion it didn't.

'And you think it was the new cleaner, Thal—something, do you?' Angie started to clear away their breakfast thing as she gazed out of the window, her thoughts drifting back to a time in Galway, in the back of Jim's old, battered car. Her back had hurt for days afterwards.

Coming up behind her, Jim put his arms around her waist, snuggling her ear.

'And what are *you* thinking about my wee darlin'?' he whispered playfully.

'Oh…you know, what we were like when we were younger.' Angie swivelled round and stood on tiptoe to kiss her adoring husband, just as the kitchen door opened and a bleary-eyed Lorenzo loped in, searching for food as always.

'Oh…really, guys?' Stopping dead in his tracks, Lorenzo backed out of the room again, unable to cope with the sight of his parents having the audacity to kiss in their own kitchen.

'Hey, get back here and have some breakfast.' Angie shouted, laughing at her red-faced son as he covered his eyes in mock embarrassment.

Working the toaster once more, Angie sat down with Lorenzo and started to tell him the big news of the day. Jim was not quite ready to hand over ownership of his story, so he sat down again and re-told the tale all over again, managing to add several new versions.

'I've asked Harry to bring in that fu— that cleaner, Thallis, Thallo, something…it was him alright, on the video.' Jim tapped a finger on the table, emphasizing his point.

Lorenzo thought he was going to be violently sick any moment as the blood drained from his head, accompanied by a faint whistling sound.

'Are you ok, love? you look very pale.' Angie was concerned, wondering if he was hungover or if he'd caught the flu from his sister.

'Um…I think I'll just go back to bed for a while…don't feel so good.' Lorenzo's knees threatened to buckle as he hastily vacated the kitchen. Angie frowned as he left, thinking of flu remedies. Jim also frowned as he left, thinking alcohol and high jinks in the town the night before.

Lorenzo made it to the bathroom just in time, as last night's kebab made a second appearance down the toilet. Dashing into his room, he flung himself on the bed, tapping out a message to Sam.

Need to see you. Urgent

What's happened?

I'm in a shit load of trouble, meet you at King Alfred's…asap?

***

'So… what's up?' The boys had gone into the park and were sprawled on a bench. Sam couldn't imagine what could have happened to get his mate in such a state; Lorenzo was always so 'together.'

By the time Lorenzo had finished his tale of woe, Sam was in hysterics and could barely breathe.

'It's not funny man. What do I do? I can't just sit back and let some poor guy get sacked, can I?' As Lorenzo sat groaning with his head in his hands, a man selling pink balloons strolled by; their resemblance to the dreaded condoms morphed into some grotesque parody in his imagination.

'Bloody hell, Rez, you can't tell him it was you!' From what Lorenzo had told him about his father, Sam imagined all sorts of terrible repercussions, not least of all his mate being grounded.

Lorenzo looked at Sam in astonishment. 'I have to mate…I have to own up.'

'So what do you need me for then? If you're gonna tell him, just tell him…on your head, be it Rez. Look what happened last time you upset him.' Sam reminded him about the awful moment Lorenzo's father discovered them smoking; he'd been grounded for a month. 'Anyway, you and Tessa, how did it—?'

Lorenzo cut him off, not wanting to go into those details just now.

'Never mind what went where, Sam, what am I going to say?' Glancing at his watch, Lorenzo was worried that the innocent Thallo/Thallis, was at that moment losing his job.

'The poor guy's probably earning a pittance and sending all his money home to his family in some godforsaken hovel in Eastern Europe,' he moaned.

After deliberating for a further hour, they formulated a plan. Lorenzo would explain to his father how Tessa had been angry with him for spending too much time with Sam and how she'd been desperate to lose her virginity before she turned eighteen. She'd given him an ultimatum, *tonight or never*. What else was he supposed to do?

***

'You?' Jim Murphy wasn't usually lost for words, but on this occasion, he made an exception. Glaring open-mouthed at his crestfallen son, Jim took a huge gulp from his whiskey tumbler.

Lorenzo had told his father he needed a word, in private, man to man. This was not something he wanted his mother to hear. Father and son were seated opposite each-other in the large sitting room; the afternoon sun streamed in the big bay window as Lorenzo gathered his courage. Ten minutes later, having made his confession, he was now awaiting his sentence. Glancing at his father in nervous anticipation, he wondered what his punishment would be.

'How did you know the password?'

Of all the questions his father could have asked, this was not what Lorenzo had expected.

'Erm…I don't know…I mean, I do know it, but I can't remember how I know.' He stammered, grateful to have something positive to say.

'And this girl of yours…she, erm…she was willing to break into *my* garage just for the chance to get into a back seat with you?' Jim hid a small grin behind his whiskey glass.

'Yeah, dad, more than willing…she said we *had* to do it that night. She even wanted to go into that field up the road, but I said no way am I rolling around in the mud in a bloody field.' Lorenzo shook his head solemnly at the absurdity of the idea, ignoring the fact that the truth was very much the opposite.

He watched his father as he returned to the problem at hand, his face revealing varying emotions. Angry, yes, for sure, but not excessively so. Disappointed that most terrible of parental put-downs, much worse than anger. But there was something else lurking behind his father's twinkling eyes, was it empathy? Humour? Lorenzo waited, his leg tapping up and down on the soft carpet.

'You know…I started this business from nothing, just fixing cars for family and friends…self-taught I was back in Galway. Then I realised there was money to be made in buying and selling…' Lorenzo fought to keep the resigned look from his face as he listened once again to his father's rags-to-riches story.

'…bought this place and never looked back, built a reputation as a good honest dealer…'

Lorenzo thought he knew where this was going; honesty and trust, that would be the theme of the lecture.

'Is this a private party, or can anyone join in?' Suddenly, the door flew open, and his mother came in. Settling herself in a comfy chair, Angie tucked her legs up under her and looked from Jim to Lorenzo expectantly.

'I met Sue in town today, and she was telling me—' Jim leaned forward, smiling at his wife as he cut her off mid-sentence.

'Lorenzo and I were just having a chat, love…you know, man to man?' Winking at Angie, Jim nodded towards the door. Angie didn't need to be told twice; the use of her son's full name was enough; she left the room safe in the knowledge that Jim would tell her all about it later.

The inopportune appearance of Lorenzo's mother had lessened the tension in the room. Jim stopped swirling his whiskey around in the glass and downed the last mouthful, slamming the glass down on the coffee table. He looked at his son, arranging his face in order to pronounce the sentence.

'Right then…' Lorenzo held his breath; he stopped tapping his leg in anticipation.

'I give you credit, lad, for coming forward and admitting it was you; that can't have been easy.' Jim refilled his glass, using the time to organise his thoughts.

'I also give you credit for taking care of your girl; I agree a muddy field isn't exactly romantic, now, is it.' Jim's mouth twitched as he remembered many a muddy field from his youth.

'No, it's not and—' Lorenzo started but was cut off by a raised hand from his father.

'You've said your piece lad…I'm not finished yet,' Jim said gravely before continuing. 'Can you imagine the embarrassment in the showroom when one of my best customers got into the back seat of that SUV…white fecking leather seats Rez…why that one of all the cars you could have chosen…' Jim shook his head, trying to suppress a grin as he remembered Harry's description of the event.

'Erm…Tess said it looked so lovely and comfortable, and me being over six foot, I thought it would be the best one.' Lorenzo shrugged a shoulder, wishing his ordeal was over.

'Okay…well, I think we've done this to death now. You're grounded for a week, Rez, now feck off out of my sight.' Jim waved a dismissive hand, ushering his errant son from the room before adding with a sly wink, 'and next time, take your fecking condoms with you, *all three of them.*'

Later that evening, relieved that his ordeal was over, Lorenzo lay back on his bed and messaged Sam.

Condom confession went well, grounded for a week, not so bad after all.

Are you going to tell the guys? The phone pinged back.

Nah, don't want anyone else knowing, so keep it to yourself, please mate.

***

Making herself comfortable on the sofa, Angie was itching to hear what was going on with Lorenzo. Jim handed her a large glass of Shiraz, pouring an equally large measure of his favourite Bushmills whiskey. He settled himself down in the big, comfy armchair opposite his wife and swirled the amber liquid around in his glass, savouring the powerful aroma.

'Well? Come on, what's going on?' Angie knew how her husband enjoyed the telling of a juicy story and was usually happy to indulge him, but on this occasion, she was impatient to know the details since it was about her beloved son.

'Right then…are you ready for this?' Jim grinned at her over the top of his glass.

Ten minutes later, Angie sat with her hand over her mouth, horrified at what their son had been up to.

'Who is this girl…do we know her? Is she his girlfriend?' Angie sincerely hoped he hadn't just taken up with some random girl he'd just met. Jim was able to reassure her that Tessa was indeed Lorenzo's girlfriend and had been for some time.

'Well at least he used protection…all three times.' Puffing out his chest with pride, Jim grinned at his wife with a dopey *That's my boy* expression. Angie was not amused.

'Oh, I see, so you're proud of our son, are you?' Folding her arms, she glared at her husband as she refilled her glass.

'Well, I'd say the apple didn't fall very far from the tree, darlin,' he allowed himself a quick smile before gazing down into his glass. Not wanting to risk falling out with his wife, Jim came and sat next to her on the sofa; drawing her in close he kissed the top of her head.

'Ach love, he's eighteen, he'll soon be off to university. Isn't it better that he gets a bit of experience?' he asked, not unreasonably.

Angie was quiet for a moment, and then he felt her shoulders heaving. Alarmed that he'd made her cry, he turned towards her.

'Ange' darlin', don't cr—' It was with great relief that Jim realized she was helpless with laughter; she tried to speak but couldn't get the words out through her fits of giggling.

'Do you remember that car you had back home, the old battered one with only two doors? We had to climb in the back seat, and I caught my foot in the seat belt getting out?' The tears were running down her face as she remembered once again.

'How could I forget darlin'…I got through three condoms!' Jim laughed, squeezing her shoulder.

'Well, at least we didn't leave ours in someone else's car.' Angie boasted proudly.

Jim was relieved that his wife could see the funny side of it, too. They both agreed that Lorenzo was to be commended for owning up and not allowing an innocent man to be sacked. On the other hand, it couldn't go un-punished.

Unaware that his parents had found the whole thing highly amusing, Lorenzo was surprised and relieved to have been grounded for just a week. His phone pinged—Alex.

Hey mate, fancy trying our luck in the pub tonight?

Nah…too much work to do, maths doing my head in…sorry mate.

'S ok, I'll try Sam, no worries.

Lorenzo felt a pang of jealousy at the thought of Sam going out with their mates without him; he hoped he wouldn't say anything about the car incident. Sitting back on his bed, Lorenzo's thoughts drifted back to Tessa and their night of passion in the back of the car. He couldn't wait to do it again. Being grounded was such a pain. Just as he was bemoaning his bad luck, a thought occurred to him…Tessa could come to *his* house…his bed.

He pictured the two of them naked, Tessa's long hair spread out over his pillow.

His phone pinged…Tessa.

Hey Rez, wanna do something?

There certainly was something he'd like to do at that moment.

Oh, hi babe, I was just thinking about you. Lorenzo hated the term babe, but he knew she liked it.

Ooh…anything nice?

Tempting though it was to send her a photo, he thought better of it. They had agreed they wouldn't get caught up in the craze for sharing that sort of photo.

Ooh yeah…veery nice

He sent her a fluttering heart emoji.

Mmmm…me too

Many texts later, it was agreed that Tessa would come to visit the prisoner at home and try to cheer him up, preferably when his parents were out.

Chapter 5

'Have you told the 'rents yet, Rez? You know they had their heart set on you going to university.' Alice peered in her mirror as she dried her long blonde hair, preparing to go out. Lorenzo was lounging on his sister's bed as they discussed the current hot topic in the house.

'That's just it, though, Ali. They had their hearts set on it, I didn't…I 'spose I just went along with it.' Lorenzo had to shout over the drone of the hairdryer.

'Come on, Rez, you knew we all thought you'd go; why didn't you say something?' Standing up from her dressing table, Alice gestured for her brother to turn his back as she pulled off her old T-shirt, replacing it with another.

'…what made you change your mind anyway?' she said over her shoulder.

'It was that guy from Octagon who came into college on a recruitment drive. They were looking for management trainees, the salary was amazing, and prospects of promotion to senior role were good. I just want some money, Ali, some independence to do what I want.'

As the heavy rain battered against the bedroom window, Lorenzo gazed out. St Catherine's Hill, normally a stunning vista from his own room, was completely invisible today.

Storm Mable, the weather people called it.

Storm uni, more like.

'What were you going to study anyway?' Ali fluffed out her hair before emptying a can of hairspray on to it.

'Business and Mark—Jesus Ali!' Lorenzo choked on the fumes from the hairspray. When he'd recovered, he continued. 'D'you know how many people I work with in the restaurant who have a degree and can't find a job? Three years wasted and a mountain of debt…what for?' Lorenzo liked this point; he'd have to remember it when he told his parents.

'But I still don't get it, Rez. Three years away…you'd have all the independence you ever wanted.'

'I just don't think I can study any more, ok Ali? The last two years of A levels have been a nightmare for me. I only just scraped through, you know.' Lorenzo hesitated, realizing he'd never admitted this to anyone before.

'Oh…I didn't realize Rez.' Ali smiled and bounded over, enveloping her beloved brother in a hug.

'God Ali, that hair stuff stinks.' Lorenzo reeled from the blonde cloud that was smothering him. Returning to her dressing table, Ali resumed her make up routine. Carefully glueing on her eyelashes, she said with a grin, 'you do know mum said I can have your room…'

Smiling to himself, Lorenzo thought that was the least of his problems as he watched in fascination as his little sister transformed herself from schoolgirl to vamp.

'Bloody hell, Ali, how much more of that gunk are you going to put on?'

'Humph...I bet your Tessa wears more than I do.' Alice pouted as she wiped a splodge of mascara off her cheek.

'Yeah, probably, and I end up wearing most of it when we—'

'Ew...too much info Bro.' Alice flapped her hand in disgust as an image of her brother with his girlfriend popped into her head.

Jumping off the bed, Lorenzo headed for the door, giving his sister's overly tight T-shirt a critical glance.

'Be careful in town, sis, there's a lot of weirdos around,' he advised wisely.

'Mmm, maybe I'll bump into Sam; he'll protect me,' she gushed dreamily.***Lounging in his room whilst aimlessly flicking through his phone, Lorenzo heard his mother's car pull up. He waited for the front door to open and for her to call out, 'any one home?' as she always did. Stuffing his phone in his pocket he went downstairs to find the kitchen full of bags.

'Oh hi, love...I've been shopping.' Angie said unnecessarily.

'Mmm yeah, you have, haven't you.' Lorenzo stepped over various bags as he headed for the fridge.

'It's pouring out there; I'm absolutely soaked…make us a coffee, love.'

'So what's all this then?' Lorenzo asked as he put the kettle on.

'Oh, it's great Rez. I managed to get everything you need for uni.' She smiled happily as she began to delve into the bags.

'You're going to need a new duvet, so I bought one and two new sets of covers.' Lorenzo thought of Mary Poppins and her bottomless bag as his mother repeatedly dived into the depths to retrieve yet another useful item.

Taking a deep breath, he gathered his courage.

It's now or never,

'Erm…Mum?' Placing a gentle hand on her arm, he tried to divert her attention away from all the goodies she'd bought.

'Yes, love? What do you think? This one or this one?' Angie held up two frying pans for his approval.

'Mum, will you just—'

When she finally realized her son was trying to talk to her, Angie stopped fussing with duvets and plates. The pained expression on her son's face told her something was wrong.

'What?' She sighed, exasperated at his lack of enthusiasm.

'I'm not going to university, Mum; I'm getting a job.' He waited.

The thunder raged outside as the sky darkened. Lorenzo thought it was quite fitting, really, as the shock on his mother's face reminded him of a scene from his favourite horror film. Angie groped for the nearest chair and slumped down, looking at all the supplies she'd bought.

'Not going? NOT GOING? What do you mean you're not going? Don't be ridiculous; of course you're going.' Lorenzo waited for the next scene to play out; he knew what was coming.

'We'll see what your father has to say about this.' Angie delved into her bag once more, rooting around whilst muttering angrily under her breath. Lorenzo headed for the kitchen, sweeping up Angie's phone from the table and handing it to her. As he boiled the kettle, he could hear Angie ordering his father home to discuss the crisis in their midst.

***

When Jim Murphy had finished his lecture, which covered everything from wasted opportunities to the state of the world in general, he sat back and asked the only question that mattered.

'So what's the grand plan, eh son? What are you going to do? Don't think you're just going to sit around—'

'I've been offered a job as—'

'A job, is it? Who's gonna offer you a job with no education? Tell me that boy?' Jim poured himself a big slug of Bushmills, the smooth burning liquid immediately soothing his rage.

'He's got his A levels, Jim.' Lorenzo was surprised to have his mother's quiet support.

'He needs a degree Ange'; he'll get nowhere without it –' Jim flicked a wrist dismissively.

'Look, dad, if you'll just let me speak for once—'

'Let you speak? Aye, I'll let you speak, go on then, enlighten me.' Jim sat back in his chair, arms braced on the arm rests.

The storm outside abated, as did the storm inside. After reiterating all their concerns about the perils of life without the prized university education, Angie and Jim reluctantly conceded defeat, agreeing to listen to their son's point of view.

Lorenzo was not used to having his parents listen with rapt attention to anything he had to say; he found it all very disconcerting. However, he ploughed on, his voice tremulous at first, but as he gained confidence, the words came easily. Ignoring the thumping of his heart, the grunts of derision from his father and the deep, sad sighs from his mother as he pitched his argument.

Disappointment...there it was again, that most dreaded of words; he could see it in their faces, but this time, Lorenzo rose above it. He didn't feel he'd let his parents down. This was his life, his choice, and he'd be damned if he was wasting three years of it, ending up with a mountain of debt for a worthless degree.

'Do you know how many people I work with in the restaurant who have degrees, Dad?' Jim shook his head sadly. Lorenzo couldn't be sure where his father's sympathy lay with the poor, overqualified workers or with the system in general.

Sam's name cropped up several times; what a great career he'd have as a dentist in stark contrast to Lorenzo, his own hard-earned A levels seemingly worthless. Lorenzo felt like he was playing a tennis match: deuce, to advantage, back and forth the ball went, his parents hoping to deliver the final coup de grace.

Silence fell eventually as Jim Murphy dramatically left the room with a defeated shake of his head. There was nothing left to say.

'I s'pose I'd better take all this stuff back then.' Angie looked forlornly at all her purchases strewn around the floor.

'I'll help you, mum. Maybe we can swap them for some work suits for me?'

'Oh...so you'll be wearing a suit for your new job?' She perked up at the idea of her scruffy son wearing a suit.

'I'll be a management trainee, mum; I need to be smart,' he grinned as his mother strutted proudly down the hall.

Chapter 6

'You all set then?' Lorenzo and Sam were in the pub nursing pints. It was a sad day for both of them as Sam was going off to Bristol the next morning. Lorenzo tried to be upbeat for his friend.

'D'you remember the first time we got served in here?' Sam swilled his beer around, a glum expression on his face.

'Yeah, how could I forget? I was bricking it.' Lorenzo shook his head, smiling at the memory, but he felt Sam's mood and added, 'Why so sad, bro? Tomorrow's your big day; you're gonna be the best dentist ever, I know it.'

'I wish I wasn't going.' Sam mumbled.

Lorenzo thought he hadn't heard right. He leaned in closer, frowning.

'I mean, I wish I could have just stayed here, Rez, in Winch.' Sam's words were slurred now after five pints, but he continued.

'My Dad's not well again, Rez; he's getting those headaches again…after his accident, you know?'

Lorenzo winced at the memory of Mike Brewer's motorbike accident a few years earlier.

They sat quietly for a while, watching a group of nervous-looking lads who'd come in, hoping to get served.

'You'll still look out for Sid, won't you, when you get the chance, I mean.' Sam suddenly said.

'Yeah, course I will; Tessa has taken him under her wing now too; she even bought him a coffee.' Lorenzo smiled. Sam fought for control of his lower lip, which was edging down at the mention of Lorenzo's girlfriend.

'Oh mate, you'll be fine. Don't forget I'm coming down the first chance I get. Maybe I'll bring Ali, she's heartbroken.'

'Aw. Ali. I love Ali…me and Ali—' Sam wobbled and almost fell off his chair.

'Come on, man, let's get you home. Don't want you to be hungover on your big day.' Lorenzo heaved his friend up, holding him under the arm.

***

Sam's mother, Julia, opened the front door and frowned at the sight of her son slumped against the door post with a silly grin on his face.

'Hey mum, Rez has brought me home, he's my best friend…did you know?' He slurred whilst patting Lorenzo affectionately on the back.

'Hmm…yes, I think I knew that, love, come on, you'd better get to bed.' Julia smiled at Lorenzo.

'Thanks, Rez, he's been a bit down in the dumps this week. His dad's not well, and he feels bad about leaving me.'

'Oh yeah, he said …I'm sorry to hear that.' Lorenzo hugged Sam one last time before handing him over to his mother.

As he walked home, sadness descended over him like a black blanket; when would he see Sam again? Would it be the same? What if Sam met someone…a guy? Lorenzo swiftly dismissed the thought, shoving it out of his head and slamming the door. Sam and Rez, Rez and Sam, the karate kids they, were called at school. WhatsApp and Instagram were great, but it wasn't the same. He walked back along the river, taking a longer route through the town.

'Hey, Rezza…come and have a drink.'

Lorenzo looked around for a face to go with the voice. Spotting Josh and a few old college friends, he went over to the pretty riverside pub garden.

'You lot off tomorrow too?' He asked, grinning around at the eager, excited faces.

'Yeah, Mac's not going though; he's got a job, so he's staying here in little old Winch.' Josh flung a heavy arm around Lorenzo's shoulders, almost sending the two of them sprawling. Lorenzo nodded over at Mac, whom he didn't know very well but suddenly felt a bond with as a fellow stay-at-home. Mac raised his glass in a gesture of camaraderie and wandered over.

'Welcome to the thicko's club, mate,' Mac sneered.

'You got a job then?' Lorenzo ignored the barbed comment as he bought himself a drink.

'Yeah, starting work next week in a luxury car-dealer. Cleaning at first, but it'll lead to sales later.' Lorenzo's heart skipped a beat; surely it couldn't be his father's company.

'What about you?'

Hesitating for a moment, Lorenzo watched as Josh and his friends downed more beer. Tempted as he was to join in, he couldn't shake off his glum mood, and anyway, it felt wrong without Sam.

'Oh…erm, yeah, I'm starting with Octagon next week, you know the insurance people? Management trainee.' Lorenzo was stinging from the thicko jibe and wanted to put Mac in his place.

'C'mon Rezza, drink up, we're celebrating', Josh staggered over, spilling his beer on the way.

'Nah mate, you're alright. I'll be off now.' Lorenzo smiled genially.

'What's up man, we not good enough to drink with or what?' Mac squared up, shoulders twitching as he started to bounce lightly on his feet.

'Ha-ha, that's not a good idea Mac; he's a black belt karate dude. Right, Rezza?' Josh swayed alarmingly, sloshing his beer as he gestured towards Lorenzo.

'Ha-ha yeah, Josh, that's right,' Lorenzo laughed, edging towards the exit. 'I'll see you later, guys.'

Lorenzo left quickly and flopped down on a bench in the park, his thoughts too jumbled to go home yet. As he sat musing on the events of the night, he saw a young couple kissing and had a sudden longing to see Tessa. Checking his watch, he texted her.

Hey babe, whatcha doing?

Oh, you know, just sitting here, waiting for a message from you, Rez. What else would I be doing?

Ffs Tess, why are you always so sarky?

Oh, piss off, Rez.

Lorenzo stared at his phone in frustration, resenting it for making him miserable. He considered flinging it in the bushes before shoving it in his jeans pocket.

As he walked, he thought about Tessa; maybe it was time to end it for good now. She always seemed to be annoyed with him these days, and he was getting fed up constantly trying to figure out what he'd done wrong. His phone pinged again—Tessa, Lorenzo hoped she'd changed her mind about coming out tonight.

FYI, I've been offered a place through clearing, so I'm off to Essex UNI next week, soooo excited!

Tessa's last message did nothing to improve Lorenzo's continuing sense of abandonment, as it seemed more and more of his friends were now leaving Winchester. She had been disappointed at not getting the place she wanted, and he'd initially felt guilty for not being more supportive whilst secretly feeling glad she wouldn't be leaving. He reluctantly messaged her back.

Hey Tess, that's great news, well done

Thanks, Rez, sorry for being arsy, good luck with the new job tomorrow.

His new job. Lorenzo's stomach clenched at the thought of it. Would they like him? Would he fit in? He worried about his new suit; was it too formal? What if everyone was in casual gear?

A car horn snapped him out of his reverie as it slowed down alongside him.

'Well, well, if it isn't the karate kid himself, where's your little sidekick tonight then?' the disembodied voice jeered from within.

Bending down, Lorenzo peered into the dark interior of the battered old Fiesta; he recognized a couple of adversaries from his school days.

'Alright, Lewis?' Considering his options, Lorenzo decided to try and talk his way out of this one, as there were three of them in the car.

'You leaving tomorrow with all the other girls, eh?' Lewis sniggered.

'Nah mate, no uni for me, got a job, earn some cash. You?'

'Erm, yeah. Got a job, haven't I.'

'Anyway, guys, gotta go, I'll see you around, yeah?' Lorenzo banged the roof of the car by way of a goodbye.

'Yeah, yeah…come and have a drink some time Rez.' Lewis shouted out the window as he roared off down the street.

Lewis and his cohorts would be the last people he'd want to drink with.

I really need some new friends. Maybe I should have gone away; this isn't going to be easy, stuck here on my own.

Chapter 7

'Right then, everyone, listen up…this here is Lorenzo, he's our new management trainee, be gentle with him.' Lorenzo's new boss, Richie, handed him an old-school paper file of passwords and company policy before slapping him on the back and disappearing, leaving him to settle in at his desk. Picking up his mouse, he played around with his computer screen, dazzled by the array of icons on the desktop.

Glancing around the large office, he suddenly felt overdressed; the other guys were all in casual gear, so he quickly divested himself of his jacket and tie. By eleven o'clock, he was desperate for a coffee, so he left the sanctuary of his desk and wandered around searching for a vending machine or a kettle.

Spotting a skinny guy with a huge beard sipping coffee, Lorenzo approached him.

'Hey man, erm, where can I get a coffee?'

'Vending machine in the corridor…out there.' Skinny Guy flicked a hand at some double doors.

'Oh, thanks…I'm Lorenzo. Rez. First day today,' Lorenzo grinned amiably.

'Yeah, so I heard. Welcome to purgatory.' Skinny Guy growled and turned back towards his screen.

As Lorenzo waited for the coffee machine to gurgle and rumble, he wandered over to the vast staircase leading down to the reception area far below. Octagon occupied the top two floors, and he decided at that moment that from now on, he'd use the stairs and not the lift; he needed to stay in training and was finding it hard to get to karate practice.

Sipping his coffee back at his desk, he picked up his mouse and began transferring figures from one spreadsheet to another. After several hours of tedium, he sat back and stretched his arms up, looking around for distraction. Everyone had their heads bent to their tasks, tapping away like little robots.

Jesus, this place is like a morgue.

By the end of the week, he was confident he'd pick it up quickly enough, but for him, it was the people that mattered; would he like them? Would they like him? So far, everyone had been supportive, especially a girl with long blonde hair called Gemma. He was wary of the bearded skinny guy, whom he'd found out was called Nick. Having told everyone to call him Rez, Nick seemed to take great delight in calling him Lorenzo, with a ridiculous Spanish accent and bullfighter gestures.

Lorenzo tried very hard to ignore the blinking email icon on his pc. this would be the ninety-fourth one today. As he gazed out of the office window, hoping for a distraction, anything would do. His phone pinged. He smiled to himself as Sam's name came up.

Hey, Bro', how's it going in the land of insurance?

Boring as hell, mate, thinking of jumping out this window

Aw, wait 'till, after Saturday, Rez, I'm coming up to Winch

Really? Thank god for that. Okay, I can hold it together 'till then

'Hey, Murphy, have you done those estimates yet, I'm waiting for them,' Richie, Lorenzo's boss, yelled across the office, his refusal to use Lorenzo's first name causing great hilarity among his colleagues. He didn't mind; he almost wished he'd thought of it himself all those years ago.

Dashing over to his PC, he clicked print and waited; leaning back against his desk, he folded his arms. Bored by the various clicks and clunks from the printer as it geared up, Lorenzo found himself staring at Gemma, who sat a couple of desks away from him. He watched as she tapped efficiently on her keyboard, stopping now and then to push her hair back over her ear.

'You know you could make a complaint about that, don't you?' She stopped tapping and looked over at Lorenzo from under a blonde fringe.

'Huh? A complaint about what?' Lorenzo snapped to attention, feeling like an idiot. She'd spoken to him…but what had she said?

'The fact that he won't use your given name silly.' Gemma smiled and slowly shook her head before pointing to the floor where, to Lorenzo's horror, the printer was regurgitating the precious documents on to the floor in a tangled mess.

'Oh…I don't mind, really; I answer to most things.' He gave her his best grin as he bent down to gather up his work before his boss saw it scattered on the floor.

'Tosser,' muttered the odious Nick from his desk a few feet away. Lorenzo looked up.

'You got a problem with me, mate—' Lorenzo could feel his grip on his temper failing when Gemma came over, bending down to help pick up the rest of the paperwork.

'Nothing to do, Nick?' she glared at him whilst handing the papers to Lorenzo.

'Oh hey Gemma, I…erm…yeah—' Nick quickly turned back to his machine.

At that moment, Lorenzo came to a realization— he really didn't like this job; Nick's pathetic jibes barely deserved the name and yet somehow seemed to put a hard edge on his growing feelings of frustration. The fact that he had to stick with it, having gone through all the hassle with his parents about not going to university, just made it harder. But at least the money was good, and he'd have some cash to splash when he saw Sam at the weekend.

As Lorenzo shuffled all his paperwork into some sort of order, Gemma handed him another errant sheet, which she'd fished out from under his desk.

'What, that guy's problem anyway?' he nodded vaguely in Nick's direction.

'Oh, never mind him, he's an idiot.' Gemma scowled before grinning at Lorenzo.

'Is it always like this? Just endless emails and printing?' he moaned.

'At least you get to print,' she said with a face full of wistful longing. She caught his eye and laughed. 'Don't worry, it does get better…after a while.'

'How long have you been here then?'

'Only six months, don't worry, it gets more interesting when they let you go out on assessments.' Gemma hopped up and sat on her desk, her long legs swinging under her, whilst Lorenzo wondered about the mysterious assessments.

'Some of us are going out for a drink after work tonight…if you're free?' she asked shyly.

Lorenzo wanted to play it cool and say he was busy. It didn't do to be too keen, after all. But then again, he *was* keen.

***

It seemed that the whole of Octagon was in the pub. Gemma was with a group of girls, and he was disappointed not to be able to talk to her alone.

'Hey Murphy, what are you having?' Richie bellowed across the crowded pub as he waited at the bar, waving his card at the harassed barmaid.

It would seem that once a month, on a Friday after work, Richie took his team to the pub and bought them all a drink. Team Building, he called it— in order to claim expenses.

'There you go, lad, get that down you.' Richie planted a pint of Fosters on the table in front of Lorenzo, patting him on the back with great enthusiasm.

'Well, Murph', you survived your first month, eh?'

Lorenzo nodded, wondering if his name could possibly get any shorter.

Richie appeared to be happy with his new recruit and, having slapped him on the back once again retreated to a corner with his fellow managers.

Two other newbies introduced themselves as fellow management trainees, and several pints later, Lorenzo had two new friends.

Malik worked in accounts, a dark-skinned guy with warm brown eyes and a heavy Yorkshire accent. Lorenzo liked him immediately as they exchanged stories of their disastrous first weeks in the new job.

'Lorenzo, what's that then Spanish?' Malik teased.

Lorenzo tried to keep the heavy sigh from showing.

'Nah mate, it's Italian, my mates call me Rez. What's Malik then, Indian?'

'Yorkshire bruv, born and bred, me.' Malik hooted with laughter as he broke into a broad Yorkshire accent.

Jinx worked in applications. Lorenzo didn't like to ask what applications did; he'd find out sooner or later, he supposed. Jinx was so named by Richie, as several things had gone wrong in his department soon after his arrival.

'Hey Rez, we're gonna go check out the scuba club at the pool on Saturday. You up for it?' Malik handed Lorenzo another pint, taking a huge slurp of his own. Scuba diving, he'd never thought about it before, and it sounded expensive. He hesitated.

An image of Lewis and his loser friends and the other stay-at-home Mac with the enormous attitude problem flitted across his mind like a portent of doom, and before he knew it, he was enthusiastically agreeing. After all, now he was earning some money, maybe he could afford to give it a try, and he was grateful for the chance of making some new friends.

Placing his drink on a table, Lorenzo turned, searching around for the toilets. As he stepped back, he bumped into someone standing behind him, spilling their drink.

'Oh, jeez, sorry mate, I'll get you another one.' Lorenzo didn't much like the look of the guy, heavy set with a murderous look on his face, but it was the body language that Lorenzo recognized. Posturing and looking for a confrontation, this was the last thing he needed tonight, with all his work colleagues watching.

'You wanna watch where you're going mate, look at the state of my fuckin' shirt.' Lorenzo flicked his eyes down; the shirt was clean. The guy took a step forward and shoved him forcibly in the chest. He was bigger than Lorenzo and taller, with an enormous stomach which overhung his baggy jeans.

Stepping back, hoping to diffuse the toxic situation, Lorenzo was aware of the hush that descended as people paused their conversations; a frisson of excitement hung in the air. He could see the odious Nick sniggering as he nudged his companion.

'Look buddy, it was an accident, alright? Let me get you—' Lorenzo tried again to reason with him, raising his hands by way of apology.

He saw the second shove coming and stepped neatly to the side, slapping the offending hand out of the way and causing the big guy to overbalance and fall flat on his face in an indignant heap. A ripple of disappointment went through the pub as the floor show ended abruptly. Feeling hugely embarrassed, Lorenzo was grateful when Malik handed him a pint with a congratulatory slap on the back. This was the first time he'd had an altercation on his own without Sam to back him up.

'Well, you're full of surprises, aren't you?' Gemma sat down beside him as Jinx and Malik made crude gestures behind her. Lorenzo grinned at her, thinking that sometimes being a superhero had its advantages.

'Ha-ha yeah…look…erm, do you want to go and get something to eat? I could do with getting out of here.' As far as Lorenzo was concerned, the evening in the pub was ruined, and he didn't want to risk another bout with his would-be assailant, who was now huffing and shrugging at the bar with a very red face. Gemma agreed, and they headed for the door.

'Hey Rez, don't forget the scuba club tomorrow at ten, okay.' Malik shouted as they made their way out. Lorenzo nodded, making phone-me gestures as they left the pub.

***

Gemma picked at her plate of salad leaves whilst Lorenzo tucked into a burger. He looked at her plate, pointing with a fork full of chips.

'How can you survive on that?' he mumbled.

'Ah…now you're making assumptions, aren't you?' Gemma pointed an admonishing finger across the table.

'I've eaten already in the pub…you were a bit too busy to notice.' She smiled.

Lorenzo certainly felt put in his place, but a pleasant tingle flickered up his spine.

She likes me.

They talked about what had happened in the pub, apparently, the guy caused trouble with the Octagon 'suits', as he called them, in the past.

'Lorenzo…Italian, isn't it?' Gemma toyed with her leaves, spooning on more dressing in a futile attempt to make it edible.

'You do *look* Italian…a bit,' she added whilst scrutinizing his face.

'Yeah, one of these days I'll get to the bottom of it, have it out with my parents, you know?'

'So you don't know why they called you that? Could it be some big family scandal…' Gemma peered at him closely and concentrated on her wine. Lorenzo liked that she was so outspoken, with no games being played.

'Mmm…it has occurred to me. My sister is blonde, and my dad has reddish hair…Oirish, you know,' he grinned at his attempt at the accent.

As the evening wore on, Lorenzo felt as if he'd known Gemma all his life. She was so easy to talk to. He found out she was a couple of years older than him, but somehow, it made her more fascinating.

'Ooh, does that make me a cougar?' she giggled.

'Well, that all depends, doesn't it.' He laughed, opening his arms by way of invitation.

Leaving the restaurant, they walked slowly back to the Octagon car park, chatting and sharing anecdotes about their lives. Gemma stopped at her car, fishing around in her bag for keys. Lorenzo hovered uncertainly, hands in his pockets; for the first time in his life, he didn't know what he should do next. Gemma's car beeped as she zapped the key fob and opened the door.

'Well, 'night Rez…I'll see you on Monday?' She turned to him and stood on tiptoes, kissing him on the cheek.

'Um…yeah, thanks for tonight,' he bent down to receive the cheek kiss. He longed to turn his head, but he knew he daren't.

Jumping in her little Blue Mini, Gemma eased it out of the car park, waving as she went. Lorenzo wasn't sure whether he was ecstatic or bereft. Did she like him? was she just being nice as a work colleague? She didn't have to kiss him. She could have just said goodnight and gone. His stomach was churning; how could he get through the weekend and wait 'till Monday to see her? What if she ignored him? Maybe he'd got it all wrong, and she didn't fancy him at all?

Chapter 8

The house was in chaos as Lorenzo stepped over boxes and piles of clothes on the floor upstairs.

'Bloody hell, what's going on here?'

Peering into an open box, he saw all his A-level textbooks.

'Ah…you're here at last. You're supposed to be helping.' Alice flounced past, buried under an armful of clothes.

'Helping with? — hey, that's my stuff.' Lorenzo made a grab for his jeans.

'We're swapping rooms…or did you forget?' Alice busily continued with her mission, dumping piles of her brother's things on her old bed.

Lorenzo had indeed forgotten. He'd been to the scuba club at the swimming pool and had decided to join. He'd come home clutching a PADI diving manual, a facemask and a snorkel, which he'd bought at the club.

'Hey guys, I've joined a scuba club. It's *amazing*. They let me put a tank on, and I sat on the bottom of the pool in twelve feet of water; it was—'

Ali shoved him out of the way once more.

'For god's sake, Rez. If you can't help, get out of the way.'

Finding his mother heading to his old room, he followed her in.

'It was great, mum, so calm and peaceful just breathing through my mouthpiece…'

'Hmm, that's nice love. Can you pass me those hangers?' Angie looked over her shoulder with a sigh.

'…I could see my bubbles drifting up to the surface…'

Leaning against the wall on the landing, he flicked through his newly acquired diving manual. The wonderful photos spirited him away to warm blue seas with brightly coloured fish darting around.

'Rez…for goodness' sake, either help or get out of the way.' His mother tutted as she bustled past, clutching more of his stuff.

'Oh no, you don't.' He jumped into action when he saw his X-Box passing by, managing to wrestle it away from his mother.

'Will you just…what the hell—?' Angie giggled as Lorenzo donned the scuba mask and snorkel before marching into his new room with his precious X-Box.

***

Struggling to get his TV and games set up, Lorenzo sat on the floor clutching various USB cables, trying each one in despair.

'God damn it, why doesn't this sodding thing fit…arggh.' He yanked the cable out and lay down, hands over his face.

'Having trouble there, big brother?' Alice lounged against the door post, grinning.

'This is all your bloody fault, Ali, wanting to change rooms, it all worked perfectly well before,' he grumbled.

Alice watched for a while before deciding to put him out of his misery. Picking up a cable with great aplomb, she proceeded to connect all his equipment; it was the least she could do, after all.

'Rez, can you come and give me a hand, love?' Angie shouted from her bedroom.

Lorenzo was grateful to be summoned away; there was only so much battering his ego could take.

'Yup. What's up?' Going into his parent's bedroom, Lorenzo found his mother teetering on the edge of a chair, reaching up to a high shelf in her wardrobe.

'Bloody hell, Mum, why didn't you call me? What are you trying to reach?'

Angie held on to him as she stepped down from the chair, indicating a box at the back of her wardrobe.

'Just leave it on the bed for me, would you love,' she called over her shoulder as she left the room.

Lorenzo took great delight in reaching things his mother couldn't ever since he was fourteen and had started to tower over her. It was a strange feeling, the gradual reversal of roles where he could take care of her; he liked it.

Reaching far to the back of the wardrobe, Lorenzo grabbed the box. It was just an old shoe box, not heavy, but pushed away into a far corner. He just about managed to get it to the front of the shelf when the box collapsed, spilling the contents on the cream-coloured carpet. Hoping nothing had broken, Lorenzo gathered up the bits and pieces. He smiled when he realised what the box contained: very old school reports, a school prefect badge, an old watch and some photographs.

Sitting on the edge of the bed, Lorenzo flicked through the photos, wondering why they were languishing in an old box in the wardrobe. Pausing to admire his mother as a young girl, he looked closer at the young man who stood with his arm around her; they were very obviously in love. Lorenzo felt his heart begin to thump; the blood drained from his head as the walls began to close in around him. Shaking his head, he forced himself to look again. There, staring back at him, was his own face. The same nose, the same easy smile. A knife stabbed into his heart as he turned the photo over, written on the back in very elaborate loopy writing, was: *Me and Lorenzo, Tuscany.*

Gemma's face popped into his head, peering curiously at him over her wine glass.

'...some big family scandal...'

With trembling hands, he stuffed the contents back into the box, making sure the photos were at the bottom where he'd found them. Leaving the box on the bed, he dashed to the bathroom, quickly locking the door before slumping down on the cold tiled floor.

As he sat on the floor, he felt as though someone had pulled the plug out of his life, and it was all draining away. Trying to control his breathing, he struggled to get his thoughts to focus. He tried to remember every conversation, every comment and reaction when he'd mentioned his strange name. It wasn't so much that he disliked Lorenzo. In fact, he quite liked it, but with Murphy as his last name, it was always cause for confusion. 'So, are you Italian or Irish?'

His attention focused on an annoying fly, its incessant buzzing breaking the silence. Was that boy in the photo his father? But that would mean–did his father know? The buzzing of the fly became more frantic as Lorenzo's eyes scanned the bathroom; he spotted it eventually, caught in a spider web in the corner. Picking up a toothbrush, he advanced on the web, determined to rescue the doomed fly. After pocking and prodding for a few minutes with the handle, he managed to release the hapless creature, who immediately flew straight down the toilet bowl.

Feeling somewhat calmer after his rescue mission, he ordered himself to stop panicking…it didn't work; his heart still pounded against his ribcage, and he thought he might throw up at any moment. Sinking back down on the floor, head in his hands, he remembered his mother crying when, as a small child, he'd asked yet again about his name. He'd grown up knowing the subject was taboo…but what now? What should he do?

Dashing back into his mother's bedroom, Lorenzo was relieved to see the box where he'd left it on the bed. He rooted around once more and retrieved the offending photo, placing it carefully on the bed, where the light from the window illuminated the vile image. Willing his shaking fingers to cooperate, he switched his phone to the camera, took a picture and quickly put the photo back in the box.

Back in his room, he shut the door and swiped to the gallery; zooming in on the image, he studied it carefully. His doppelganger was a lot older than him, maybe mid-thirties, and his mother looked to be late teens. Suddenly, he understood Angie had been a teenage girl seduced by an older man, an Italian she'd somehow met on a holiday to Tuscany. But what happened? Did he leave her? Maybe he didn't even know about the pregnancy. He desperately wanted to dash in and confront his mother, demand the truth, but the repercussions would be horrendous. He knew he needed to calm down and think clearly.

His phone pinged…Sam.

Hey Bro' my train gets in at 2 ish, meet you in the Bishops?

Oh, God, mate, do I need to talk to you!

Erm…ok, should I be worried?

I'll tell you later.

Lorenzo gazed at his phone, willing to give him the answers he needed. The message from Sam had severed the last thread holding him together; this time, as the tears welled up, Lorenzo let them flow.

Chapter 9

Sam fought his way through Winchester High Street, dodging the excitable tourists who thought nothing of blocking the entire pavement to get the right selfie shot. He ducked out through one of the side streets and took a shortcut to the pub through the cathedral grounds, all the while keeping an eye out for Sid.

Feeling the emotion rising as he walked through their old haunts, he remembered his younger self and the times he'd spent there with Lorenzo when they were kids; it seemed so long ago now. He thought about those feelings of confusion and isolation and wondered how he'd ever got through it. How many kids must be going through it all now, some with no one to talk to or willing to support them. He still hadn't told his parents he was gay, not that he was worried about it…not really; he had every faith that they would support him. It was his oafish brother Dan he was worried about.

Entering the pub, Sam adjusted his eyes to the gloom as he scanned around for Lorenzo. He wondered what had happened to upset his friend so much, probably something to do with bloody Tessa no doubt. Spotting Lorenzo at the bar, he went over.

'Hey Rez, what's up, man?'

Lorenzo turned around, pulling his friend in for a hug.

'God am I glad to see you,' he groaned.

Sam had never seen Lorenzo look so distraught; he was now fairly sure this wasn't about Tessa. Patting his friend on the shoulder, he guided them to a quiet table at the back. Lorenzo downed half his pint before lifting his eyes to look at Sam across the table.

'So, what's happened Rez?' Sam waited as Lorenzo wrestled with his emotions.

'Jesus Sam, I don't know where to start…it's all gone to shit…my whole fucking life gone up—'

Sam interrupted him.

'Woah there…just breathe, bro, start at the beginning.' Sam leaned forward, his hand on his friend's arm.

Lorenzo wasn't sure where the beginning was exactly, but he managed to get the gist of it across despite the wracking sobs that were threatening to engulf him. Sam listened intently, trying not to look too horror-struck as his friend struggled with his words. When the sorry tale came to an end, Lorenzo looked up at Sam, pleading for a solution, knowing Sam didn't have one.

'Can I see the photo?' Sam asked gently.

Lorenzo wanted to fling the thing across the floor but handed over his phone with a grimace.

'Jesus, I see what you mean. It could be you in twenty years' time.' Sam peered closely at the image.

They went over it all again, Lorenzo feeling calmer now that he'd shared his angst with Sam.

'Thank god you're here, man. I don't know what I would have done.' Sniffing loudly, he tried to gain control of his breathing; the last thing he needed right now was to lose it in the pub.

'Well, as far as I see it, you have two options: speak up or keep quiet. As soon as you say something, your world will change…believe me, I've been there.'

Lorenzo frowned, shaking his head as he imagined the fallout.

'On the other hand,' Sam continued, 'if you don't say anything, you suffer in silence keeping your big secret.'

The pub was filling up, happy chatting people without a care in the world, or so it seemed to Lorenzo.

'How can I go back home? Live there as if nothing's happened?'

'Look, why not come and stay with me in Bristol for a few days? You could call in sick to work, couldn't you?' The words slipped out before Sam had time to formulate a plan; he didn't care though, Lorenzo needed him.

***

Over the next few days, Sam showed Lorenzo around the university campus, introducing people as they roamed around. It was clear to Lorenzo that Sam had made a new life for himself, he was surprised to feel a small twist in his guts each time he was introduced to yet another of Sam's friends. A pretty, shy girl called Chloe had accompanied them a few times. Lorenzo could see the way she looked at Sam and wondered what was going on there. Sam would put his arm around her and kiss her cheek. Guiltily, he felt himself hoping that Sam wasn't gay after all, that maybe he was bisexual and things in his life weren't so different after all. He couldn't shake the thought, resolving to ask Sam before he left. He felt a deep, growing regret at not having gone to university. Maybe it wasn't too late; it would get him away from the lie that was his life back home. Maybe he'd look up some courses for next year, find something here at Bristol with Sam.

Lorenzo was glad of this time away; chewing it all over with Sam had helped get his head in some sort of order. He realized now that storming into his parents, demanding answers, wasn't the best way to go.

'So you're sure you're okay?' They were sitting on Sam's bed in his cramped room. Lorenzo had decided after four days that he needed to go home.

'Yeah mate, I'm fine…got a sore back from sleeping on your floor, though.' He grinned.

'Have you made up your mind? What you're gonna do?' Sam handed him a cup of coffee with a warning to avoid the huge crack running down the side.

'Yup…I'm keeping shtum for now, gonna play detective for a while.'

Sam nodded in agreement, looking down to check his messages as his phone pinged yet again.

'You're popular today, mate.' Lorenzo grinned as he tried to stop the coffee from seeping out of the crack in his mug.

'Yeah, sorry, it's Chloe. She wants me to go to some sort of fashion show.'

'Oh yeah? So what's the deal with you two?' Lorenzo sipped his coffee as he glanced over at Sam.

'We're just mates, Rez, don't get any—' Someone was banging on Sam's door, and he wrenched it open. Lorenzo could hear laughing voices in the corridor outside before Sam came back, shaking his head with a smile.

'So where were we? Oh yeah. You and Chloe…' Lorenzo persisted, knowing he was pushing his luck, but somehow, he couldn't stop himself. Seeing his friend so happy in his new environment had somehow highlighted his own bad decisions.

'Just friends, like I said.'

'But you seemed so close so…'

'So…what Rez? You think I'm *what*? Over it? Outgrown it? Fuck's sake Rez, I expected more from you.' Sam snatched Lorenzo's cup, pouring the coffee into another mug, he handed it roughly back to his friend.

'I'm gay, Rez…get over it.'

Lorenzo knew he should stop but somehow just couldn't.

'I know, I just…I thought maybe…'

'Maybe what?' Sam's voice was rising, his cheeks flushed and red. 'Maybe I'd changed? Maybe I was wrong? Maybe I'd made some big mistake, and I'd fucked up my life just like you have.' Sam went over to the sink and began aimlessly wiping down the top; he knew his last comment had stung and couldn't bear the look on his friend's face.

'What?' Lorenzo spluttered, the sharp barb slicing through his core.

'What the hell's that supposed to mean?' Lorenzo stared at Sam's rigid back, desperate to make sense of what was going on.

'I'm sorry, Rez,' Sam muttered eventually, in a voice choked with emotion. 'That came out all wrong.' He turned to face his friend; a stony silence fell between them.

'Jesus man, that was—' Lorenzo shook his head as Sam interrupted.

'I just…I need your support, mate; it's hard, you know? I'm just a bit sensitive about it all.' Sam managed a watery smile.

'A bit?' Lorenzo forced a laugh. 'Mate, I thought you were going to come at me.'

Sam flicked an eyebrow.

'We should sell tickets if we ever put on that show.'

Lorenzo made himself smile back, his mind desperately trying to piece together what had just happened.

***

On the train on the way home, Lorenzo had a knot in his stomach. He knew he'd blundered with his crass comment and hurt Sam's feelings, but what to make of Sam's comment 'fucked up my life just like you have'? Was Sam right? Had he fucked up his life? He had regrets about university for sure, but for Sam to throw it at him like that really hurt. They'd never fallen out before, and he'd hated having to leave with bad feelings. He resolved to choose his words more carefully in future if their friendship were to survive.

The train rumbled its way through the countryside; Lorenzo dropped his head back and closed his eyes. The knot in his stomach was easing off, only to be replaced with a tightening in his chest as he remembered why he'd gone to Bristol in the first place.

As he dozed, he tried to formulate a plan for when he got home. Stage one, he'd ask for his birth certificate, say it was for a diving permit or something. Stage two would depend on the name on the certificate. Stage three—he was saved from stage three by a very loud rendition of Highway to Hell as a young lad threw himself into the seat next to him, his head invisible under massive headphones. Lorenzo smiled to himself, feeling very old.

Chapter 10

Weeks turned into months, and Lorenzo still hadn't asked for his birth certificate; he began to think that maybe it would be better to just live with the uncertainty. Strangely enough, it had been Tessa who'd made him reconsider. She was home for a few days, and they'd agreed to meet up. Lorenzo told her all about the Tuscany photo and the turmoil he'd been in since he'd found it.

'Oh my god, Rez, that's terrible. It must have been such a shock.'

They were sitting in Zizzi's eating pizza, and Lorenzo had gone over the whole story again, this time without the overwhelming emotion from the first telling of it.

'Can I be honest, Rez?' Tessa looked down at her coke, playing with the straw before she looked up.

'Erm…yeah, 'course.'

'Does it really matter?' Lorenzo's thunderous face gave her the answer to that question.

'But I mean…they brought you up, they love you, done everything good parents should do, why rock everyone's world? There's a reason they don't want you to know; maybe they're waiting for the right time.' Reaching across the table she held his hand, rubbing her thumb soothingly over his clenched fist. He felt a flush of old emotions.

'I'm sorry I've been such an arse Tess,' he said tentatively. 'Can we, maybe, start again?'

'No, Rez,' she said without missing a beat. 'It's over; we have different lives now, and anyway, I've met someone so—' She smiled, and Lorenzo knew it was for the new guy in her life, not for him.

***

It was the last Friday of the month, and the Octagon team were in the pub once more. Malik, Jinx and Lorenzo were celebrating gaining their first PADI diving qualification.

'Hey Rez, Liz says they're organizing a diving trip to Malta, what 'd you think?' Jinx flopped down on a seat beside him, excitedly waving his phone.

'Wow, yeah, sounds great, count me in.' Lorenzo leaned over, trying to read the email.

'Where the hell's Malta?' Malik asked.

'Dunno, mate, but I'm going.' Jinx shrugged.

Gemma came over to join them, pulling up a chair beside Lorenzo.

'Is everything okay with you?' she whispered, putting a gentle hand on his arm.

'Erm…well, I've had a few problems at home, with my family, you know?'

Lorenzo shrugged. He hadn't wanted to talk about it at work, his safe sanctuary away from it all. He'd been disappointed that their meal out hadn't progressed to anything. Gemma had been distant at work, and he assumed she wasn't interested. Now, as her hand rested on his arm, he should have been feeling optimistic, but even Gemma couldn't cure the dull ache in the pit of his stomach.

Jinx thrust his phone in front of Lorenzo, a long finger pointing out Google's latest proclamation. 'Malta, Island of the Knights Templar. What the hell's a knight templar?'

'God, you're so bloody ignorant, mate. The Knights Templar guard the temples don't' they.' Malik informed him with great authority.

Lorenzo shook his head in despair, chuckling as Jinx stood up to declare a debate. An official debate meant that all phones were put away, and anyone having a sneaky peek at Professor Google would have to buy a round.

'Malta? You know Richie's wife is from there.' Gemma commented as all heads turned to look at Richie. 'I'd love to see it; it always sounds so romantic, a little island in the Mediterranean with swaying palm trees…mmm.'

The boys all turned their attention to Gemma now, wondering how diving could be classed as romantic.

Chapter 11

Sam wandered into the communal kitchen, searching for alcohol and distraction. He found the former in the fridge after rummaging through various unidentifiable items belonging to his housemates and the latter sitting at the kitchen table. Chloe, whose room was two doors down, was halfway through a bottle of red wine as she gestured for Sam to sit beside her. After rooting around in the fridge, Sam emerged triumphant with one can of lager; he frowned in consternation when he spotted a post-it note stuck on the side, a dire warning for anyone daring to drink Gregg's beer.

'Bloody cheek.' He muttered, opening the can, 'This isn't even his kitchen.' His eyes flicked briefly up to Gregg's room on the floor above.

'I said he could use ours; he doesn't like his lot upstairs, and anyway he's doing cookery and nutrition. Much more useful than studying teeth,' Chloe opined with great authority before adding: 'Has your friend gone back to Winchester?'

'Yeah, he's gone,' Sam growled irritably.

'What's happened, I thought you two were *best mates?*' Chloe's emphasis on the last two words only served to increase Sam's dark mood.

'If you must know, my *best mate* wanted to know if I was "still gay."' Sam slurped down more beer in the vain hope of erasing Lorenzo's thoughtless remark.

'I mean, I've known Rez my whole life, and he asks me that.' He shrugged whilst, shaking his head sadly.

Chloe hesitated a moment.

'Well, you've known *him* your whole life,' she said tentatively, 'but he hasn't known *you,* has he? You weren't even out to him until what, a few months ago?'

Sam glanced at her.

'I suppose,' he nodded. 'But it hasn't been easy for me either. Remember Callum?'

'How could I forget?' Chloe said drily, rolling her eyes and sipping her wine.

'Ok, ok, he wasn't ideal, but he was my first real boyfriend,' Sam winced slightly at the memory. 'So hot, but just so…out there, you know? So…'

'Gay?' said Chloe with a raised eyebrow. Sam laughed.

'Yeah. Gayer than I was ready for at the time, I think. Still. I learned a lot.'

'Bet you did. So did the rest of us, eventually. You remember that time on the bridge?' Chloe shuddered.

'When you tried to kiss me?'

'That's the one.' She slurped her wine. 'You could have told me before…would have saved a lot of embarrassment.'

Sam sighed and stood up.

'Oh right…so I should inform every girl I meet that I'm gay, just in case she has designs on my body, or I could hang a sign around my neck.'

'And anyway,' he said heavily as he headed back to the communal fridge in the forlorn hope of finding something to eat. 'I was too busy learning the rules of the big gay world and how to stay safe from the Neanderthals.'

Squatting down, he peered into the compost heap that was their shared fridge. Finding nothing remotely edible that didn't require cooking, he stood up, brushing his long black hair back with an exasperated sigh.

'The what?' Chloe asked flatly.

'Callum's word for the intolerant masses baying for our blood. That was one of his rules. Assume everyone not at a Pride event is a Neanderthal until proven otherwise.'

'I love it when your hair falls in your eyes like that.' Chloe slurred randomly.

Rolling his eyes at the alcohol-fueled comment, Sam eyed the almost empty bottle and suggested they go out; he could do with letting off steam in a club or something.

'I know…my friend Saira is putting on a fashion show tonight. We could go?' Snapping out of her melancholy, Chloe jumped up and grabbed her phone, excitedly scrolling through her contacts.

'A what?' Sam said, aghast at the very idea.

'Free food and booze.' Chloe had no idea if this was true, but she warmed to her theme. 'Oh, come on, misery guts, it'll be fun.' She nudged Sam with her hip.

'Free food, you say?' Sam's stomach growled in eager anticipation.

'Would the food be before the fashion thing or after?' He wondered how long he would have to endure the spectacle of prancing girls parading down a catwalk.

'Oh, for god's sake, Sam, we can get a kebab on the way if you're in imminent danger of total collapse.' Grabbing her bag, Chloe touched up her lipstick as they headed out the door, grabbing an umbrella as it was starting to rain.

As they walked into town, Chloe quickly messaged Saira, who reserved them two seats. She explained that Saira was doing fashion design and creative arts. She'd put on a few shows and was gaining a reputation for her exotic designs. Sam feigned interest, but all he wanted to do right now was get drunk and forget about his row with his friend.

They arrived just as the first model came down the catwalk. Saira shot Chloe a disapproving look as they took their seats. Sam had been dreading it, thinking it would be full of 'arty' types he didn't know. He was right, in that he didn't know any of them, but intrigued when he realized this was no ordinary fashion show. The models were extraordinarily beautiful, exuding a kind of old-world charm and glamour. The outfits on show reflected the theme; sequins and glitter sparkled as each model paraded past.

'Why didn't you tell me?' Sam whispered to Chloe.

'Would you have come?'

'Probably not.'

Chapter 12

Backstage after the show, Saira introduced them around, and Sam found himself surrounded by the most exotic people he'd ever met. Saira herself floated around in a cloud of emerald green hair, which Chloe assured him was her own. Diamante's sparkled and champagne glasses clinked amid a haze of heady perfume. He stood mesmerized, as if apart from the colourful world which surrounded him.

'Who's that?' Sam was intrigued by a very tall drag artist wearing a tight gold shimmery dress. Her platinum blonde hair was piled on top of her head, with wispy tendrils falling to her shoulders. She seemed to know everyone and sashayed around, working the room confidently.

'Oh, that's Maxine…tonight anyway.' Saira laughed as she called Maxine over to introduce her.

'Hullo darlings, did you like our little show?' Maxine asked in an overly theatrical voice.

'Erm…yeah, it was…um,' Sam stumbled over his words as he tried to control the tingling in his spine. Chloe giggled beside him, throwing a conspiratorial glance at Saira. Handing them all a glass of champagne, Saira disappeared to organize her outfits, and Sam found himself inexplicably drawn to the costumes hanging on racks, running his hand down the soft, silky gowns. He watched in fascination as fluttering eyelashes were peeled off and elaborate wigs removed. His hand strayed up to his own thick black hair; maybe he should let it grow…just a little bit.

'Are you one of Saira's models?' Maxine asked, squinting at Sam through inches of glittery eyelash.

'No…um…I'm doing Dentistry,' he mumbled, trying to quell his rapid pulse.

'Ooh, really? What do you think of these babies, eh?' Maxine flashed an identical row of gleaming white perfect teeth for his inspection.

'You see this one here?' A long red fingernail tapped on the tooth in question. 'I asked my dentist to—' Just as Sam's heart sank at the inevitable dental questions, he was saved by Saira, who dashed back in a fluster, her green hair now tied back in a functional ponytail as she complained that two of her backstage hands had disappeared.

'Are you two free by any chance?' I really need to get these girls out of their costumes, and Zoe and Mark have gone AWOL,' she pleaded.

Quickly ushered into the dressing room, Chloe and Sam found themselves surrounded by yards of gold lamé, glitter, exotic wigs and piles of discarded clothes. Maxine teetered over on her very high platforms, asking Sam to help with a zipper that was stuck. Kicking off her shoes, she gestured to the offending zip and suddenly shrank six inches in front of him.

'Bloody hell, how can you walk in those?' Sam laughed as he struggled to free the zip.

'I don't walk darling, I glide…serenely,' she drawled with a wry smile.

After much tugging and pulling, Sam managed to free the zip and help Maxine peel out of her dress. He was amazed at the padding underneath. Maxine grabbed hold of the top of the body suit, pealing it down, boobs first. Breathing a deep sigh of relief, she carefully placed it in her box on top of the towering shoes.

Having divested themselves of their gowns and wigs, the models were now seated at their dressing tables, removing the elaborate make-up with huge dollops of cream.

'Drinks anyone?' Saira shouted to no one in particular.

Chloe begged off as she had some errands to run, so Sam found himself in the pub, drinking with the now de-dragged Max and his boyfriend, Kyle. It had been such a shock to see Max without the drag; he could pass for a pretty girl even without it. When he'd first emerged from the changing room wearing skinny jeans and a T-shirt, Sam hadn't recognized him; pale blonde hair with deep green eyes and killer cheekbones, even his voice was different. Kyle sat quietly as Max hugged his beer, chatting excitedly about his next gig.

'Do you not … Erm…?' Sam asked Kyle, not sure of the terminology and not wanting to offend anyone.

'Me? You must be joking, mate, I wouldn't have the balls to get up there, and anyway, I couldn't hope to look this fabulous.' He lifted Max's hand, kissing his palm.

'So what's your story, Sam…are you out?' Max took a sip of his beer, peering over the glass at Sam.

'Yeah, came out when I was seventeen. Mostly.' Sam was relieved to be on safer ground again.

Sam felt comfortable enough to exchange coming-out stories with Max and Kyle. He realized how lucky he'd been once he'd heard Max's story.

Kyle clutched his hand reassuringly as Max recounted his teenage years living rough on the street.

'My Father was a troubled man, Sam. I don't know what went on with him when he was a child, but he had something to prove…how tough he was or how *manly* I s'pose. Whatever it was, he couldn't possibly have produced a son like me.' Max took a gulp of beer as the telling of his story took its toll. Sam waited in silence, unsure what to say. He glanced at Kyle, whose slight smile reassured him Max was okay.

Max continued. 'Eventually, of course, he threw me out. I was an embarrassment; I think he even doubted I was his son at one point, even though I was the spitting image of him.'

'I expect that was his problem, love…he wanted you to be like him,' Kyle put in gently.

'When I was about thirteen, he sat me down for a chat. I thought maybe it was going to be the usual father-son sex talk, but he told me bluntly that I had 'till I was seventeen to pull myself together and that if I *hadn't grown out of it* by then, I'd be out on my ear…and so I was.' Max sniffed and rubbed his nose vigorously whilst trying in vain to retain a modicum of control over his emotions.

'Jesus, Max, that's awful, how did you—? Sam struggled to hold on to his own tears as he tried to imagine Max's life as a teenager. 'What about your mum … didn't she try and stop him? Or was he—'

Max raised a hand, cutting him off.

'My stepmother wasn't in the least bit interested, Sam. All she wanted was for her loving husband to stop venting his rage on her every night.' Max waved a hand dismissively.

Sam thought fleetingly about his own parents; he was pretty sure they wouldn't react as Max's did; they had no idea he was gay. In fact, he himself hadn't realized it as a younger teenager, unlike Max.

'So what happened after he threw you out? How did you get by?' Sam asked the question, but deep down, he knew what the answer would be.

'Well…I lived in various squats for a while, trading the one thing I had to offer to get some money. I was a good-looking boy. Blue eyes, blonde hair, I had plenty of offers.' Max said sadly, smoothing back his hair as he remembered.

'…But then I met my saviour.' Leaning in close to Kyle, Max laid his head gently on his shoulder. 'Kyle found me one night, fast asleep behind some supermarket bins.'

'Oh, so…he wanted—?' Sam looked from one to the other, making a conscious effort to close his mouth lest it betray his thoughts.

'Oh…no darling, not like that…Kyle worked with a local charity. He was out checking up on us young ones; that was ten years or so ago.' Max looked up at Kyle to share a kiss.

'Ah, okay erm…I'm so sorry, man; it must have been awful.' Sam shook his head sadly.

Pulling slowly away from Kyle, Max fixed Sam with a contemplative look. Feeling slightly intimidated, Sam leaned back a little, away from that intense, searching gaze. He felt like Max could see his very soul, all his secret hopes and dreams. Kyle rolled his eyes; *here we go again,* planted a kiss on the top of Max's blonde head, and declared he was off to the bar.

'Yes, it was awful, Sam, but I am who I am because of what happened to me. That story is what I express every time I go on stage. Maxine is the light that grew out of that darkness. She's the strength I needed, the confidence I wore like amour, the beauty and perfection I never felt inside. Now I serve her to the world every time I put on that makeup.' Max sat back, flashing those perfect teeth, except this time, the smile looked like a challenge to the world in general. *Come for me*, that smile said, *I can take all you've got.*

'And I live for it,' he added, more softly, with a grin. 'Never forget, Sammie, people like us don't get to choose our families. But we get to choose who we are, and if our family doesn't want us, well fuck 'em, we make our own family.' He gave Sam a sidelong, knowing glance.

'You'd be welcome in ours…if you ever wanted to try. You're so beautiful, Sam, you'd make a gorgeous queen; I saw you looking at those frocks.' He grinned before nudging Sam with a friendly elbow.

'What?…nah, not my thing Max,' Sam protested, his hand drifting up to brush a stray lock of hair out of his eyes as he tried to explain further. 'I mean, I don't need … erm well, it's like you said, for you, Maxine is your amour against the world, right? But I don't need that, Max.' Sam shrugged, dismissing the preposterous idea.

'Maybe not.' Max said thoughtfully, still holding him with that discomforting gaze. 'But what if *this* is your amour. Perhaps you've been wearing it for *years*.' Max swept a languid hand down Sam's torso.

Sam looked deep into Max's eyes, allowing those last few words to circle for a while before settling. He tried to respond, but his mouth was dry; something about Max's words had hit him hard, somewhere he hadn't realized existed, deep inside him that maybe, just maybe, yearned to be free. A peculiar feeling of elation tingled up his spine as he realized he was smiling.

'You don't have to put a label on it, you know. This isn't a novel that has to fit a certain genre. Just be yourself, wear a little make-up every day, drag up once a month, or don't…whatever floats your boat.' Max shrugged a shoulder, trying to lighten the atmosphere.

Wiping his palms on his jeans, Sam fought to control his rising excitement. Could he? Just a little bit to satisfy a yearning that had suddenly gripped him.

Kyle returned with the drinks, frowning as he saw Sam and Max leaning close, deep in conversation. Taking a sip of his beer, Sam tried to stop his hand from shaking.

'It took me many years to find my own thing, Sam, something I could do just for me—' Max broke off when Kyle came back; sensing his mood, he reached over, planting a kiss on his cheek.

They stayed until the last orders, by which time they'd exchanged numbers. Sam promised to attend Max's next show, still protesting it wasn't his scene. Kyle winked at him knowingly and patted him on the back as they left.

***

As the months passed, Sam and Chloe became great friends with Max and Kyle. Sam decided to move out of his university accommodation, and he and Chloe were now sharing her two-bedroom flat. Saira had begged Sam to model for her, and he'd tentatively agreed on condition he wouldn't be *dragged* too much.

Chloe had volunteered for leg waxing duties, and Sam now found himself stripped down to his boxers and reclining on the sofa. As he watched Chloe stirring a pot of bubbling wax, he felt the panic-rising droplets of sweat gathered on his top lip.

'Erm…is this really necessary? I mean, couldn't I just wear tights or something?

Chloe advanced towards him, carefully placing her bubbling cauldron on the table. Sam squirmed away into the far corner of the sofa, pulling his legs in under him.

'Oh, come on, Sam, Saira will kill me if I present you with hairy legs.'

'Bloody hell, Chlo,' I'm not an exhibit at Crufts,' Sam whinged as he unfolded his legs and lay back with one arm over his eyes.

As she waited for the wax to set, Chloe let her eyes roam over Sam's half-naked body; when she got to his chest, she sighed.

'Hmm, we really should do something about your chest, you know.' She trailed her fingers through the dark, silky hairs, feeling the hard muscles underneath.

'Don't even think about it, Chlo.' Sam said menacingly as he flicked her hand away.

'Right then…ready?' Grabbing one end of the now-hardened wax, Chloe yanked the strip up Sam's leg, holding it up triumphantly for inspection.

'Jesus Christ, Chloe, what the fuck?' Sam screamed in agony whilst clutching his throbbing leg.

'Look how much came off Sam, lets do another one.' Returning to her bubbling cauldron, Chloe began stirring.

Sam declared he'd had enough, and after likening Chloe to one of Macbeth's witches, he jumped off the sofa he pulled on his jeans, mumbling about finding a razor as he stomped off into the bathroom.

Later that evening, after he'd heard Chloe go out, Sam opened his special drawer, taking out a black wig and a box of make-up. Chloe had shown him how to apply foundation, lipstick, and eyelashes. The latter he wasn't too sure about as he felt they were a step too far, although they did serve to complete the look. He tried to ignore the box on top of the wardrobe, even though he was longing to retrieve it.

He and Chloe had been round to Max and Kyle's for dinner one night when Max beckoned him into the bedroom and handed him a box.

'Look, I know you aren't ready for this yet, and that's cool, but just keep it under the bed or something…just in case you need to scratch that itch.' Max smiled and sat down on the bed as Sam opened the box.

'Jesus Christ, Max, what the fuck?' Sam was horrified when he saw the flesh-coloured padding; he thought it resembled some sort of limbless corpse from a horror film.

Max winked and left the room, allowing Sam time alone with his thoughts. Stealing a sideways glance at the soft body form, Sam reached out, running a hand over curvaceous hips and breasts. His heart pounded as he allowed himself a glimpse of a possible future…could it be?

As their evening wore on and more champagne was consumed, Sam gradually warmed to the idea, so much so that with Chloe's help, he ordered a beautiful black silk dress and shoes. Chloe had giggled at the thought of teaching him to walk in the high heels.

Sitting now in front of his mirror, Sam reached for his hairpiece; turning it over in his hands, he gently teased the long black strands out before clipping it carefully into his own hair. He applied the deep red lipstick, rubbing his lips together and savouring the creamy texture. Flicking his head, he enjoyed the feel of his hair as it brushed his bare shoulders. He'd practised his hair and make-up several times before and had resisted the siren call from the box on the wardrobe, but tonight, he was ready. The box slid down into his arms like a willing lover, his mouth dry with anticipation. Lifting the lid carefully and with great reverence, his heart pounded as he retrieved, first, the black dress, holding the soft, silky fabric to his cheek. He studiously avoided looking at the flesh-coloured body form as he stepped into it, even though he knew he couldn't wear the dress without it.

Fifteen minutes later, Sam steeled himself to glance in his mirror, expecting to be appalled at how ridiculous he looked. He squinted through his fingers, gradually moving his hand away as the vision in his mirror appeared. He gawped in shock at the beautiful girl looking back at him. She had silky black hair, just curling onto her shoulders, with a wispy fringe that swept her eyebrows. Her full lips parted, the red lipstick emphasizing perfect white teeth. Deep blue eyes gazed out through long, dark eyelashes. Fascinated by the image in the mirror, Sam watched, mesmerized, as the girl ran her hands sensuously down her hips, slowly smoothing out her dress. Her hands moved up, caressing her small breasts, causing the silky fabric to shimmer under her hands.

'Oh my God,' the girl said with a hesitant smile.

'Nice to meet you, Samantha,' he whispered back.

Chapter 13

It had been difficult at home for Lorenzo, trying to act normal, not wanting to face the usual inquisition from his parents. It usually went along the lines of:

'Everything alright, love?'

'Yup. Great.'

'You know you can talk to us, don't you?'

'Yeah, Mum-thanks.'

'I mean, if there's something bothering you…'

'Mum, I'm okay, alright.'

Except, of course, this time, he'd have to add, *'Apart from the fact that my dad's not my dad, you were seduced by an old Italian perv, and my life has gone down the toilet.'*

His mother knocked on his door, bustling in with a pile of ironed shirts. She began arranging them in his wardrobe. Lorenzo sighed as he glanced up from his laptop.

'Mum, I can do that…Mum! Will you just leave them on the bed?' he hadn't meant to shout, but he knew it was just her excuse to come in and check on him.

'By the way, your grandma is coming to visit next weekend, you will be here, won't you?' she said. It wasn't a question.

'Oh, what? No, Mum, you know she hates me.' He groaned at the thought of it.

'For goodness sakes, Rez, she doesn't hate you. My mother doesn't hate anyone. She's just a bit…prickly sometimes.' She laughed as she shut the wardrobe door.

Lorenzo thought prickly didn't quite do it, more like a porcupine that had swallowed a wasp in his opinion. It was just the strange way his grandmother looked at him sometimes as if she wanted to rip his head off. He wondered if it had anything to do with his real father. Groping around on his bed for his phone, he quickly sent out a WhatsApp to his diving group.

Anyone up for a dive somewhere next weekend?

He wanted to add, 'preferably with an overnight stop,' but didn't want to appear desperate. The phone pinged back almost immediately. Liz was organizing a trip to Stoney Cove, a flooded gravel pit somewhere up north. She said he could train towards his next qualification. Whilst a dive in a muddy gravel pit didn't exactly light up his world, it was better than facing the wicked witch who was his grandmother.

'Ah…Mum,' he called into the kitchen before dashing out the door, 'I'm really sorry, but I'd forgotten about a dive I'd agreed to go on next weekend.'

***

'So…underwater navigation. Is that, like, just finding my way around?' Lorenzo and his instructor, Liz, were having a coffee in Winchester.

'Yeah, I'll place a few things around on the bottom and give you the coordinates to find them using your compass…easy, really.' Liz grinned, taking a huge bite of her blueberry muffin.

'And we'd need to stay over?'

'Well, yeah, really. It's a long drive, Rez, and we can do more dives the next day; you could log a couple of wreck dives.'

'Great, count me in.' Lorenzo pinged his deposit over to Liz with relief; he'd be away when the wicked witch came.

Malik and Jinx came bounding in like a couple of over-excited puppies. After searching around for Lorenzo and Liz, they slid in beside them.

'Hmm, this looks cosy.' Malik nudged Lorenzo as Liz raised her eyebrows with a sigh.

'Shall I put you two down for Stony Cove as well?' Liz looked from one to the other expectantly.

'You can count me out…don't fancy freezing my balls off in a gravel pit. I'll wait for the warm sea and sunshine.' Malik laughed.

'I'm gonna get a Maltese phrasebook…learn a few words.' Jinx announced.

'Hmm, good luck with that; they all speak English, you know.' Liz tutted before continuing, 'Anyway, you'd never be able to learn it. It's too hard, mainly Arabic.' She said with a dismissive wave of her hand.

Another hour passed, during which Liz described the various dive sites in the Maltese Islands. The boys left Liz to her paperwork and fired up with stories of deep shipwrecks and shoals of exotic fish. They walked down to the pub.

Winchester was heaving with tourists as usual, so Lorenzo suggested they go to the Bishops Tavern. Malik and Jinx weren't local boys, so Lorenzo took great pride in showing them his hometown. As they cut through the cathedral grounds, a wave of nostalgia washed over him. This was their place, his and Sam's. Would it ever be the same between them?

'Hey Rez, look at this…this guy's a knight! Like the Templars!' Lorenzo looked around to find Malik taking a selfie with a statue of a knight in armour.

'Bloody hell, Mal, you're turning into a sodding tourist.' Lorenzo snapped out of his melancholy, laughing along with Malik.

***

The week dragged slowly for Lorenzo as he tried to keep a low profile at home. Angie had forgiven him for absenting himself at the weekend when his grandmother would visit. Lying face down on his bed, he clicked through various dive websites, gazing longingly at photos of people diving with turtles in the Red Sea. His phone pinged: Sam.

Hey Rez, there's a party here on Saturday, it'd be great if you could come.

Lorenzo breathed a sigh of relief tinged with disappointment; he'd liked to have seen Sam, as things had been strained between them since Bristol. Part of him was longing to go. He knew he needed to apologize and make things right between them. At the same time, he knew he couldn't let Liz down for the dive trip.

Sorry mate, can't make it. Going diving to get away from Grand High Witch

K, no worries. Everything alright at home?

Yeah, I haven't said anything.

There was a pause. Lorenzo saw the "typing" icon appear and vanish several times as Sam hesitated on the other end.

Really sorry, Rez. About last time.

Lorenzo let out a short laugh of relief.

Nah, mate, I was out of order; you were right to be pissed.

I wish you could come; it'd be great to catch up.

Can't really back out now, mate, I've paid for the trip

Ok, well, maybe see you soon

Lorenzo put his phone down, feeling like a weight had been lifted; he and Sam were okay.

***

Sitting at his desk on Friday, Lorenzo got a message from Liz telling him the diving trip had been cancelled as there had been some emergency at Stoney Cove, so they'd shut the dive centre for the weekend. She assured him he'd get his money back. Lorenzo didn't care about the money; he just needed to get away for the weekend. The spectre of his grandmother floated before his eyes.

Scrolling back through his messages, he re-read Sam's invitation and was about to reply when a thought occurred to him. What if he just turned up? He'd surprise Sam, and he'd be so pleased to see him. It would prove to Sam that he really was sorry.

Chapter 14

Stepping off the train at Bristol, Lorenzo checked his phone for Sam's new address, trying to remember the name of the girl he'd moved in with. No more stupid remarks about her this time, he told himself. He'd been miserable without Sam in his life, and this was his chance to make amends.

As he followed his GPS along Sam's road, Lorenzo hoped they'd have a chance to spend some time alone to catch up. Looking at his watch, he smiled, realising that his prickly Grandmother would be arriving in Winchester any moment. He hoped she'd be annoyed he wasn't there to pay homage.

Arriving at last at number 56, he gazed up at the big old house looming over him. As he walked down the overgrown path, he looked around indecisively, still clutching his phone. His finger hesitated over Sam's number; maybe he should have let him know he was coming after all. Someone came out the front door just as his resolve was failing, so he slipped in, following the stairs up to flat number 2.

'It's open.' A voice shouted from within. Lorenzo breathed a sigh of relief as he recognized Sam's voice.

He walked in cautiously, feeling like an intruder in the unfamiliar flat. A long corridor led to what looked like a sitting room. A photo caught his eye, him and Sam posing as teenagers in their karate Gi's. As he gazed at the photo,' a girl emerged from the kitchen clutching a bottle of wine.

'I hope you brought some booze, coz we—' The girl froze, staring at Lorenzo in horror as if she'd seen a ghost.

Lorenzo stared back at the stunning girl in front of him. She had black hair, falling in soft curls to her shoulders, her eyes were deep blue, framed by long dark eyelashes. She was wearing a figure-hugging black dress which accentuated her curves, and a short white denim jacket finished the look. Lorenzo held his breath, realizing that he was looking at the most beautiful girl he'd ever seen. His mouth went dry, and he knew he must have looked like a complete idiot. Forcing himself to pull it together, he took a deep breath.

'Hi, I'm looking for—'

She cut him off, walking slowly towards him.

'It's me Rez'

Lorenzo frowned, his thoughts racing around in his head as they tried desperately to make sense of what he was seeing. He knew who was talking to him, but his eyes belied the logic. The girl turned and walked into the sitting room, beckoning him to follow. He hesitated in the hallway, slumping back against the wall.

Jesus Christ, Sam, what's going on?

Steeling himself, he walked gingerly into the room; the girl was standing with her back to him, gazing out of the window. Lorenzo studied her, hoping that somehow, he'd made a mistake and she'd turn out to be a friend of Sam's. As his eyes drifted down to her soft, round hips and pert backside, he wanted badly to be right.

'You should have told me you were coming, Rez.' She turned around and smiled, that shy smile he'd known all his life.

Lorenzo swallowed, his throat suddenly dry.

'Jesus, Sam, what the hell's going on? Is this a fancy-dress party?' Lorenzo knew this was more than fancy dress, but until he heard otherwise, it was all he had.

The girl left the room, returning with two cold beers. Handing one to Lorenzo she sat down opposite him and waited. Lorenzo opened his beer and chugged half of it down, grateful to have something to do with his hands as he studied his friend.

'I'm sorry you found out like this…it wasn't–' The girl's hands twisted nervously in her lap.

'Found out what exactly?' Lorenzo's heart thumped as he asked the question, knowing yet not wanting to hear the words.

'Oh god, this is so hard for me, Rez—' She dropped her head down, her hair hiding her face.

'Are you...transitioning? Is that it?' Lorenzo wasn't at all sure if this was the term he was looking for, but it seemed a reasonable question as he struggled with his composure.

'No, no...nothing like that.' She smiled, waving a hand dismissively.

'So...what then?' Lorenzo took another huge swig of beer, grateful for the calming effect of the cold alcohol.

'I don't know Rez, it's —' Lorenzo cut her off.

'Just tell me, Sam, I'm going crazy here.' Lorenzo paced around, arms flailing in confusion as a welter of emotions threatened to undo him.

She took a shuddering breath.

'Okay, so I'll try Rez, but I'm still trying to understand it myself...just...don't judge me, okay?' The beautiful girl with Sam's face poured a huge slug of wine for herself and took a deep breath.

'When I first came here, it was so exciting. I had the freedom to really explore my sexuality, you know? I had a couple of boyfriends and learned what it's like to be 'out', the good and the bad. I had to learn to really be *myself*...ha! Sounds crazy, doesn't it? After years of hiding it, suddenly, I had the chance to shout it from the rooftops. It should have been great, Rez, this was my chance to find myself at last—' Taking a huge glug of wine, she tried to control her shaking hands.

'So…erm, what went wrong, Sam? I mean, why this?' Lorenzo swept a hand towards her.

'I wasn't happy Rez. Here I was, a gay guy in a young city…I should have felt on top of the world. But somehow, I just didn't. Something was missing. I was so confused; then I met some people…erm…drag queens, you know?' She hesitated, watching his reaction.

'Drag queens…you mean those guys that dress up and go on stage n stuff?' Lorenzo frowned, unable to see any connection between them and Sam.

'Yeah. But that isn't me, Rez,' she smiled, flicking a wrist in dismissal.

'One of them, Maxine, you'll meet her later. She took me under her wing and sort of helped me find a way to express a different part of myself…she's been a good friend.'

'I thought *I* was a good friend, Sam.'

'You're my *best* friend, Rez, but would you have been able to help me with this?' Sam smiled shyly.

'No…you're right there. Your life is so different now, Sam…I don't see where I'd fit in, I—' Lorenzo stared at the floor as the realization hit him that he was no longer part of Sam's life.

'Please Rez, I'm still me, can we —' the front door banged, and loud, raucous voices filled the air. The girl turned her head, sighing as the party guests began to arrive.

'Come on, we can't talk here.' She stood up and headed for the door; Lorenzo followed, still grieving for their lost friendship.

They left the house and walked down the road to a small pub around the corner. Sam went to the bar, and Lorenzo glanced around, realizing she seemed to know everyone; he felt out of place here, in Sam's world. As she came back with their drinks, he felt a sudden tightening in his stomach when he saw some guys looking appreciatively at her.

Jesus, Sam, do you know what you're doing?

'Is this your local?' Lorenzo asked, trying to bring the conversation back to some sense of normality.

'Our nearest one anyway.' Samantha smiled, taking a sip of her wine.

'So…erm…this is, what? Just for fun? Now and then?'

'Yeah, it's just an itch I need to scratch sometimes, Rez. The hair, the make-up, the clothes, they make me feel good, confident…you know? It's like a part of me that stays inside most of the time, but sometimes she needs to come up for air.' She searched his eyes, pleading for understanding.

The door burst open, and several laughing people fell in; glancing around, they spotted Samantha and came tumbling over.

'Hey Sammi girl, why aren't you at home playing hostess? We were just on our way over.' A tall, slim girl with amazing purple hair flung her arm around 'Sammi girl'. Lorenzo looked on in bewilderment.

'Mmm hullo gorgeous, Sammi's been keeping you a secret, hasn't she?' Purple haired girl swayed seductively over to Lorenzo, scrutinizing him through long glittery eyelashes.

'Hands off, Saira, this is my best mate from home. Rez—Saira.' Sam made the introductions quickly, all the while glaring at Saira to back off.

'Okay, okay, don't get your panties in a twist; we're going.' Saira and crew bought several bottles of champagne before sashaying out the door.

'I'll see you later, *Rez from home*,' she winked back over her shoulder.

Lorenzo grinned in spite of himself, thinking this might be fun after all.

As he looked at his friend, he felt a strange sense of admiration for making a new life, something extraordinary they'd never experienced in sleepy Winchester. Could he be part of it?

'You know, you really do look fantastic in that get-up, Sam.' Lorenzo touched her hair fleetingly before snatching his hand away.

'Thanks, Rez, but erm…could you call me Samantha or Sammi when I'm dressed up?' She played with a beer mat as she looked over at him through long black lashes.

'Oh, sure. Is that part of…the thing?' Lorenzo was completely out of his depth but was worried they might fall out again if he put his foot in it.

'Yeah. When I'm Samantha, I'm a different person…I think I might sit my exams as Samantha; she's cleverer than Sam,' she said solemnly.

'What… really? Is that—' Lorenzo realized she was laughing at him and shaking her head.

Glancing at her watch, Samantha stood up, saying they'd better get back to the house, or Chloe would kill her. On the short walk back, she hooked her arm in Lorenzo's.

'So…we're okay, Rez? I mean, you don't mind too much?' She asked hesitantly.

'Mind? It's not up to me to mind, Sam—antha, it was just such a shock, you know? I just…I don't know how I'd fit in with all this stuff. I'm just a boring cisgender straight guy from sleepy Winchester.' Lorenzo shrugged, not at all sure if he believed his own words, but they seemed to fit at that moment.

Samantha reached up on tiptoes and kissed him on the cheek.

'You're a lot of things, Rez, but never boring.'

Lorenzo tried not to react to the unexpected electricity that shot down his spine when she kissed him.

***

The music blasted down the street as they arrived back at the house, throngs of happy people gathered on the steps outside. They headed upstairs, stepping over reclining bodies draped on the stairs. Lorenzo breathed in deeply, the unmistakable smell of marijuana seeping into his lungs.

'Don't worry, that's one thing I'm not into.' Samantha smiled at him, squeezing his hand as they went in.

'Sammi, where the hell have—oh, sorry.' Chloe shouted above the din of the music.

'Rez, isn't it? This is great; Sammi didn't say you were coming.' Chloe grabbed Lorenzo and dragged him into the kitchen, thrusting a beer into his hand.

'Chloe, hi. We met last time I was here.' He shouted above the din.

'Yeah, Sam moved in a couple of months ago. Made sense, really.' she smiled, looking up from under her lashes.

'So, erm, you're not, um—' Lorenzo could have kicked himself; he really needed to get with the jargon if he wasn't going to look like a complete prat tonight.

'Haha, no, I just like hanging out with them all; they're fun. Me and Sam met everyone through Saira.' Chloe tipped her head, nodding towards the girl with the purple hair who was swaying seductively to the music, a bottle of wine was her dancing partner.

'Yeah, we've met,' he said, gazing at the lone dancer.

Saira looked over and reached her arms out, beckoning him to dance with her. Never one to refuse an invitation from a pretty girl, Lorenzo glanced at Chloe and shrugged apologetically.

'Well, you might as well. Saira always gets what she wants anyway.' She pouted, pouring herself another glass.

Saira slipped into his arms as if she belonged there, pulling him in close. She still held the bottle of wine in her hands behind his back.

'Tell me your story,' she whispered. 'I want to know all about you, Lorenzo.'

'Oh, so you know my name already?' He grinned, amused by the exotic girl in his arms.

'Mmm, I make it my business to know important things.' She said mysteriously

As they danced and talked, Lorenzo wondered where this was going; he had his answer a couple of minutes later when Saira left him to get more drinks; the next time he saw her, she was dancing with someone else. He smiled to himself, thinking he'd probably had a lucky escape.

He wandered back into the kitchen searching for a beer when a delicate bejewelled hand appeared as if from nowhere, offering him a glass of champagne.

'So you just *have* to be the infamous Rez. I'm Maxine,' she drawled.

He looked up slowly, his eyes taking in a very tight gold lame dress. So this was the drag queen that had helped Sam find his Samantha. She had to be at least six foot four as she loomed over him. He automatically looked down, checking out the towering heels, okay, five-ten then, but even so.

'Yup, that's me. Not too sure about the infamy, though,' he laughed, beginning to feel more confident amongst these exotic birds with their spangles and glitter. Now, he knew a little of their backstory.

'What do you think of our girl? Isn't she just a darling?' Maxine looked lovingly at Samantha, blowing her a kiss.

Lorenzo grimaced at the *our girl* comment, feeling inexplicably possessive; he'd known Sam far longer than this preening queen.

'I know you and Samantha go way back, and from what she's told me, you were there for her when she needed you.' Maxine sipped her champagne, studying him over the rim. 'I wish I'd had someone like you in my life all those years ago,' she continued with a half-smile.

He frowned, unsure how to respond to such a personal revelation.

'Oh really? What—' he was saved by a guy coming in behind Maxine and wrapping his arms around her.

'Kyle, darling, there you are. This is the gorgeous Lorenzo, isn't he just delicious?' She leaned back into her boyfriend's chest, turning her head for a kiss.

'Don't look so shocked, mate; she's harmless.' Kyle laughed, rolling his eyes. 'C'mon you, leave the poor boy alone.' Kyle took Maxine's arm and led her off in search of some food.

Chloe caught his eye and waved her glass by way of invitation, smiling with amusement, he went over, leaning back against the kitchen counter beside her.

'You know, I've heard all about you,' she slurred, leaning her head heavily on his shoulder.

'Oh yeah? What have you heard?' He grinned, beginning to enjoy his celebrity status.

'Well, you're his best friend *ever*, and he came out to *you* first.' She prodded him in the chest to emphasize her point.

'Yeah, that's—'

'But,' she interrupted him with a raised finger, 'You didn't know about *Samantha*, did you, huh? So that makes *me* his best friend too, doesn't it?' Chloe's eyes suddenly filled with tears, and she sniffed loudly.

'I thought when we first met, you know?' She snuffled through her blocked nose.

'Oh, right. You fancied him.' Lorenzo nodded with an understanding grin.

'I'm over it now, but sometimes–' She flapped her hand in front of her face as only girls can, trying to dismiss the unwelcome emotion.

'He was always too good looking for his own good.' Lorenzo grinned, remembering their teenage years.

'Hey, my two best friends in the whole world,' Samantha came teetering into the kitchen, towing a very handsome young man by the hand. She threw her arms around Chloe and Lorenzo, leaving her guy hovering and waiting to claim her back.

'I'm so happy you two are getting on. My life is complete,' she said theatrically, throwing an arm in the air and spilling her drink in the process.

'Rez, this is…what d'you say your name was?' she asked her guy, hanging on to him for support.

'James,' he laughed before tugging her off to dance, one arm possessively around her waist.

Lorenzo's mind was in turmoil as he watched Sam disappear off with James. Who was this guy?

Does he think Sam's a girl? How do they know who's a boy and who's a girl? How the hell does that work?

He couldn't help thinking that life in his world was a lot simpler, but then that was the problem, wasn't it? Life outside the box wasn't easy.

Ed Sheeran's 'Perfect' was playing as Lorenzo slouched against the wall, hugging his beer. He was watching Samantha and James slow dancing, she was still hanging on to him, her arms wrapped around his neck. Lorenzo didn't like the way James kept pulling her in close, hip to hip. A dark mood descended over him, and a muscle in his jaw began to twitch; he knew he should leave; he was out of his depth here. He glanced around the room as he sipped his beer, trying to force his tightly coiled body to relax. His eyes kept drifting back to Samantha, pulled by some invisible force. Chloe came over and slumped against the wall for support, sliding down it until she was sitting on the floor. Lorenzo squatted down beside her.

'Who's that guy with Samantha?'

'Wha—' Chloe lifted her head long enough to glance up.

'Dunno, but he's very cute,' she mumbled before passing out on the floor at his feet.

Lorenzo scooped her up, carrying her to her room before placing her carefully on the bed. He briefly considered leaving the party at that point; he was overwhelmed by unfamiliar emotions, and he was very drunk, but coming out of Chloe's room, he spotted Samantha and James leaving the flat. His chest tightened protectively, and his heart began to pound. He followed them down the stairs and out through the back door into the garden.

Ordinarily, Lorenzo would have been impressed with what they'd done to the garden; pretty lights were strewn through the trees, and flaming lanterns cast an orange glow down the garden path as they wound its way into the darkness. The still night air was heavy with the scent of jasmine; Lorenzo found himself thrashing through bushes and shrubs, narrowly missing an ornamental pond, as he struggled to keep up with Samantha and James. Eventually, he heard voices coming from a small gazebo tucked away at the bottom of the garden, someone shouting in distress. He ran towards the gazebo and found Samantha trying in vain to squirm out of James's grasp, her dress torn during the scuffle. Giving vent to the rage he'd been controlling all night, Lorenzo stormed into the gazebo and wrenched James away, punching him square on the jaw. Samantha flopped down on a bench, her head in her hands as Lorenzo started in on James again.

'Rez, no, leave it!' she shouted in panic.

As Lorenzo turned around at the sound of her voice, James used the opportunity to escape, thrashing away through the bushes before disappearing into the dark.

'Jesus, Sam, what happened?' Slumping down beside her, Lorenzo waited for the adrenaline to diffuse. As it did so, the alcohol kicked in, making his head swim. The scent of jasmine was intoxicating, the small white flowers invisible in the dark of the night. Samantha rested her head heavily on his shoulder, and he put his arm around her, pulling her in close.

'I wasn't…I mean, I didn't want to—' she snuffled through her tears.

'I know…I know Sam,' he whispered.

Samantha lifted her head, a deep blue gaze looking up at him through wet lashes; she smiled her shy smile as he turned towards her. His heart began to pound, and he struggled to breathe…then he reached for her, pulling her in close and kissing her deeply.

For a moment, Samantha returned the kiss, her arms wrapping around Lorenzo's neck as their bodies moved closer.

'Rez…no, stop.' She pushed him back before scooting away along the bench, needing to put a distance between them.

Lorenzo shook his head, squinting through unfocused eyes. The fog cleared slightly, and reality came crashing in, like an uninvited guest. He jumped up, staggering back, horrified at what he'd done.

'Sam? Oh no, oh my God…I'm so sorry. I don't know what—' He covered his face with his hands in a futile attempt to block out what he'd done.

'Rez, it's okay…it doesn't matter, we can—' she pleaded.

'It's not okay, Sam, what the hell just happened? Jesus Christ…it's not okay.' Lorenzo swallowed hard, trying to quell the tears that were threatening to flow as he sat down with his head in his hands. The overpowering scent of jasmine was choking his lungs as he tried to breathe.

'This is bad, Sam, really bad.' He kept his head turned from her, focusing instead on the intricate pattern of the gazebo trellis work.

'I've never felt—I mean, not like this. You're my best friend.' He jumped up again, pacing around, desperately trying to sober up and make sense of it all.

'Can't we just forget it ever happened, Rez? We're a bit drunk and—' Samantha put her hand on his arm, pleading. He flicked it away as if her very touch would undo him.

'Forget it happened? You're fucking kidding, right? No, no, this is it, Sam, I can't do it. If this is what you want,' he waved an arm in the general direction of the house, 'then you do it without me. It's too hard for me, Sam, I can't—' His voice cracked as he tried to control the overwhelming sadness engulfing him.

Lorenzo left the gazebo, wracked with feelings of shame and disgust, to find his way back through the garden. His head was spinning as he tried to rationalize what just happened. James suddenly appeared from nowhere and was startled to see Lorenzo again; he held his hands up, apologetic.

'I'm sorry, man…I didn't mean—'

'Ever heard of consent, mate?' Lorenzo interrupted, resisting the urge to punch him again.

James grinned, shrugging his shoulders cockily.

'Yeah 'course, but she did. Why else would she have—'

The punch knocked him back into the pond with a satisfying splash, followed by copious swearing.

As Lorenzo waited, fists still clenched, he hoped the little creep would come back for more. His thoughts raced around in his head like cars on a track and he tried to slow them down, capture them. Finding a small window of clarity, he realized he needed to get away.

Looking down at his phone, he checked the time. It was 3 am, and he didn't know where to go. He collected his bag from Sam's flat and mercifully made it out without any awkward questions. Setting his GPS, he made his way through the dark streets to the station and curled up on a bench to wait for the first train. He was sober now but wished he wasn't.

The 5.00 am out of Bristol trundled its way slowly out of the station as Lorenzo huddled in his seat, curled into the window. Ignoring his phone as it screamed for attention, he glanced down at his jeans, torn and muddy from rampaging around the garden in the dark. He briefly considered going to the toilets to clean up, but then he realized he didn't give flying stuff what anyone thought. He'd lost his best friend, probably for good, and it was his own fault. He'd crossed a line, and he couldn't see a way back.

Chapter 15

'Oi, Murphy, have you got those reports for me yet?' Lorenzo's boss, Richie, yelled across the room, clicking his fingers impatiently.

'No, I haven't, I thought you said next week?' Lorenzo sighed; Richie seemed to be on his case at the moment.

'Yeah, I did last week.'

'Twat.' Nick sniggered as he walked past. Lorenzo whirled around, ready to confront him, when Gemma caught his arm and steered him away to get a coffee.

'Don't rise to it, Rez. Everyone knows Nick's a tosser,' she grinned, closing the door to the coffee room.

'What's up with you anyway? You've been miserable for weeks.' She handed him a coffee and leaned back against the worktop.

Lorenzo was confused about his relationship with Gemma. Was she just a work colleague, or was there something more? She always seemed to be interested in the minutiae of his life, but that could just be a girl thing.

'Tell you what, come out for dinner, and I'll tell you everything.'

'Every single thing?' her eyes narrowed as she waited for his answer.

'Hmm, could take a few dinners to cover it all.' He grinned.

***

A loud crash thundered out from the kitchens, and the restaurant erupted with cheering and clapping. Lorenzo and Gemma were seated in a cosy corner of what had become their favorite restaurant. A candle on the table flickered its orange glow as Gemma played with the melting wax. This was their second dinner date, which Gemma had dubbed Project Tuscany. Lorenzo had decided not to say anything about Sam; that night was firmly locked away, and he was trying to throw away the key.

'Right then, series one, episode two. Have you said anything to your parents yet?' Gemma smiled as she settled in to hear more of Lorenzo's family dramas.

Two bottles of shiraz later, and Lorenzo was emotionally drained; having analyzed and dissected it all once again, he felt like it wasn't happening to him like it was a story he'd read about. Gemma sipped her wine, her head cocked to one side as she absorbed the story.

'So…you still think this Lorenzo guy in the photo is your father?' Reaching across the table she gently took his hand.

'What else can I think Gemms? It's the only obvious conclusion, isn't it?' Lorenzo swallowed the lump in his throat and turned his head away, unable to bear the pain reflected in Gemma's eyes.

'…But he's so much older than her.' Gemma studied the photo' squinting at the enlarged image.

'Yeah, I think it must have been a holiday romance; maybe he was a local, working the bar or something. Came on to a pretty naïve English girl? Wouldn't be the first time that has happened, would it?' Taking a gulp of his wine, Lorenzo thumped his glass down, the impact causing their cutlery to jump as it hit the table.

'Sorry. Sorry Gemms, I'm not great company when I talk about all this crap.' Lorenzo sighed, then tried to smile, but it didn't quite work.

'I want to know Rez. I hate to see you so unhappy. I'd like to help if you'd let me.' She looked at him shyly, pushing a long lock of blonde hair behind her ear. Lorenzo grinned as the errant lock of hair escaped once more; he longed to reach over and tuck it in, just to feel the silky texture.

He realized that whilst it was very flattering that this beautiful girl was happy to sit and listen as he opened his life up, he wanted to know more about her and hear her stories, too. They'd kissed after their last date, and he was hopeful something would come from their blossoming friendship.

'So, are you saying you want to cheer me up?' He wiggled his eyebrows suggestively.

'Hmm. I s'pose I walked into that one, didn't I?' She laughed before cocking her head to one side.

'Do you love your parents, Rez?' She looked up at him from under her lashes.

Lorenzo frowned, jerking his head back in shock at the crass, hurtful question.

'What? Of course I do, that's a—' Gemma raised her hand, cutting him off.

'So the only question should be, does your father know? He brought you up, loved you and cared for you. He is your father, Rez.'

'You don't understand, Gemma, I can't—'

'I'm adopted Rez. I understand.'

Stunned into silence, Lorenzo looked at her across the table; he struggled to compose his face, aware that his mouth had dropped open. His thoughts flashed back to all their dinner dates, how self-indulgent he'd been, droning on about his family when all the time she'd gone through much worse. Or so he assumed. She smiled, sensing his discomfort.

'I'm sorry Rez. I didn't mean to just spurt it out like that, it's just—'

'I know, I know. I've been an arse, ranting on about my own problems; why didn't you tell me before?'

Gemma reached for the dwindling candle again, squeezing the melting edges in as the flame flickered angrily at the intrusive fingers.

'It's not something I feel the need to tell people, Rez. Their first reaction is to feel sorry for me as if my life has been something less because of it. I have a lovely family; my parents are great. I have no idea who my biological parents are, and I don't really want to know. It's not—' Gemma looked up and smiled at their waitress as she cleared their table, plonking a dessert menu in front of them. Lorenzo looked at her quizzically, then told the waitress they would have the bill.

'…I can only speak from my own experience, Rez, and I can't imagine my life being any better for searching for my birth parents. Maybe it would help you to think of it in those terms. Anyway, you know who your Mum is.'

They paid the bill and left the restaurant, strolling through Winchester high street in the balmy summer evening. Cutting down along the river towpath, they stopped to look down on the clear, cool water as it babbled over the ancient stones below.

'Thank you,' he whispered into her hair.

Turning towards him, Gemma reached up on tiptoes to kiss him, his arms folded around her as he pulled her in close as the kiss deepened. A memory bubbled to the surface from deep within, another kiss, a gazebo in a garden and a girl with black hair. He pulled away, desperate to banish the unwanted image in his head.

'Erm…are you okay Rez? What's wrong?' Gemma put her hand on his arm, the gesture seeming to pull him back to reality.

'Oh jeez…I'm sorry, Gemms. Just too much wine, I guess.' He shrugged, attempting a smile that didn't quite reach his eyes.

'It's all been a bit heavy tonight, hasn't it?' She hooked her arm in his as they strolled towards the taxi rank.

'Yeah, I must admit, it doesn't exactly make for a relaxing evening, does it?'

'Next time, come round to me; I'll cook for us.' Gemma kissed him lightly before jumping into her taxi.

Lorenzo strolled home slowly, berating himself for ruining the moment by the river. The scent of jasmine filled the warm night air, fueling the memory he was desperately trying to erase. Was that night with Sam going to haunt him every time he kissed someone? It hadn't happened the last few times he'd kissed Gemma. Why tonight? Maybe it was the wine. He resolved to stick to beer from now on.

***

The early morning sun peeped in through a gap in his curtains and was shimmering across his eyes as Lorenzo emerged from sleep, lost in those first few moments of bliss before reality crashes in, bringing with it angst and despair. He reached an arm out for his headphones, adjusting the volume to drown out the radio from downstairs; Ed Sheeran's 'Perfect' was playing, stabbing at his heart as he recalled the fateful night at Sam's.

Going over it all again, he tried to understand what had happened and why, alternating between blaming himself and blaming Sam. They'd both been very drunk, but that was nothing new; he and Sam had spent many happy nights getting hammered, but he'd never, ever felt that way about him. Starting from the moment he entered the flat, he replayed every word, every movement, agonizing as each new memory surfaced. He had reached for Sam. As much as he'd like to blame Sam, Lorenzo knew the guilt lay with him. He wished it had been the other way around; he would have forgiven Sam, but he couldn't forgive himself.

A small unwelcome twinge nibbled away at the back of his mind; like a little burrowing beetle, he refused to let it in, shutting an imaginary door in its face. Was he being truly honest with himself?

For months after that night, Sam had texted and left numerous voicemails, pleading with Lorenzo to respond. Even Chloe contacted him through Facebook, wondering why Sam was so miserable; he hadn't responded and had blocked Sam from all his media, unable to cope with seeing him. He added cowardice to his list of failings, along with guilt and shame.

His thoughts returned to last night and the kiss with Gemma; he chuckled to himself wondering why kissing seemed to be the root cause of all his troubles recently. Removing his headphones, he crossed to the window and pulled back the curtains, the sunlight dazzling him as he peered out. St Catherine's Hill rose high against the deep blue of the sky. He could just about see the walkers trekking up from the car park; some of them had backpacks and walking poles. He remembered running up there with Sam in their karate training days, no backpacks or poles for them, just a bottle of water when they reached the top, laughing and panting as they collapsed on the grass. He smiled at the happy memory just before the little red devil with the pitchfork stabbed him in the heart.

Patting his stomach as he stood in front of his mirror, Lorenzo frowned as the flesh wobbled slightly. He knew he needed to get back into karate training; he was working towards his second Dan black belt but was finding it difficult to get to the classes whilst squeezing in his scuba training. Flexing his muscles in the mirror, he wondered what Gemma would think, she'd offered to cook for him at her place, did that mean? He promised himself he'd go to the gym a few times next week, just in case.

'Hey Rez, you coming down or what?' his sister bellowed up the stairs. Ali had been insufferable lately as her birthday loomed closer. It seemed to Lorenzo that the whole world was overrun by squealing teenage girls…well, his house, anyway.

Arriving in the kitchen on a mission to find food, he was momentarily dazzled by pink glittery banners strewn across the table proclaiming Eighteen in very shouty letters. Ignoring the fluttery gaze of several preening girls, Lorenzo foraged in the fridge, emerging with three eggs and a slice of pizza, which he ate whilst breaking the eggs into a pan. As he waited for the omelette to cook, he leaned back against the kitchen counter, enjoying the admiring glances from his sister's friends.

'We're having a joint party, Rez; the three A's. It's gonna be great.' Ali had been best friends with the girls for as long as Lorenzo could remember;

their names all began with 'A', and they'd made a pact never to allow any other girls to join their group unless their name began with 'A'. Lorenzo had laughed, and their parents had worried, thinking that sooner or later, the gang would have to diversify, but it had never happened; the three 'A's had reigned supreme. Annabelle, Abby and Alice had surprised them all.

Lorenzo sat down with his omelette, smothering it in tomato ketchup before tucking in. Last night's pasta and salad were all very well, but he had muscles to feed; he needed protein.

'How's the party arrangements going, girls?' He glanced around at the excited faces.

'We're just making a list of names for invites; what's Sam's address at Bristol Rez?' Ali waited, fingers poised on her keyboard, unaware of the large black pit that had opened under her brother.

The realization hit him like a thunderbolt. Of course, she'd want Sam there; he was like a second brother to her; she'd even wanted to marry him at one point.

Aware of the happy, eager faces waiting for his response, Lorenzo played for time, chasing his food around the plate and chewing slowly. He could hear the girls babbling about Sam in the background, how good-looking he was and what a shame he was gay, each one of them convinced they had the charms to seduce him, dissolving into giggles as they connived ever more bizarre tricks to snare him.

'Well?' Alice tapped her hand on the table, impatient for an answer.

'Erm…I'll—' Lorenzo was forever grateful as his phone pinged a message from Jinx.

Don't forget holiday meeting at 2 pm.

Lorenzo's fingers worked fast; Phone me, NOW

The phone rang, and he quickly snatched it up. Ali glared at him, her brow furrowed and her lips pursed as she tapped the table impatiently. She knew her brother very well. Following a very heated conversation with a perplexed Jinx, Lorenzo shrugged an apology to the party girls, claiming an urgent appointment as he made a hasty retreat.

Back in the sanctuary of his room, he flopped on his bed, one arm flung over his face in a futile attempt to block out the world.

Would this nightmare never end? The ripples from that night were turning into giant waves, and Lorenzo was drowning.

Chapter 16

The university dental surgeries buzzed with the incessant whine of high-speed drills, the moulded plastic head in Sam's lap stared up at him with dead eyes. Chloe glanced over, grimacing as she attempted to extract a large molar from her plastic patient.

'Don't worry, this won't hurt a bit,' she giggled, patting her patient's forehead.

Today, they were under the watchful eye of The Vulture, the hapless tutor, so named because of her huge red nose and baggy neck, which wobbled when she shook her head. The Vulture wandered over, peering into the open mouth of Sam's dummy. Chloe watched as the tutor plucked an instrument from Sam's tray, thrusting it into his hand, her scraggy neck quivering with rage. An altercation ensued, and Sam stormed out, sending his patient rolling under a chair.

Alarmed at Sam's behaviour, Chloe immediately put down her forceps and started to pack her instruments away. She paused as the Vulture wandered over, tapping a small mirror on her upturned palm. The tutor shook her head sadly as her eyes followed Sam's departure.

'Go then. Talk some sense into him before he blows his career.' She flicked her hand dismissively. Chloe nodded her thanks and picked up her bags.

'And Chloe? Don't let him drag you down, too; you have the makings of a great dentist.'

Chloe dashed out, needing to catch Sam before he hit the bars. She knew where he'd be and ran to their local pub. Sure enough, he was there, halfway through his second pint.

'If you're here on a mission to save me, forget it, Chlo'. I'm fine.' Sam attempted a smile, succeeding in raising one corner of his mouth.

'I wish you'd talk to me Sam, I'm worried about you, ever since—'

'D'you want a drink then or what?' Sam interrupted her, sliding his chair out and heading to the bar. He returned with another beer and a diet coke, placing it in front of her with a sigh.

'Look, Chlo', I really appreciate that you're concerned, but I just need to work this out myself, alright? Me and Rez, we just got our wires crossed. It'll be fine, don't worry.' Sam downed the rest of his pint, then set to work on the third.

'You shouldn't have come out, Chlo', the Vulture will mark you down.'

'She's worried about you too, Sam, she—'

'Oh, for god's sake, why can't everyone just mind their own bloody business.' Slugging back the rest of his beer, Sam slammed the glass down on the table.

'Go back, Chlo', please. Just let me sort out my own life, okay?' He stomped out of the pub, leaving Chloe to stare after him in frustration; tears filled her eyes as she realized she had no idea how to help him.

After wandering around aimlessly for a while, Sam found himself in the park, slumped on a bench clutching a beer. His eyes rested on a group of mothers playing with their children, their squeals of delight highlighting his own misery. As he opened a can and took a swig, he felt the hostile glare from the women as they subconsciously moved closer to their children. Sam was about to move away but changed his mind; why shouldn't he sit in the park? Okay, the beers in the middle of the day probably gave the wrong impression, and he hadn't realized he was sitting opposite the children's playground. His brow furrowed as a thought occurred to him; if it was Samantha sitting here, they probably wouldn't have looked twice. Sam had not yet been out on his own as Samantha; he suddenly felt a yearning for his box on top of the wardrobe, untouched since that fateful night.

As his feeling of discomfort grew, under the wave of disapproval from the mothers in the park, Sam reluctantly moved away to another bench; this time, he sat and watched a large dog delightedly chase after a frisbee, his long pink tongue lolling out of his mouth.

He smiled wistfully to himself, missing his own big furry dog. He longed to go home for a visit but that usually meant meeting up with Rez, going to their pub, reliving old times. He couldn't bear the thought of being in Winchester and not seeing him. It would just be wrong. He'd tried several times to contact his friend but had had no response.

Opening another beer, his thoughts returned to that fateful night in the garden. Sam's memory of events was very fuzzy; he knew he'd been in the gazebo with some guy and that things had got out of hand; he remembered Rez dashing in and punching the guy, *my very own knight in shining armour*; he smiled a wry smile wondering how it had all gone so wrong. Sipping his beer, he suddenly felt a thump on his leg as a large bundle of fur clutching a frisbee crashed into him.

'Sorry mate, he's just a puppy. No manners yet.' The dog's owner came dashing over, grabbing his collar before hauling him away.

'Ah, you're alright.' Sam grinned as he patted the slavering mutt's head.

He continued his reminiscing, painful though it was, focusing on the kiss, trying hard to recall the details; he'd gone over it time and again; who instigated it? He knew he would never have come on to Rez; the thought had never crossed his mind, all those years together, and he'd never ever—suddenly, a light breeze washed over him, bringing with it the sweet aroma of Jasmine, and he knew. It was Rez…he'd reached for him, pulling him in. Sam remembered kissing him back, remembered the heady scent of Jasmine as it entwined around the gazebo. Closing his eyes, Sam allowed himself to re-live the moment. He'd returned the kiss, moving into Rez's arms as if it was the most natural thing in the world, feeling as though he belonged there. His heart pounded, and his chest tightened as his memory replayed the forgotten images aided and abetted by the intoxicating scent of the breeze. He remembered being lost in the embrace, their bodies responding as they moved closer. Sam chased the image as it threatened to drift away; he watched the scene play out, realizing it was him who'd pulled away, their moment of madness ending as quickly as it had begun.

He inhaled deeply, desperately trying to remember what had happened next. The memory surfaced slowly, reluctantly. Rez had jumped up, horrified at what he'd done.

'Hey man, are you okay?' Sam snapped out of his reverie, looking around in confusion as he tried to locate the source of the intrusive voice. It was the guy with the dog; his brows were furrowed in concern as he looked down at Sam.

'Oh, hi. Yeah, just having a bad day, you know.' Sam sat up straight and wiped his eyes, embarrassed to feel tears on his cheeks.

'Must have fallen asleep,' he mumbled.

'Okay, well, if you're sure you're okay?' the guy called to his dog and put him on the lead before strolling off down the path.

Sam sat for a while, trying to compose his thoughts before moving off. He briefly revisited the event once more, relieved that it was him who'd broken the embrace first.

But the worst image of all, the one that was burning him up inside, was the look of disgust on Rez's face when he'd realized what he'd done.

***

Chloe gazed around the dressing room, the glitz and glitter making a mockery of her sullen mood. She glanced over at Maxine, watching her facial contortions as she applied yet another layer of makeup.

'Come on then, kiddo…spill.' Maxine raised an eyebrow and paused for a moment to glance at Chloe through her giant mirror.

'Don't you ever get sick of all this Max?' Chloe waved an arm around the dressing room. Maxine sighed and put down her make-up brush, swivelling around in her chair.

'I s'pose this is about our gorgeous girl again?'

'He's not a girl, Max, he's a guy and…and—' Chloe choked on her words, knowing Maxine could see through her charade.

'And you're in love with him.' Maxine said gently.

'What? Don't be ridiculous. You know Sam isn't interested in me like that,' she sat back, folding her arms crossly.

'We can't help who we fall in love with, kiddo, mother nature has to get her kicks somehow.' Maxine's lip curled in a wry smile as she reached for Chloe's hands, holding them gently in her own.

'I'm just so worried about him, Max, ever since that party at our place. Something happened between him and his friend from back home, but he won't tell me. Just shuts me out. How can I help him if he won't let me in?' Chloe's voice quivered as she clutched Maxine's hands.

'Ten minutes, girls.' Saira shouted as she poked her head round the dressing room door, stabbing her watch by way of demonstration. Her hair was bright blue today, and she flicked it back, lifting an eyebrow at Chloe. Chloe grinned, holding up her thumbs in approval.

Maxine glanced up, waving Saira away with a dismissive wave of her bejewelled hand.

'Look, Chlo.' I really need to go; I promised Madame S I'd lead the girls out tonight. Don't want to let her down. There's a scout coming from TV and she wants to impress her, something about a TV series about us gorgeous gals.'

'Madame S? That's so funny, poor Saira, she tries so hard.' Chloe managed a watery smile and gently pulled her hands free from Maxine's.

'Tell you what, why don't Kyle and I invite you two over for supper, and we can interroga— I mean, talk to Sam and see if we can get it out of him.' Maxine stood up, arms outstretched for a hug as she towered over Chloe on her six-inch heels. Grateful for the hug, Chloe moved in, wrapping her arms around Maxine's waist as her head nestled under the large, soft bosom. Chloe left the dressing room as Maxine made a 'call me' gesture.

Arriving back at their flat, Chloe headed straight for the kitchen, sighing with relief as she spotted Sam's shoes and socks carelessly abandoned in the hallway. As she filled the kettle, her eyes fell on a half-empty bottle of vodka on the kitchen table.

Following a trail of discarded clothing to Sam's room, she found him face down on his bed, snoring quietly. She hovered uncertainly in the doorway before deciding to go in and check on him. Satisfied he was breathing okay, she tilted his head slightly just in case he was sick.

Sitting down at his desk, she studied him for a while, noting he needed a haircut as his thick black hair curled down over his neck. Feeling like some sort of perverted voyeur, Chloe knew she should leave the room, but she was mesmerized as her eyes travelled down his body. Having thrown off his shirt and jeans, Sam was still wearing his boxers, so she didn't feel it was too indecent to sit and admire that which she couldn't have.

As she did so, Chloe thought back to her conversation with Max. Am I in love with Sam? Maybe just a little bit. Can you be just a little bit in love? Wasn't there a song about that? Maybe you could since there was a song about it.

Pondering on this, the object of her unrequited love stirred, flipping over onto his back. His snoring increased, and his breathing was laboured. Worried he might choke if he was sick, she went over to the bed to turn him over onto his front again. Gripping one shoulder, she tried to heave the dead weight but couldn't get him to move. Sam grunted and shrugged off her efforts irritably. Chloe stood back, her lips pursed in concentration, wondering how she could get him to move.

As she looked at his slumbering form, her eyes drifted down his slim, muscular body. She watched his chest rise and fall as his breathing deepened.

Her gaze drifted down his legs, and she smiled to herself, remembering the day she'd tried to wax the thick dark hair; he'd shrieked in pain and stomped off, saying he'd shave them. He'd obviously not bothered with that either, as the hair was now thick and dark once more.

Sam grunted and turned his head towards her, his eyes still closed in sleep.

She had always envied his long dark eyelashes, much too pretty for a boy, she'd thought. She remembered his friend's comment at their party. Sam had always been far too good-looking. She leaned in and kissed him chastely on the forehead, wiping a strand of hair away from his face.

'Sleep well.' she whispered before leaving the room.

Chapter 17

Lorenzo was listening to his favourite Troye Sivan track whilst making a sandwich in the kitchen. Suddenly, his earphones were yanked out, and Troye's voice quickly faded. He looked around in alarm as his father loomed over him, his face contorted with rage.

'Answer your mother when she talks to you.'

'Jeez, Dad, you nearly ripped my head off. I didn't hear her, did I?' Lorenzo looked at his mother, his hands held out in exasperation.

'Sorry Rez. It's just that I never get a chance to talk to you these days; you're always out, and when you are here, you're cosseted away in your room.' Angie glared at her husband, a warning shot across the room; *keep out of it.*

'What did you want to talk about.' Lorenzo asked brusquely as he sliced a banana onto a layer of peanut butter sandwich.

Angie glanced at Jim, who raised an enquiring eyebrow.

'Erm, I just wondered when you were getting back from your diving holiday. You know it's Ali's birthday party that same night?' Angie asked tentatively.

'So you do know when I'm getting back then?' Lorenzo asked, not unreasonably, he thought.

'Watch your tone, my lad.' Jim interjected over the top of his newspaper.

Lorenzo took a bite of his sandwich and scrolled through his phone.

'I don't appreciate you looking at your bloody phone when I'm trying to have a conversation with you, Rez, ' Angie said irritably.

Lorenzo sighed and held up his phone, showing her his boarding pass with the flight times.

'Oh. Well, that's okay; you should be here in plenty of time for the party.' Angie looked over at Jim, grimacing at her faux pas.

'Yeah, well, that's if I decide to go.' He said with a nonchalant shrug.

'You're bloody going whether you like it or not.' Jim barked; this time, Angie was grateful for his support.

'What? What do you mean? You can't *not go*. Ali would be devastated. Sam's going to be there; you'll want to see him, surely?' Angie was really worried now; there must be something very wrong if he didn't want to go to the party.

Lorenzo's stomach tightened at the mention of Sam's name. Ali must have got hold of him somehow, maybe through her friend's older brother. What the hell was Sam thinking, even accepting the invitation? He suddenly laughed out loud as an image of Samantha arriving at the party popped into his head. That would put an end to the three 'A's big plans to seduce Sam.

'Why don't you want to go? I don't unders—' Lorenzo cut his mother off with a sharp wave of his hand.

'I just don't okay, Mum?' He snapped.

Angie's patience deserted her at that point and she gave vent to her frustration.

'What the hell's going on with you, Rez? Has something happened at work? Is it a girl? Come on, we've always been open and honest with each—'

'Open and honest? Oh right, just like you're open and honest with me, eh mum?' Lorenzo grabbed his phone and earphones and stomped out.

Angie and Jim sat in stunned silence for a moment, trying to make sense of their son's angry words.

'What the hell was that all about?' Angie looked at her husband, hoping to find the answer written on his face. It wasn't. Jim was as puzzled as she was. They'd had the conversation a couple of times in the last few months, wondering what was going on with Lorenzo. Usually a happy, easy-going character, he'd suddenly become morose and bad-tempered with them. They'd assumed a girl was to blame; maybe a relationship had gone wrong. Angie was proud of the fact that her son was always able to talk to her honestly and openly about his life without fear of condemnation. Whatever was upsetting him now must be pretty bad.

'It must have something to do with someone who's going to be at the party.' Jim poured himself a whiskey, tilting the glass towards his wife. Angie shook her head; she needed a clear mind.

'Did you see how his face changed when you mentioned Sam? Could they have fallen out somehow?' Angie's lips pursed in concentration as she tried to follow the timeline. 'And why did he laugh so suddenly…what was so funny?'

'Hmm. Let's see now, he went to Bristol that weekend your mother came down, didn't he?' Jim took a swig from his glass, frowning as he concentrated on the dates.

Angie jumped up and grabbed her phone, scrolling through the calendar with an elegant finger.

'Yes, that's right, he was supposed to go on a diving trip but went to see Sam instead. I remember I was annoyed at him leaving when Mum was coming down.' Her brows knitted as she remembered yet another row.

'Well, can't say I blame him, love; your mother's not exactly nice to him, is she?' Jim's eyebrows rose knowingly.

'Yes, I know Jim, and you know why. He's the spitting image of—' Alice interrupted, bounding into the room with great excitement at something she'd seen on YouTube.

'Oh my god, Mum, you just have to see this.' Plonking herself down beside Angie, she began to tap on her keys.

Angie and Jim shared a resigned look…later.

***

Back in his room, Lorenzo lay on his bed and replaced his headphones. Troye was still singing.

Tell me we'll make it through

Please don't leave me

Now I'm vulnerable, so sad and alone

Listening to the lyrics, a fog gradually cleared from his brain as the epiphany unfolded. Why am I being such an idiot? Sam's my best mate, more like a brother, really; surely I'm big enough to move on from my mistake?

He knew Sam had forgiven him and had wanted their friendship to continue but could they just forget it ever happened? It had been such a shock to see him dressed as a girl…a beautiful girl. But what if it happened again? What if they were drunk and Sam was Samantha? He knew it was Sam who'd pulled away first; what if he hadn't? Lorenzo had agonized over the what-ifs ever since that night, but tonight, with Troye's encouragement, he messaged Sam.

Hey buddy, how are you doing?

Having sent the message, he stared at his phone, willing it to ping back but worried in case he'd pushed Sam away for good. Clicking absently through diving websites, he tried to focus on his upcoming holiday. Liz had booked them into a dive school that had accommodation, assuring them that the 'Après Dive' was always great fun. Ordinarily, he wouldn't have been able to afford to stay on-site, but for some strange reason, his grandmother had sent him a cheque for £1,000. She'd given Ali the same for her birthday, so Lorenzo was surprised to receive something, too. He'd often wondered why his grandmother was so cold towards him; he knew it was something to do with his father, but why take it out on him? It wasn't his fault that his mother had got herself pregnant by some Italian lothario.

Lorenzo had planned, once he'd had it out with his parents, to try and trace his biological father. He couldn't decide whether to give him an almighty punch in the face or give him a hug, the former giving him the most satisfaction. He imagined turning up at his father's work, or maybe his house and the look of horror on his face as the realization hit him. Lorenzo would say, 'Hullo, Dad'. Or maybe he'd try a covert mission to get to know him first, although the resemblance to Lorenzo senior would render that plan not quite so covert. But first, he needed to confront his mother, demand to know the truth….and what about his father? How much did he know? Did Angie have an affair? It wouldn't be unusual for a guy to bring up another man's child as his own. The dates all worked; they'd been married for twenty-two years, maybe she had been pregnant with him when they married.

As Lorenzo agonized over dates and events, his phone pinged; he reached for it, hesitating for a moment when he saw Sam's name, realizing how much he wanted him back in his life.

Not great tbh mate, great to hear from you though, I ...erm, don't really know where to start ...are we okay?

I hope so, I'm sorry Sam, I know it was all my fault, I was so disgusted with myself I just couldn't face you.

We were very drunk Rez, it doesn't matter who did what, let's just move on...if we can?

Of course we can, I love you man, can't lose you over this.

Lorenzo punched the air in jubilation before messaging back, telling Sam about his diving trip and how he'd be arriving back on the morning of the party. They arranged to meet in the Bishops Tavern at 7 pm that night. His stomach flipped at the thought of having to talk about that night in Bristol, but it had to be done before they could move on.

Glancing at his watch, he realized he was running late; he and Jinx were meeting in town to get some last-minute holiday stuff. He dashed downstairs, hearing the drone of conversation from the kitchen. As he popped his head in, his parents stopped talking, both heads turning simultaneously.

'Just so you know…I'll be going to the party,' he said to no one in particular.

Angie's eyebrows shot up in surprise before knitting together in a suspicious frown. Jim's expression didn't change at all. He just glared at his son and sniffed loudly.

'This isn't over, my lad; you owe us an explanation.' Jim used his 'my house, my rules' voice, the one that meant business. Lorenzo was about to fire back but didn't want to get into another argument. He let his father have the last word as he headed out the front door, resisting the temptation to slam it very hard.

As he walked into town, Lorenzo had a spring in his step; he felt as though he wanted to skip along the road like a little child. Everything was going to be great now that he and Sam were back on track. A couple of small niggles threatened to mar his good mood; what if their friendship had changed? What if Samantha was a permanent part of Sam's life? Did it matter anyway? So many what-ifs. Lorenzo shut the door on his doubts; even his family dilemma didn't seem so insurmountable now.

Chapter 18

Lorenzo gazed out of the small window as the jet soared into the sky, leaving Gatwick airport far behind. The flight to Malta should take around four hours, the captain had announced the temperature was 37 degrees. Malik was seated in the middle seat next to Lorenzo, his incessant chatter beginning to get on his nerves.

The buzz around their two rows of seats was palpable as the boys tried to contain their excitement. Jinx was sitting behind them with their club instructor, Liz, who smiled indulgently as she fielded all their questions.

'Will we be on boats Liz, or just walk straight in like?' Malik had swivelled around in his seat, struggling to peep through the gap to the seats behind.

'It all depends, Mal. Deffo boats if we go to Gozo.' Liz smiled indulgently, enjoying her mother-hen role.

'Gozo…wow. Where's that?' Malik's excitement grew as Liz described the small, quiet island north of Malta. Lorenzo smiled to himself; he'd read all about Gozo and was hoping they'd get a chance to go.

'You know Mal, there's another island in between Malta and Gozo called Comino, apparently, there's a cave you can swim through.' Lorenzo couldn't resist flaunting his superior knowledge but soon regretted it as Malik erupted with shouts of whooping. Liz passed a very battered old

PADI dive magazine through the gap, tapping a finger on an article about a Blue Lagoon.

'You know, I'm really worried about my ears, Liz.' Jinx pulled on his ear lobe by way of demonstration. 'It still feels blocked.'

'Didn't you have them syringed…like I told you?' Liz sighed, shaking her head.

'Yeah, I did, cost me a fortune, too, coz the nurse at my surgery doesn't do it anymore.'

'Well, we'll just have to wait and see how it goes then, stop worrying, you'll be fine.' She patted his hand reassuringly.

As the flight ploughed its way south, Malik was absorbed in the ancient magazine, constantly nudging Lorenzo to point out anything about Malta.

'Rez, mate, look at this…St Paul was ship-wrecked here; they named a bay after him. Isn't that great?' A long, slim finger stabbed at the article.

'St Who?'

'Bloody hell, Rez, don't you know anything? St Paul. Like the cathedral.'

'Oh, right…him.' Lorenzo mumbled. 'How come you know about *him* then, I thought you were Hindu.'

'Nah mate, don't let this Brown skin fool you…I'm a good Catholic boy.' Malik grinned as he crossed himself piously.

'Yeah? My bad for assuming then, do you go to church?' Lorenzo twisted in his seat, seeing his friend in a new light.

'Not anymore. I did when I was a kid, but it stays with you. That's why I never tell lies, Rez; I'm scared of going straight to hell if I die, man.' Malik shook his head as the fear of everlasting damnation contorted his features.

'You'd better go to confession before we dive then…just in case of sharks.' The look of horror on Malik's face had Lorenzo curled up with laughter.

The drone of the engines had a soporific effect on everyone, and they soon settled down, each lost in their own vision of what the coming week would bring.

***

As the plane bumped down and coasted to a halt, the eager passengers were out of their seats and scrambling about collecting their belongings. Overhead lockers were flung open as bags were swept down in a frenzy. The cabin crew watched the scene unfold with fixed smiles, having seen it a thousand times before. Finally, all movement ceased as they waited for the doors to open, grumbling about being kept waiting.

Lorenzo inched his way down the aisle, trying to be polite, allowing others to join the line in front of him. However, having made little progress after twenty minutes, he decided he'd been gallant enough for one day and joined the masses, barging his way through.

Stepping out of the plane, Lorenzo felt like he was being hit by a blast from a hundred hairdryers. The hot air blew around his face as he descended the steps onto the tarmac, the ground shimmering in the blinding sunlight. As he waited for the others to catch up, he wondered how he could possibly put on a wetsuit in this heat.

Leaving the airport far behind, the little minibus clattered its way through the narrow back streets. The driver honked her horn every few minutes at some perceived insult by another driver as she swung the vehicle in and out of parked cars. Lorenz's first impression of Malta was that it was noisy and crowded but somehow charming. He gazed with awe at the baroque limestone churches, their huge domes dominating each village. The sun dipped lower in the sky, bathing the ancient stonework in a golden glow as the mini-bus ground to a halt with a squeal of tyres. Their driver jumped out, introducing herself as Melissa, as she began opening the doors for their luggage. Gazing around the long, narrow street with tired eyes, Lorenzo saw nothing resembling a diving club. *Maybe we're not staying on site after all.*

'Okay, upstairs, first floor....' Melissa opened a heavy wooden door impatiently, ushering them all inside whilst shouting at an irate driver in Maltese.

Malik sidled up to Lorenzo, looking around apprehensively at the narrow, dark hallway being indicated by their host.

'Erm, what d'you think, bro', doesn't look much like the brochure, does it?'

'I really don't care, mate; I just want a beer and a bed.' Lorenzo groaned, picking up his bag.

They all traipsed up the narrow stairs, bags bashing against the walls as they went. Melissa stopped at the first room along a dark corridor; opening the door, she gestured impatiently, shooing Lorenzo and Malik in. The room was basic but adequate for their needs. Two single beds with a massive dark wooden wardrobe between them, a very ornately carved chest of drawers and an en suite bathroom. The floors were marble, with an intricate diamond pattern of reds and blues. Lorenzo thought it looked more Egyptian than Maltese, but then he didn't know much about either. An enormous ceiling fan swirled lazily above them, dispersing the hot air from one side of the room to the other.

Just as he and Malik were beginning to regret staying 'on site,' Liz stuck her head round the door.

'Beer's downstairs anyone?' Ordinarily a reasonable question, but on this occasion, she feared for her life as the stampede to get downstairs almost floored her. Jinx met them in the dark, dingy passageway as Liz appeared, grinning at their expectant faces.

'Cold beers, Liz…where for god's sake?' Jinx spun around, looking for a pub or restaurant, but could see no sign of life apart from a mangy cat who hissed at them.

Tapping the side of her nose, secret style, Liz rang the doorbell of a very battered old wooden door. As the boys waited in trepidation, the door swung open to the sound of laughter and clinking glasses. A very tall guy with a huge beard stood back to usher them in.

'Welcome to Ghar Id Dud dive club, guys, first beer's on the house, don't drink too much as we're off early tomorrow.' He grinned, slapping Malik on the back with great enthusiasm.

Lorenzo was never so grateful for a drink as he was that night; opening his throat, he emptied the ice-cold liquid down without pausing for breath. Two more followed in quick succession before he and Jinx decided to explore the dive club. From the inauspicious entrance at the back, the club fronted onto smooth white rocks. The sun was beginning to sink beneath the horizon, but they could just make out the dark, inky sea lapping gently against the rocks.

Heading back into the club, Lorenzo was looking around for Liz when his eyes fell on their driver, Melissa, who was sharing a passionate kiss with another girl. As she surfaced for air, she spotted him and beckoned him over to join them. Lorenzo looked longingly at a table of loud laughing guys but pulled a chair out and sat down with the girls.

'Erm…I was looking for—' Lorenzo tried to keep his eyebrows under control as Liz extricated herself from Melissa.

'Oh, Liz. Hi, I was just wondering what the plan was for tomorrow.' He managed to get some coherent words out as Liz stood up, kissing the top of Melissa's dark head.

'Come on, let's go and find Josh; he's your guide for tomorrow.' Hooking her arm in his, she led him to one of the small lecture rooms at the back of the club. The big guy with the beard was signing off some log-books as they walked in, the hum of conversation dying down as people left for the night.

'Hey Liz, did you find Mel? She's been looking for you.' Josh grinned.

'Yeah, we're good, thanks Josh. Rez here, and Malik and Jinx are with you tomorrow, yeah?' Liz peered down at the list in Josh's hand as he ran a finger down, ticking off names as he went.

'Yup, Gozo tomorrow…up early guys, for the ferry.' Jinx and Malik suddenly materialized, Malik bouncing around like an over-excited puppy.

'How are your ears now Jinx?' Liz rested a caring hand on his shoulder.

'Yeah, great now, Liz; I think it was just the flight.' Jinx pulled on his earlobe just to be sure.

As they left the club, the soft night air wrapped itself around them like a warm embrace. Trudging back up the narrow, creaking stairway, Lorenzo hoped the air conditioning was working in their room. It was, and he flopped back on his bed, grateful for the cooling breeze. His thoughts turned to Liz and her amorous embrace with Melissa; he couldn't decide what had surprised him most, the fact that she knew Melissa or the fact that she was gay. Or was he assuming too much? Maybe she wasn't gay at all…and anyway, what did it matter? He resolved to try and have a chat with her during the holiday, maybe he'd tell her about Sam and about their kiss.

Closing his eyes, Lorenzo tried to ignore an ache deep inside as images of a gazebo and a beautiful girl with black hair replayed across his memory. Soon Sam, I'll see you soon.

***

The three friends bobbed around on the surface of the water; Lorenzo shielded his eyes from the ferocious glare of the sun. Their dive guide, Josh, gave them some last-minute instructions before they let the air out of their buoyancy aids and slowly descended; the water slid over them like a soft blanket, sealing them off from the outside world above. Lorenzo's eyes followed his air bubbles as they ascended, mushrooming up to the surface. He checked around for his buddies, Josh gave the 'OK' signal, and they all responded appropriately. This dive wasn't going to be a deep one, as it was their first, so they levelled out at 25 meters. It was still shallow enough for sunbeams to shimmer on the brightly coloured fish as they darted in and out, protesting at the intrusion of uninvited guests into their gently swaying world of blue.

Back on the boat, Josh fired up the motor, and they were off, speeding across the waves and heading for a small beach cafe in a secluded cove. They all clambered off the boat and crunched their way up the pebbly beach where tables and chairs were laid out. The smell of cooking wafted on the warm breeze, garlic and herbs, fish and no doubt, chips. Lorenzo spotted Liz waving to them, so they joined her and several others he recognized from their club.

'Soo, how was it?' She asked, pulling off her wetsuit bottoms.

Lorenzo was about to reply when Malik jumped in, describing in great detail every sea creature he'd encountered. Liz smiled indulgently but turned her gaze to Lorenzo.

'How about you Rez? Was it all you'd thought it would be?' Shrugging off her wetsuit top, Liz managed to grab a breast as it made a bid for freedom from her bikini. She grinned as she adjusted the straps.

'Erm yeah, the water's so clear…a bit scary though.' Lorenzo ordered his eyes to focus on her face before continuing.

'… it just disappears into the dark blue; I couldn't help wondering what was out there, you know?' he shook his head, imagining all sorts of enormous monsters.

'Not much out there actually, Rez, only a few—' Just then, a waiter arrived with a huge tray full of food.

'Oh, I haven't ordered anything yet.' Lorenzo peered at the food, grateful for the distraction from Liz in her bikini.

'Oh, don't worry, no need to order; they only do Ftira's here. Tuck in.' Liz picked up a huge slice of something resembling pizza but was much thicker. Lorenzo followed suit, munching his way through a second helping; he tasted olives, capers, tuna and onions.

'Bloody hell, these are amazing.' He nodded appreciatively to Liz, who grinned through a huge mouthful.

The diving club was buzzing as everyone milled around, getting their books signed off and exchanging anecdotes about their day. Lorenzo was clutching a much-needed cold beer whilst looking up a strange creature he'd encountered, keen to know what it was.

'Lionfish.' Liz tapped a finger on a beautiful fish, which, at first glance, appeared to have brown feathery wings.

'Yeah, that's it. Did you see it?' Lorenzo turned to her, pleased that he could now put a name to his mysterious fluttering fish.

'I don't think I saw that particular one, but yeah, there are a few around the Med. Never touch it though, Rez, they're venomous.'

As Liz leaned in closer, Lorenzo could feel her breast pushing against his arm; his thoughts returned to the pebble beach when she had taken off her wetsuit.

'Do you want to go for a drink later? There's a nice little bar I know off the tourist track.' Liz asked as if reading his mind.

Momentarily lost for words, Lorenzo picked up his beer in an attempt to smother his confusion. Images of Liz locked in an embrace with Melissa adding to the mix.

'Is everyone going?' He asked, looking around the room for Jinx and Malik.

'I thought it would be nice, just the two of us.' Liz smiled and shrugged a shoulder.

***

They were sitting on the smooth limestone rocks, throwing pebbles into the sea, having abandoned the bar as it was too noisy. Brightly coloured fishing boats were bobbing around on the flat, calm waters as the sun began to set. Lorenzo leaned back, resting on his elbows, his eyes closed as he listened to the chattering call of the cicadas in the trees behind them.

'Hey…sleepy head.' Liz nudged him with her elbow and handed him the bottle of vodka they'd been sharing.

'What? Sorry, Liz, it's just so peaceful here. Well, apart from those noisy little bastards up there.' He reached for the bottle, taking a large swig.

Snuggling in closer, Liz lifted Lorenzo's arm, placing it round her shoulders, her hand resting on his thigh.

'I 'spose you're wondering about me and Mel?'

'Erm, now that you mention it. But it's none of my business really, is it, Liz?' Taking another swig from their bottle, Lorenzo thought that, in fact, he was very interested in Liz's relationship with Mel.

Her hand moved higher on his thigh, slowly, gauging his reaction.

'Sometimes it's nice to have the best of both worlds…don't you think?' she whispered, her lips warm on his ear.

'A few months ago, I would have disagreed with you, Liz, but now…' He shrugged, trying to ignore the fire she was igniting in him.

'Why, what happened?'

'Not now.' Lorenzo turned to her, his lips finding hers in the dark.

Much later, as they were strolling along the seafront, Lorenzo had told her his story; : Sam, the kiss in the gazebo, the punching of the hapless James. He told her of their long friendship and how Sam came out to him that day in Winchester. She listened intently, only interrupting to clarify a point.

'So…you never had feelings for Sam before? Not even a little smidgen of attraction?' she teased, nudging him with her elbow.

'No, never, I can honestly say I never ever thought of him like that; he was…is…my best friend.' Lorenzo shook his head.

'But when you saw him dressed as Samantha?' Liz pushed gently.

'If you could have seen him, Liz, he…she, was beautiful, the most beautiful, sexiest girl I'd ever seen. Even when I knew it was Sam, my Sam, somehow it felt like she was mine…my girl, my Samantha. It just messes with your head, Liz. What does it mean? What does that make me?' Liz tugged him over to a bench overlooking the sea, where he sat with his head in his hands, agonizing over the unanswered questions.

'Don't be so hard on yourself, Rez; we're only human. We don't all conform to what it says on the packet.' She reached up, softly stroking his hair and continued.

'So what…you kissed a beautiful girl when you were drunk? Would you have kissed her if you'd been sober?'

'No, of course not.' He shot back irritably.

Strolling further along the pretty promenade, Liz told him about her relationship with Melissa. They'd met when Liz was doing her instructors' course at the dive club four years earlier. Mel was gay, but Liz had never given much thought to her own sexuality. As their friendship grew, so too did their need to be together. Like Lorenzo, Liz had never considered herself gay until her first kiss with Mel. She knew what Lorenzo was going through, albeit with the added complication of Sam being Samantha. She did concede it must be one hell of a dilemma. Walking further along the promenade, Lorenzo was intrigued by a stunning fortress jutting out over the sea. Liz explained it was built by the British a few hundred years earlier but was now a very popular restaurant; she promised to take him some time. Lorenzo imagined knights going in and out of the massive wooden doors, their armour clinking in the sunlight; Liz interrupted his reverie.

'Do you think maybe you've always loved Sam—' she held her hands up in defence as Lorenzo's eyes narrowed dangerously.

'Just hear me out, Rez…okay?' She said quietly before daring to continue.

'Maybe you did love Sam, as a friend loves a good friend…with your head and your heart not physically, then, when you saw Samantha, the physical side kicked in, and what was missing was suddenly there, it all fitted together like a jigsaw.' They had stopped walking. Lorenzo leaned against the ornamental balustrade and stared out over the ink-black sea.

'So where does that leave me, Liz? I'm in love with someone who doesn't exist; Samantha isn't real, is she?' He sighed in frustration.

Chapter 19

'Oh, come on, Sam, please, it'll be fun.' Chloe had been pleading with Sam to go with her to another one of Saira's fashion shows. He'd agreed to go when she'd asked him a couple of weeks ago, but now, suddenly, he'd said no.

They were sitting in Costa sipping frothy cappuccinos before the start of their Oral Surgery lecture. Sam leaned over, gently wiping a creamy moustache off Chloe's top lip.

'I'm going to Winchester Chlo' to an 18th birthday party.' Even saying the words set Sam's heart thumping. He'd been in such a quandary when Rez's sister invited him.

'Oh, who's that then?'

'Rez's younger sister, Ali, I've known her since she was a kid, always had a thing for me.' Sam smiled at the memory as he continued. 'I wasn't going to go but Rez messaged me, said he was sorry, wants to talk about what happened, you know? at the party.' Sam looked up at Chloe under his lashes and decided he needed to tell her.

'So what did—' Chloe started, but Sam raised a hand.

'I should have told him Chlo about Samantha.' Sam grimaced, acknowledging the mistake, then continued.

'That night at our party, the look on his face when he realized who I was.' His eyes misted over as he remembered the awful moment.

'But it wasn't your fault, Sam, he—' Chloe reached for his hand as Sam cut her off.

'Just…let me say it, okay?' He pleaded.

'I went into the garden with some guy, I dunno, Josh, James, something like that, my memory's a bit fuzzy. Anyway, things got a bit heated, and I changed my mind and wanted to go back in, but he pulled me into the gazebo, you know, the one with all the jasmine growing around it?'

'Yeah, the one right down at the end past the pond.' Chloe smiled.

'My dress got torn in the struggle with the guy, and I suppose I must have called out or shouted at him coz the next thing I know, Rez arrives, crashing through the bushes like some sort of demented superhero and punches the guy to the ground.' Sam smiled at the memory.

'Aw, your very own knight in shining armour.' Chloe said dreamily before adding.

'…So what went wrong, Sam?'

'I dunno, Chlo, it's all such a blur; I remember shouting at Rez to leave James…Josh, whatever his name was, alone coz he was really going for him, you know?' Sam gazed down at the table, spinning his spoon around as he struggled to find the words.

'We sat down on the bench, you know, the one with the dragon carving on it?' He glanced up at Chloe.

'Yeah, done by some student many years ago, so I was told.'

'And we kissed Chlo; I don't know who kissed who first. I think he pulled me in, but we just melted in together like it was the most natural thing in the world. It feels weird putting it into words like it's no big deal, '*so what you kissed someone when you were drunk*'. But it is a fucking big deal, Chloe, coz it's ruined our friendship.' Sam watched her carefully, gauging her reaction.

'Erm, how? I mean, what sort of kiss was it, Sam?' Chloe asked, hesitating in case she'd got the wrong end of the stick.

'A lovers kiss, Chlo, deep, passionate, and, at that moment, I wanted him more than I've ever wanted anyone.' Sam's breathing faltered as he desperately tried to control the tears, threatening to embarrass them both.

'And now? Do you still want him, Sam?' She asked gently.

'What? No, of course not; bloody hell, what do you take me for? He's my best mate.' Sam immediately regretted his harsh response to a reasonable question.

'Sorry, sorry Chlo, I just, I wish I knew how he felt. I guess I'll find out soon enough.' He managed a wry smile and continued. 'I've been so miserable, Chlo', well you know, you've had to put up with me.'

'Well, if you want my opinion, I think Rez was out of order ignoring your messages, Sam; it was just a misunderstanding after all, wasn't it?'

Sam frowned, his thoughts racing. Just a misunderstanding? Is that all it was? No, it was much more than that; it was something they'd both wanted to happen. The realization made his stomach flip. Although he did concede he was very drunk, Rez, on the other hand, was not, as far as Sam could remember.

'My stomach's been in a knot for days, going over and over everything; what would he say? Could we salvage our friendship after this?' Sam sat back, gazing up at the ceiling.

'I wish you'd told me, Sam, maybe I could have helped, somehow.' Chloe smiled.

'You're a good friend, Chlo.' Sam picked her hand up, kissing the back of it.

Later that night, Sam lay on his bed wrestling with his demons once again. Samantha called to him from the box on top of his wardrobe; he'd readily given in to her ever since that night, needing the comfort she gave him.

Reaching up for the precious box, Sam carefully resurrected Samantha; he wondered for the hundredth time why he felt this irresistible need for her. Smoothing down her black leather skirt, Samantha gazed at herself in the full-length mirror. Her soft black hair fell in waves to her shoulders. Peering at herself one last time, she selected a lipstick from her make-up box, *a touch of rose*. Samantha steered away from the gaudy reds that were a favourite of Maxine's, preferring a more natural look instead. She thought back to a conversation with Maxine a few weeks ago.

'Where's the point in being a bloody Drag Queen if you're not going to dress up darling?'

Samantha smiled to herself in the mirror as she remembered.

'But I'm not a fucking Drag Queen, am I? And anyway, I thought we didn't do labels…'

She'd been pleased with herself for standing up to Maxine, but sometimes, in her darker moments, she found herself searching for answers.

Plucking up courage, she'd decided to go shopping; she hadn't been out on her own yet, needing the security of Chloe or Max. As she opened the front door and gingerly stepped outside, she almost expected passers-by to stop and scream imposter at her, in the event nothing of the sort happened.

Arriving in town, she headed for the clothes shops; excitement was building as she flicked through the rows of dresses and skirts. She watched as young women her age prowled around the racks, touching, sometimes holding up items to check in the mirrors. Suddenly she panicked, realizing someone had spoken to her.

'Erm, sorry?' she smiled, willing herself to stay calm; a girl was holding up two sweaters and gazing at herself in the mirror.

'Which one, the Blue or the Grey?' she asked.

'Oh, er …the grey, I think.' Samantha smiled, suddenly aware of her deep voice. The girls' eyes widened momentarily, but she smiled and put the blue sweater back on the rack as she went off to the checkout.

'Thanks, hon …I love your skirt, by the way.' Checking the full-length mirror, Samantha admired her leather skirt. It really was rather gorgeous, she thought; maybe I'll just find a nice top to go with it for Ali's party. As she wandered around enjoying shopping for the party, an image kept popping into her head; Rez, with a look of horror on his face when he saw Samantha sashaying into the party. Filing away the unwanted image, she sighed and went up the escalator to the men's section.

Browsing through the shirts, Samantha realized with horror that she needed to pee. The toilets were up on the top floor in the home section, so she traced her steps back to the escalators. As the stairs rumbled slowly upwards, she began to panic about entering the ladies' toilets. It had never been an issue before as she had only ever been out with Chloe and Maxine, and the toilets in their local pubs were unisex. Stepping off the escalator, she headed for the dreaded toilets, hesitating as she approached the entrance, male to the left, female to the right. Her heart thumping wildly, she turned towards a display of towels, browsing nonchalantly through the array of colours on offer. Flicking her eyes over to the entrance, she could see some women coming out; how many were still in there? Sweat was glistening on her top lip; she needed to go in very soon. Eyeing up the disabled toilet, she briefly considered going in, but the thought of an irate person waiting to go in was too much to bear. Two more girls came out, and none had gone in. Samantha approached the entrance just as an elderly man with a child arrived. The girl went in, and the man took up position outside, arms folded across his chest as if guarding the entrance. Nodding to Samantha conspiratorially, he gestured to the ladies' door.

'You can never be too careful, can you? Lots of weirdos around these days.' He stated knowingly.

Samantha smiled and nodded in agreement, terrified that if she spoke, she would be put firmly in the 'Weirdo' category. Dashing into the first empty cubicle, she bolted the door and slumped down with relief on the seat, waiting for sounds from any occupied cubicles. Satisfied she was alone, she released her bursting bladder with a sigh. Smoothing down her skirt she waited in her cubicle, safe in her little sanctuary behind the locked door. Sounds of hand washing and dryers faded away to silence. Listening carefully for sounds of other occupants, she gingerly slid back her bolt and headed quickly over to the sinks, washing her hands before dashing out the door with a sigh of relief.

***

'So…what did you get?' Chloe rummaged through the carrier bags from Samantha's shopping trip, emerging with a button-down black shirt and a pale pink silk top. 'Hmmm, so who's going to the party then, Sam or Samantha?' she asked, posing with one then the other in the mirror. Samantha pulled off her wig and unhooked her bra, flinging both across the floor.

'Bloody hell, Chole' I don't know; I bought both just in case.' Sam flopped down on the sofa with his head in his hands. 'After what happened last time, I don't think Rez would ever want to see Samantha again, but I had to get something for her, didn't I?' Chloe sat beside him, reaching for his hand as she'd done so many times, wishing she could find the words to ease his pain and wishing he could feel for her what he felt for his best friend.

Chapter 20

Lorenzo ran his fingers through the soft black hair as their lips met, warm and soft. The kiss deepened as the plane touched down with a jolt, pushing him against his seat belt. In bleary eyed confusion, he stared out the window, trying to reconcile the images outside with the image in his head. He shifted uncomfortably in his seat and glanced around, expecting to see knowing smirks from his fellow passengers. He needn't have worried; most of them had leapt to their feet, opening and shutting overhead lockers in a desperate bid to escape the confines of the plane as soon as possible. He looked at Malik, still, sound asleep in the seat beside him. Lorenzo stayed in his seat, watching in bewilderment as people tried to make their way to the front of the aisle, pushing and shoving their way through. He closed his eyes again, trying to recapture his dream, trying to remember who he'd been kissing.

'C'mon man, we have to go; we'll be left behind.' Lorenzo felt a sharp nudge in the ribs as Malik struggled with his seat belt.

'Why are you in such a rush Mal? There's nowhere to go.' Lorenzo yawned, stretching out his cramped legs. He suddenly remembered with a jolt that tonight was Ali's party, the night he was meeting Sam. Sitting up straight, he tried to clear his head as many and varied scenarios swirled around, re-run after re-run of what Sam might say, what he might say. Would it be alright after tonight? Could they move forward? Forget the night in the garden? His stomach was in knots at the thought of losing Sam; they had to resolve it…had to.

Arriving home at last, Lorenzo was relieved to find the house empty; remnants of party preparations were strewn around the kitchen so he assumed everyone was at Abby's house preparing for the party. Abby had persuaded her wealthy parents to hold the joint event at their house. Ali had told him all about it at great length one day. They had a huge garden that sloped down to the river, with its own mooring for the family cruiser. Against his better judgement, Lorenzo had been impressed. He'd wondered fleetingly if a romance with his little sister's friend would be out of order, concluding a few seconds later that it most certainly would.

Lugging his suitcase upstairs, he plugged his phone in before flopping down on his bed and falling soundly asleep. Several hours passed before his phone beeped and buzzed, demanding attention. Reaching out blindly, he grabbed the phone and checked for messages, of which there were many. His mother, then Ali, then his father, Gemma …and Sam. For an agonizing moment, Lorenzo couldn't breathe. Had he changed his mind? Was he cancelling? Tapping Sam's name, he dared to read the message.

Hey Rez, hope you had great holz, can't wait to hear all about it, see you in the Bishops at 7.00

Allowing himself to breathe again, Lorenzo quickly sifted through the other messages; they ranged between '*Are you home yet?*' to '*Can you come down and give us a hand, Rez?*' Smiling to himself as he headed for the shower, he realized he was grateful to Ali for inviting Sam. He'd make it right; tonight was going to be great.

It was 4 o'clock, and Abby's driveway was awash with vans, all bearing logos advertising their various services. Catering, flowers, bunting. Following a gravel path round to the back garden, Lorenzo spied a large marquee shimmering in the sunlight. A huge banner proclaimed *Happy Birthday Three AAAs* as people scurried here and there busily preparing the garden for the night's festivities. Lorenzo wandered around, unsure of his role in the preparations, when he heard his name being called.

'Rez, what bloody time do you call this? Get over here and hold this for me.' His father was up a ladder trying to attach yet another string of lights to a huge tree trunk. Lorenzo ran over, squinting up at his father.

'Dad, what the hell are you doing up there? These guys are being paid to do that.'

'Oh yeah…feckin useless is what they are, here catch this.' Jim threw down a large hammer, almost hitting his son on the head.

'So, you didn't get eaten by sharks, I see.' Jim grinned down at his son.

'Rez, oh, thank god you made it in time.' His mother rushed over hugging him and commenting on his deep suntan. As she stepped back, she glanced up at her husband, who was balanced precariously on one leg as he threw another string of lights over a tree branch.

'I told you I'd be here in good time Mum; how are—' Lorenzo noticed the look that passed between his parents.

'What? What's wrong?' he asked, frowning. Angie quickly smiled, reaching up to gently touch his cheek.

'Oh, nothing, Rez, it's just, you look so handsome, I'm so proud of you.'

Confused about his mother's sentimental comment, he was about to ask her what she was so proud of when his heart froze. Striding towards them was his grandmother; she smiled as she approached, the smile gradually fading as she got closer.

'Bloody hell, Mum, I didn't know the wick—Grandma, was going to be here.' He groaned.

'Stop it, Rez, be nice.' She nudged him with her elbow.

'Oh, Lorenzo, how are you?' Grandma scrutinized him with her usual dismissive air but pulled him in for a hug for appearances. Lorenzo looked over her head at his mother, his eyes pleading for a rescue. Angie smiled, her eyes misting over when Lorenzo's silent plea shook her out of her reverie.

'Come on, Mum, let's go and find Ali, she's so excited about her party.' Angie extricated a stunned Lorenzo from her mother. He watched them walk away as his grandmother leaned into Angie, resting her head on her daughter's shoulder as they walked.

Jim wandered over, following Lorenzo's gaze as the two women disappeared into the huge marquee.

'Alright, son?' Jim asked, too casually for Lorenzo's liking.

'Did you see that, Dad? What the hell's going on with those two, first Mum, then Grandma?'

'Ach, pay them no mind, son, who knows what goes on in a woman's head.' Jim flicked his wrist, dismissing the strange world of the female mind.

Lorenzo wasn't convinced, something was definitely off, but today wasn't the day for demanding truths. Looking at his watch, he realized he'd need to get home and get ready to meet Sam.

Chapter 21

'What time's your train?' Chloe asked between mouthfuls of burgers.

'I want to get the 3 'o'clock if I can; gonna surprise my folks before I meet Rez.' Sam had bought Chloe lunch by way of compensation for not going to Saira's fashion show; he hadn't wanted to go anyway and was grateful he had a genuine reason not to.

'When will you be back?' She asked casually.

'Probably late Sunday; all depends on my odious brother, really. If he's there, I won't hang around for long.' Sam glanced at his watch and swigged the last of his coffee.

'I really should go, Chloe; I'll see you tomorrow night.' As they stood up, Chloe moved in for a hug.

'I hope it goes okay with Rez Sam; I've hated seeing you so unhappy.' Sam kissed her cheek, grateful for the support.

'Yeah, me too, Chlo', he's always been there for me, the brother I never had.' Sam shrugged a shoulder.

'A bit more than just a brother though, eh Sam?' Chloe smiled, touching his cheek gently.

'Really Chlo'? And you wonder why I didn't tell you what happened, eh?' Sam gently removed her hand from his cheek.

'I'm sorry, Sam, I didn't mean—'

'I'll see you tomorrow, Chlo'.' Sam headed for the door with a dismissive wave of his hand.

The sun was glinting off the river as he skipped down some steps, smiling to himself as he watched a mother duck fussily herding her babies into the shallows. Feeling calmer now, he decided to take a shortcut home along the towpath. Fishing his phone out of his pocket, he stopped beside the railings and messaged Rez.

'On my way, see you at 7 pm, Bro.'

Just as he was about to click send, Sam heard the unmistakable sound of screeching brakes behind him; he looked over his shoulder as the car sped towards him, the driver frantically turning the wheel in a futile effort to control the skid. Leaving the road, the car careered into Sam, smashing him against the metal railings; his phone flew from his hand, plunging into the depths of the river. The pain exploded he descended into darkness.

***

Preening in the mirror, trying to decide what to wear, Lorenzo felt a jolt of recognition. Grabbing his phone, he scrolled through his photos until he found the hated image. The likeness was even more pronounced now that he had the same deep suntan as the man in the photo. Flopping down on his bed, Lorenzo scrutinized the image once again, convinced now that this man was definitely his father; he reasoned this would account for the bizarre behaviour of his mother and grandmother. Forcing himself out of his melancholy, he fixed his hair in the mirror, inexplicably pulling a long strand down over his eyebrow, just like his father's. Hating himself for re-creating the pose in the photo, he lay on his bed, thoughts swirling around in his head like a tumble dryer. Tomorrow, I will solve this once and for all, but for now…Sam.

Waking up with a start, Lorenzo realized he'd fallen asleep; he grabbed his phone in a panic; it was 7.00. Flinging himself off the bed, he dashed around, gathering up his clothes, stopping only to message Sam.

'I'm so sorry man, I fell asleep…on my way'

His door opened slightly.

'C'mon Rez, we're going now.' Ali popped her head in to check he was decent before entering his room with a dramatic 'Ta Da,' twirling around in a very low-cut tight dress, her arms outstretched for full effect.

'So, what think you, big brother?' She pouted in his mirror for a while, fixing her hair. Lorenzo wondered how she didn't poke her eye out with the extra-long fingernails.

'You look amazing, Ali, have a great party, got to dash, I'll be there later.' He kissed the top of her head and ran out of the house, leaving Ali open-mouthed.

Having run almost the whole way to the Bishops Tavern, Lorenzo burst into the pub, his eyes scanning every nook and cranny for Sam. He checked in the toilets, but there was no sign of Sam.

'Idiot, stupid fucking idiot.'

Fishing his phone out, he checked for messages, nothing from Sam and his message hadn't been read. Thinking that maybe Sam had given up waiting and had gone on to the party, he ran from the pub, berating himself all the way to Abby's house.

Music and laughing voices floated over the treetops; the party was in full swing. He headed for the marquee, his eyes searching for Sam amongst the throng of happy people.

'Oh, you're here at last; where's Sam then?' Abby rushed over, looking around for Sam as she handed him a beer.

'Erm, I seem to have lost him, have you—Happy Birthday, by the way.' Lorenzo bent down and kissed her cheek, immediately regretting the intimate gesture as Abby snaked her arms around him, pulling him in closer.

'Wow, how many have you had then?' He laughed, realizing she was pretty drunk. He quickly made his escape, heading over to his mother, who was in deep conversation with his grandmother. The two women looked up as he approached; his grandmother's eyes were moist, had she been crying?

'Ah Rez, my beautiful, beautiful boy, give an old lady a hug.' She reached out to him, her eyes soft and misty.

He had no choice but to bend almost double to allow the thin, pale arms to wrap around him. Her bird-like head barely came up to his waist. Shocked by yet another unexpected embrace, Lorenzo stared wide-eyed at his mother, the unasked question written all over his face.

'What the hell's wrong with everyone today?'

Angie just smiled at him, pointing at her glass of champagne with a shrug. So, the grand high witch was drunk, too, interesting. As she released her grip round his waist, she reached up, placing a soft hand on his cheek.

'So handsome, just like him.' She murmured before Angie quickly took her arm and led her off to find Ali. Lorenzo squinted after them through narrowed eyes – this was the first time anyone had ever mentioned Him directly. What's it got to do with her anyway?

The bastard was my father; why is she so upset that I look like him?

Telling himself this was not the time to brood over the issue, he ran to catch up with Angie, but she hadn't seen Sam either.

The rest of the party passed in a blur for Lorenzo as he had to accept that Sam wasn't there. He watched from a distance as the three A's blew out candles on a three-layered cake, and everyone sang Happy Birthday. Looking at his watch, he decided to give it another hour and then go round to Sam's parent's house; maybe he'd gone round there after waiting in the pub.

Grabbing another beer from a passing waiter, Lorenzo realized he felt quite drunk; as he watched the happy party revellers dancing and enjoying themselves, his black mood threatened to engulf him once more. Leaving the marquee, he wandered out into the vast, sprawling garden; the scent of jasmine assailed his senses, reminding him of another garden and another place and time. Finding a secluded seat, he flopped down, his head spinning.

'Hey son, everything alright?' Jim Murphy appeared, clutching a tumbler full of whiskey; he sat down. He knew his son well enough to know when something wasn't quite right; Lorenzo had always been the life and soul of any party; looking at him now, Jim knew something bad had happened.

'Son, a word full of meaning, wouldn't you think, Dad?' Lorenzo glanced angrily at his father and took another swig from his tin. Jim swirled the golden liquid around in his glass, frowning as he considered his son's words.

'What's happened, Rez?' Jim rested a hand on his son's shoulder, concerned by the personal attack.

'Grandma's drunk, you know.' Lorenzo shrugged off the hand resting on his shoulder.

Jim wondered what the old witch had been saying to him, dropping more of her poison, no doubt. Lorenzo sat forward, elbows resting on his knees. He looked back over his shoulder, the puzzled expression on his father's face cutting through his heart like a knife.

'I know, Dad, I know you're not my real father.' His voice broke in the saying of the dreaded words. He tried to hold back; this wasn't the time or place to have the conversation that would change his life forever, but somehow, a dam had broken, and he couldn't control it. The whole story just seemed to fall out of his mouth like a cascading waterfall through his tears: the finding of the photograph in his mother's box, his grandmother's obvious dislike of him, and his strange name.

'Son, no, you've got it –' Jim had listened quietly as Lorenzo gave vent his bottled-up emotions.

'You can't deny it Dad. I'm the spitting image of my father Lorenzo; she even named me after him, for god's sake.' His breath came in huge gulps now as he struggled for control. A gentle breeze brought the sweet scent of Jasmine once more. Lorenzo jumped up, needing to escape from the suffocating aroma. He walked briskly down a small gravel path, his father's footsteps crunching on the gravel behind him.

'Rez, please, stop.' Jim laid a hand on his shoulder and spun him around, holding both his arms to stop him from escaping again.

'Listen to me, I am your father. It's a long story, Rez and your mother should be the one to tell it, but not here on your sister's birthday.' Jim stared into his son's eyes, concerned for the hurt he must have been feeling when none of them knew.

'After the party, okay? We'll sit down and tell you the whole story, but please, Son, believe me, I am your dad.'

Chapter 22

The aroma of hot buttered toast wafted through the kitchen. Angie always felt that heavy emotional discussions needed toast and butter; an array of conserves was laid out on the table. Grandma had been packed off to bed, and Ali had decided to stay over at Abby's house. Lorenzo and his parents were now seated around the kitchen table, the hated photograph propped up against a jar of marmalade, like an accused in the dock.

'So, who is he then, Mum?' Lorenzo flicked a dismissive hand at the handsome, grinning man in the photograph. Angie picked it up and looked lovingly at it; tears filled her eyes. Lorenzo had waited for this moment ever since he'd discovered the photo. He could hardly breathe, and his heart was pounding.

'He is my father Rez, your grandfather.' She smiled a watery smile, took a deep breath, and told the story.

'When grandma was a girl of eighteen, she and some friends went on holiday to Tuscany. This was the '70s, free love and flower power and all that, but God help you if you got pregnant, which is exactly what happened.' Angie reached over and plucked another slice of toast, slathering a huge dollop of strawberry jam on top.

'So the girl in the photo—' Lorenzo asked, puzzled but knowing the answer already.

'Yes, the girl is grandma; I looked just like her at that age; that's why you thought it was me.' Angie grabbed Lorenzo's hand, stroking the back of it with her thumb before continuing.

'I'm so sorry, Rez, I had no idea you'd seen that photo; I haven't seen it in years.' Angie glanced at her husband, feeling his disapproval at her carelessness with the photo. For once in his life, Jim Murphy stayed quiet; this was his wife's story to tell.

'Go on, son.' Jim nodded to his son.

'It was the day we changed the bedrooms around. You asked me to lift a box down from the wardrobe, and there it was; I have to say, Mum, my world fell apart that day.' Lorenzo smiled sadly, thinking about all the months he'd worried for nothing, wishing that he'd said something at the time.

'But why the secrecy? Why wasn't I allowed to know?' Lorenzo spread a huge dollop of jam on his toast, finding comfort in the sticky sweetness.

'My thoughts exactly, son; I always said keeping secrets is—' Jim was cut short by a sharp glare from his wife.

'Grandma's pride, shame at what had happened, she just didn't want you two to think badly of her, she made me promise Rez.'

Several cups of tea later, the story was revealed, dissected, and analyzed. Lorenzo now understood his grandma's strange attitude towards him over the years. Now, lying on his bed, hands behind his head, he thought about her predicament all those years ago.

She'd met Lorenzo on her holiday and had quickly fallen in love with the handsome dark Italian. His parents had owned the hotel they were staying in, and he'd offered to show her around. He'd told her he loved her and would wait for her to come back a few months later. However, when she discovered she was pregnant, her parents were horrified and wouldn't let her return to Tuscany. Angie was born, and grandma got married, going on to have 2 more children. When Angie found out about her real father when she turned 18, she was determined to go and find him in Tuscany.

Lorenzo senior had been shocked but overjoyed to discover he had a daughter; he'd written several times to grandma but never had any response. Assuming their romance was over, he'd met and married a local girl, going on to have two children. He and Angie kept in touch ever since, with Angie naming her first child after him.

Lorenzo felt a longing to visit his look-alike grandfather, wanting to get to know him, man to man. Angie had said he was in his 80s now and quite frail, but maybe something could be arranged now that he knew the truth.

The photograph that for so long had haunted him was now propped up against his clock. He had it zoomed in on his phone as much as he could, but the image was too distorted. Lorenzo felt confused; he should be ecstatic, but the truth of his grandma's love affair brought with it a sadness, all those wasted years his grandfather didn't know he had a daughter.

Switching off his light, he smiled to himself.

I'm named after my grandfather.

Chapter 23

Sam had got used to the incessant beeping; it had become a comfort to him, something he could focus on when he couldn't hear the whispered voices. Now, suddenly, something had changed; he could hear the voices clearly, and he was aware of someone leaning over him just as the beeping stopped. His body was moving from side to side; someone was shaking him.

'Can you hear me? Can you open your eyes for me?' The voice was soft and gentle, it reminded him of his mother when he was a child. Sam didn't want to open his eyes; he was happy floating in his warm, soft cocoon. Feeling himself being pulled back from his safe place, he resisted, resenting the interruption to his reverie. The pain hit him like a red-hot poker, surging through his body as if he was on fire. He was aware of shouting out, angry at whoever was causing his suffering.

'No …no, please stop. I can't –' Sam flailed around, desperate to put an end to the searing pain.

'Open your eyes.' this time, the voice wasn't so soft and warm. It was gruff, demanding in its authority. Feeling he had to obey this new demand, he slowly tried to organize his thoughts, pulling the pieces in one by one and trying to make sense of what was going on. His eyelids flickered open as he took a tentative peep through his lashes, afraid of what he might see if he opened them fully. He felt a darkness descend and began to panic.

'Am I blind?

'Don't worry, we've put some dark glasses on you, just 'till you get used to the lights again.' The soft voice was back, and a warm hand stroked his. Tentatively, he opened his eyes once more, slowly taking in his surroundings. In an effort to make sense of what he was seeing, he shifted position. The pain surged once more, but he pushed through it, determined to sit up.

'I'm in hospital.' He wasn't sure if he'd spoken out loud or just thought to himself.

'Yes, you've been in an accident, a car hit you, do you remember?' Sam turned his head towards the voice. He couldn't be sure who had spoken as several doctors and nurses stood around his bed. Flopping back against the pillow again, he forced himself to remember. Thoughts raced through his head: his beloved dog, his mother, Rez, Chloe, Chloe, he'd been with her in a café; he remembered the ducks on the river…the screech of brakes, then nothing.

'How long have I been here?' He croaked, his words catching in his parched throat. A nurse handed him a cup with instructions to sip the water when he really wanted to gulp it down in one.

'Four days. Can you tell us your name? We couldn't find any ID on you.' The nurse smiled, gently prizing the cup from his hand. Suddenly realizing no one knew he was there, Sam looked around, desperate to find his phone, needing to message everyone; he thought about his dental studies, groaning when he realized, he had an oral surgery exam on Wednesday.

'What day is it?' Easing himself further up in the bed, he looked at the nurse who was busy adjusting a beeping machine next to him.

'Tuesday.' She turned and looked over her shoulder.

'Oh God no, I have to get—argggg.' Sam fell back on the bed as the pain seared through his legs once more; the nurse handed him a device, telling him to click the button if the pain got too bad. The morphine haze descended as the pain fell away to a slight ache once more.

'Have you got my phone? I need to tell everyone where I am.' He mumbled.

'We don't have it; it must have fallen in the river when the car hit you; you were found on the riverbank.' She shrugged, seemingly oblivious to the catastrophe that had befallen her patient. As Sam pondered on how to get in touch with everyone, he went back over the events of Saturday afternoon, as much as his morphine-fogged brain allowed. He'd met Chloe in a café, she'd upset him …why? What had they—he tried to slow his tumbling thoughts down to decipher more clearly …Rez! He'd been going home to Winchester to meet Rez to patch up their quarrel.

'Oh fucking jeez, no, Rez.' His arm flopped over his forehead, trying to banish the thought of his friend thinking he'd stood him up.

'I really need to find a phone.' He mumbled, struggling to get his tongue to cooperate with his brain.

'Plenty of time for that.' A stern male voice boomed as the doctor approached his bed, picking up the notes hanging on the end.

'We'll get you a phone, Sam, but first, let's talk about your injuries.'

Sam was about to protest when it dawned on him, injuries? Was he hurt badly? The pain in his legs was just a throbbing sensation in the far distance now; surely it can't be too bad. The doctor spoke softly now, explaining as if to a child Sam didn't want to listen. He just wanted to float in soft oblivion as the doctors' words swirled around him as if in slow motion.

The soft white light seemed to drift around. Sam wanted to hold it, feel it, but each time he reached for it, he couldn't quite grasp it. It settled now on the end of his bed; his hand reached out slowly, carefully so as not to frighten it away. The voices came again, annoying him when he was trying to concentrate.

'Sam, open your eyes, you have a visitor.' This was the soft voice; he liked obeying the soft voice. Gradually, he pulled himself back, away from the pursuit of the white light, and forced himself to surface; the pain intensified as he focused on opening his eyes.

'Sam, can you hear me? It's Rez.'

His heart pounded on hearing the voice, could it really be him? Opening his eyes now, squinting through his lashes in case he'd been wrong, Sam thought he'd never seen a sight so welcome as his best friend sitting beside him. Tears filled his eyes as he reached out to grab Rez's arm.

'Oh god, Rez, am I glad to see you, how did – I mean who—?'

'Well, it was a bit of a detective game, mate. I went to see your parents to see if they'd heard from you, and I messaged your friend Chloe on Facebook. Between us all, we figured out something must have happened to you.' Lorenzo looked around with interest at the drips and machinery surrounding his friend.

'I was on my way to the train Rez, fucking car smashed into me, crushed my legs.' Sam flicked a hand across his legs in disgust.

'How long will you be in? …I've been waiting over a week for that beer.' Lorenzo grinned.

Sam shrugged, his face betraying the casual gesture.

'Dunno mate, there's still another operation they need to do on my knee. Apparently, it isn't responding to treatment; some bits of metal still in there, I think.'

The silence grew heavy as they looked at each other, neither knowing what to say next. Lorenzo reached over, tentatively taking Sam's hand. He needed to touch him, hold him, somehow mend his broken body.

'I'm sorry Sam, about …everything.' Lorenzo kept his eyes downcast, looking at the bandaged hand resting in his.

'I've been torturing myself ever since that night. I don't—.'

'Rez, can we just forget about it, move on?' Sam pleaded.

Lorenzo smiled and nodded his head.

'Yeah, if you're okay with that, on one condition.' His mouth twitched as he tried to control the grin.

Sam held his breath, this was it, the moment which would define their friendship. Lorenzo leaned over, brushing a long black lock of hair away from Sam's face.

'…you get your hair cut; you're beginning to look like her.' Lorenzo chuckled, but the touch of that soft black hair brought the memory flooding back.

Sam laughed, theatrically flicking his hair over his shoulder.

'What with this stubble?'

The softly-spoken nurse came over, rattling a cup with pills in it. As she leaned over to adjust Sam's drip, she smiled at Lorenzo.

'Is he a good patient nurse?' Lorenzo favoured her with his seductive, lopsided grin whilst quietly sliding his hand out of Sam's.

'Yeah, he'll do…keeps talking in his sleep, though, muttering about his dog…Rus, Riz…something like that.'

Sam lowered his eyes as he caught the look of smug satisfaction on his friend's face.

The next forty-five minutes passed quickly as they relaxed into their familiar teasing banter. Lorenzo regaled Sam with stories of his diving exploits in Malta, many of them augmented with man-eating sharks and dinnerplate-sized jellyfish. He neglected to mention his night on the beach with Liz. They talked about Sam's accident and how Lorenzo found out about his Italian Grandfather.

'So that's why your grandmother was weird with you all these years, coz you looked like him? That's so sad.' Sam shook his head.

'Yeah, I almost feel like I want to go and see him, make up for lost time …you know?'

'Let's do it …when I get out of here, let's go find your long-lost Italian grandad.' Sam's eyes lit up, his face aglow with enthusiasm. He'd refused to think about his future, his missed exams, but suddenly, now he had a purpose, something to work towards.

Lorenzo was already making plans; he'd only been home from Malta for a week, so maybe he could squeeze in another holiday towards the end of the summer. Glancing down at the metal cage encasing Sam's legs, he frowned.

'How long will you be in here?'

Sam was about to reply when reality loomed into view in the shape of a wheelchair being pushed by a very bored-looking porter.

'Right then, buddy, radiography for you.' He quipped whilst pealing back Sam's blankets. Lorenzo hadn't given much thought as to what was lurking beneath the cage over Sam's battered legs. He tried to compose his face, working hard to control the wave of horror that was seeping through his body. The metal rods piercing the flesh stood to attention, tall and proud and very shiny. Sam's legs dangled at the end of them like a hapless fish that had been harpooned. Lorenzo watched silently as the efficient porter manhandled Sam out of the bed and into the wheelchair.

'Erm, how long will he be?' He asked, clearing his throat as he tried to maintain his composure.

'Not sure, mate, these things can take a while.' The porter tutted, sucking his teeth.

Sam reached out, grabbing Lorenzo by the arm

'You go, Rez, you can't sit here for an hour waiting for me.'

As the porter turned the chair around and started to wheel him away, Sam looked back in time to see his friend wiping away a tear.

'You two together like?' Asked the porter.

'Nah, he's my best mate.'

'Oh yeah? Whatever you say, buddy, you're the patient.' The porter quipped with a grin.

***

The Winchester train rumbled its weary way home. Lorenzo was usually fascinated by the view into people's back gardens. He'd always liked to face backwards as it gave him longer to look at something that caught his eye. On this occasion, he hadn't been looking at all; his mind was going over and over his hospital visit with Sam. It had only been a week since his accident, the same day he'd found out about his Italian grandfather, he wondered fleetingly if both events had occurred at the same time, immediately shrugging off the pointless analysis, what would it matter anyway. It was strange, though, that such momentous life-changing events had happened to both of them on the same day.

He knew it was wrong, almost obscene, but he'd been relieved when he'd finally found out why Sam hadn't turned up for Ali's party. Relief soon gave way to overwhelming panic when he'd found out about the accident; taking the day off work, he'd dashed to the hospital as soon as he could. He told himself that Sam was okay, his legs would heal, and their life would resume as normal. What was normal, though? There was no denying a line had been crossed that night in the garden, could it happen again? He thought about the hospital visit. When he'd first arrived, Sam had been asleep, unaware that anyone was there. Lorenzo had pulled up a chair and gazed at his friend, his heart full of longing, his hand desperate to reach out, to caress.

He allowed himself to look, really look, at the beautiful face, long black eyelashes, and softly curling black hair. Lorenzo had smiled quietly as he thought about their teenage years and how hard it must have been for Sam when the girls came on to him. Sam had moved in the bed, mumbling as if having a conversation with someone, as if aware that someone was watching him; he'd turned towards Lorenzo, his hair falling over his face. Lorenzo tried not to think about how he'd felt at that moment, tried not to think about the surge of emotion that had threatened to undo him; this was his Sam…or was it Samantha?

The train slowed to a crawl, allowing an express to thunder past, and he gazed down into the back gardens with interest. A woman was walking down her garden carrying a tray of food before handing it to a young man who was sitting in a shaded area under some trees. As Lorenzo peered more closely, he realized the young guy was in a wheelchair.

Oh Jesus is that going to be Sam's fate?

The train began to move, quickly leaving the young man in the wheelchair far behind. Thinking back to his conversation about his grandfather, Lorenzo remembered Sam's excitement at the idea of going to Tuscany. Maybe they could, when Sam was better, if Sam got better.

Shoving the unwanted image to the back of his mind, Lorenzo's thoughts turned to work; since he'd been back from holiday, he'd felt even more disgruntled and bored. His boss, Richie, seemed to find fault with everything he did, accusing him of being distracted and not concentrating, which, Lorenzo conceded, was probably true. He was distracted, mainly by Gemma, who was fascinated by the story of his grandfather and wanted to talk about it at every given opportunity. Very soon, the whole office was buzzing with excitement about Lorenzo's long-lost Italian grandfather; even the odious Nick managed to refrain from acerbic comments whilst still managing to maintain his customary smirk.

Lorenzo wondered now, as the train pulled into Winchester, whether he should try and find another job; it wouldn't look too good on his CV, though Octagon management trainee jobs were very highly prized. Stepping off the train, he resolved to up his game at work and try to get a better review from Richie.

Chapter 24

'You'll be able to get an EU passport, you know.' Malik grabbed Lorenzo's arm, almost spilling his beer.

They were sitting in the garden of the Bishops Tavern, and Lorenzo had told Malik and Jinx the story behind his Italian grandfather.

'Oh man, this is amazing, we could all go…where's Tuscany? Is it on the coast, we could go diving?' Jinx immediately whipped out his phone, searching Google Maps for Tuscany. Ever since they'd got back from their diving trip to Malta, Jinx had not stopped talking about it; Lorenzo thought the whole of Octagon must have heard about the leatherback turtle and how it surfaced for air right next to Jinx when he was diving. He'd tried to follow it as it plunged down into the deep blue depths, but Liz had tugged on his fins to pull him back.

'So what will you do, Rez, gonna go see him?' Malik sipped his beer, intrigued by the new turn of events in his friend's life.

'I'd really like to mate, but since I've just got back from one holiday, I don't suppose the old bastard will let me have another week off.' Lorenzo played with his beer, swirling it around before finishing off the last mouthful. As it was his round, he swung his long legs over the bench seat and headed into the bar. His eyes adjusted to the dark interior of the pub. It seemed wrong somehow that he was here with his workmates; this was his and Sam's pub. As he waited to be served, Lorenzo gaze wandered over to where he and Sam had sat at the last time they were here. He realised with a jolt that was the last time they'd sat and had a beer together. Sam had been going off to university the next day and had been very drunk, saying he didn't want to go. Would things have been different if he hadn't gone away? Maybe he wouldn't have been hit by the car; maybe he wouldn't have needed Samantha if he'd stayed here with me.

'Hey Rez.'

Lorenzo was jolted out of his melancholy by the giggling voices at the bar beside him. His sister Ali and her posse of girls had just been served and were heading out to the garden. It still felt weird seeing his little sister being served in the pub; he immediately morphed into 'protective older brother' mode. He couldn't help wondering if he would always feel that way. Collecting his drinks, he followed the girls out to the garden, marveling at how they could walk on their heels without spilling a drop. As he manoeuvred his way through the crowded garden, he wondered if Ali would come over to their table, he hadn't encountered this scenario before and wasn't too sure he liked it very much. He was much relieved to see the girls settling down at a table further down the garden, hopefully, Ali wouldn't come looking for him.

She'd been very excited when their parents told her about their Italian grandfather, laughing about their starchy and stuffy grandma who had been a naughty girl in her youth. Angie had pointed out that poor grandma had lived through some traumatic times in her youth, her own parents being very strict and controlling, denying her pleas to be with Lorenzo. Angie had to remind them that on no account must Grandma know that her secret had been revealed.

Lorenzo's feelings towards his grandma had changed since his discovery; he felt closer to her somehow, knowing what she'd gone through and finally understanding her attitude towards him. He'd begged Angie to allow him to talk to her about it all, but Angie had forbidden any mention of it to Grandma.

'…what do you think Rez, wouldn't that be amazing?' Lorenzo hadn't realised that he'd drifted off into his own little world and was now jolted back to the conversation around the table, which was about Liz, their diving instructor. It would appear that she was buying the diving club in Malta. Jinx was now furiously searching his phone for dive clubs for sale.

'Erm, what would be amazing?' Lorenzo sipped his beer, trying to catch up.

'If we all ditched Octagon and bought a diving club, Liz has done it with her friend Melissa from Malta.' Malik, who wasn't usually enthused by such endeavours, seemed to be very taken with the idea. Lorenzo laughed and shook his head.

'We're just beginners, we'd need to be instructors or something, and we'd never get a business loan for something like that, we'd—' Lorenzo paused as he spotted Ali and her friends weaving their way through the garden towards them. As she approached their table, he looked up, resigned to having his day ruined. ***

Opening his emails, Lorenzo counted forty-three new ones in his inbox, all screaming for urgent attention. Most were from Richie asking why he hadn't responded to several earlier emails. Lorenzo typed back:

If you didn't send me so many fucking emails asking me to reply to your email, I might be able to get some work done

Then he hit delete.

'Having a bad day, Rez?' Gemma placed a mug of coffee on his desk.

'I just don't get why he has to send me emails when he sits in the same room as me, Gem; why can't he just come over and explain what he wants?' His hands flew up in frustration.

'By the same token, you could go over and ask him?' Gemma suggested, not unreasonably. Lorenzo knew it was his pride preventing him from asking questions, preferring to figure things out for himself.

The weeks and months dragged on; Lorenzo conceded defeat and had started to ask Richie for help, which, to his surprise, was offered with great enthusiasm. He no longer dreaded going to work but was still tempted to look for another job.

'You and Richie seem to be getting along better, word has it, you're the new golden boy.' Gemma laughed one night as she stirred a saucepan full of Bolognese.

'Ha, nah, he just thinks we've bonded coz his wife is Maltese, likes to give me advice on all things Maltese.' Lorenzo was lounging on her sofa, scrolling through diving photos. 'Look at this, Gemms, isn't that cool.' He held up a photo of a diver with a turtle in Malta.

'It does look nice there, maybe we could go…have a holiday?' Gemma asked tentatively.

'Erm, mmm, maybe.' Lorenzo said guardedly, whilst reading his messages.

'This is just so annoying.' He moaned, flinging the phone down in frustration.

'What's wrong?' she handed him a steaming mug of coffee before sitting down beside him.

'I've been trying to arrange to go to Bristol to see my mate Sam; you know the one who had the car accident?'

'But he's been home from hospital for ages, hasn't he?' Gemma frowned before adding, 'a bit weird, isn't it?'

'Yeah, it is, I bumped into his mum in town. She hasn't been able to get hold of him either. He did say he'd moved in with his friend Chloe into a ground floor flat, suitable for a *wheelchair*.' Lorenzo could barely say the last word as an image popped into his head: Sam in a wheelchair.

'I've messaged his flatmate Chloe a few times through Facebook to see if I could make a surprise visit, but she just keeps putting me off. It's so bloody annoying. I mean, what if she's keeping him away from everyone, like a prisoner or something.' Lorenzo's eyes were wide with horror at the possibility.

'There was a movie about that wasn't there, *Misery*, that was it, a woman had a guy tied to a bed and was torturing him.' Gemma looked at Lorenzo in alarm. 'You have to go there, Rez, rescue him, message this Chloe woman, and demand to see him.'

Walking briskly home, Lorenzo was fired up with all sorts of heroic rescue scenarios, ranging from untying a tortured Sam from his bed to carrying him, fireman style, over his shoulder down a ladder.

I'm coming, Sam, I won't let you down.

Chapter 25

'I told you, I'm not hungry,' Sam muttered.

Chloe carried the tray of cold food back to the kitchen, scraping the plate into the bin yet again. Her phone pinged; it was Maxine.

'How's our girl doing?'

Chloe felt a stab of irritation. *Their girl* Sam was being a pain in the arse, if truth be told. She tapped furiously at her phone, grumbling about her patient's refusal to go out or to eat proper food.

Sam had taken to ordering in when Chloe was out, relishing the small amount of independence it gave him. He was finding her constant fussing over his diet very irritating. Chloe had morphed into nurse mode as soon as he'd come home from the hospital, offering to help him shower and get dressed, something he vehemently refused. Feeding him was another one of her obsessions, even though he told her he'd already eaten.

'Have you done the module the Vulture gave you?' Chloe called from the kitchen.

Sam picked up his crutches and heaved himself on to the sofa, grabbing his PlayStation control on the way. He refused to answer and increased the volume of his game. He knew he was being a shit, but he couldn't help it. He also knew he was depressed, but the knowing of it didn't do anything to alleviate it. He could see the dreaded wheelchair folded up in the corridor, as yet unused. Chloe's frustration at his refusal to let her push him out in it hung over them like a black cloud. He reached down for a beer from a pack on the floor beside him.

'Well?' Chloe persisted, fully aware that her nagging would result in another snappy response.

'Jesus Chlo' can you just drop it, I'll do it when I'm ready, okay?'

'The Vulture says you're falling behind, Sam.' She knew she was pushing her luck but had to try.

Sam continued to stare at the TV screen, stabbing at the control panel as his character raised his sword in bloody victory. He waited for admonishment, daring her to make a comment. She obliged.

'If you're drunk tonight again, Sam, you can sleep on the sofa; I'm going out with Max.' Chloe headed for the front door, slamming it on her way out.

Sam slumped back on his cushions, draping an arm over his head he gave his tears free reign. He was awoken by his phone pinging; it was Rez, asking yet again if he could come to see him. It was ironic really, Rez was the only person in the world right now he wanted to see, but he wasn't ready yet to emerge from the dark cocoon he'd woven himself into. Reaching down for another beer, he checked the time; too soon for another dose of painkillers, although the fire surging through his legs begged to differ. Chloe's comment about falling behind had hit a nerve; the principal had suggested he take the rest of the year out to recover and restart the following

September, but Sam had pleaded to do the medical side and catch up on the practical when he could go in on his crutches. They reluctantly agreed to let him try, with the proviso that he completed all his assignments on time.

Grabbing his crutches, he manoeuvred his legs slowly and carefully until he could stand; his left leg could take some weight, but he'd been told on no account must he put his right foot to the floor. Checking his balance, he hobbled into his room, easing himself down carefully on the chair. He waited to allow the pain and dizziness to subside before firing up his laptop. *Tooth loss due to gum disease* shouted at him from the screen, along with a particularly lurid picture of a pretty girl with no teeth. Very soon he was absorbed in his essay, grateful that at least he could still type.

***

The pub was filled with loud, happy people, they seemed to be celebrating something, a birthday maybe. In stark contrast, Chloe and Max sat in their dark, gloomy corner, nursing their beers and talking about Sam. Chloe was grateful that, for once, Max had turned up in jeans and a sweatshirt, having decided that Maxine's frivolity wouldn't be appropriate on this occasion. As a nod to Maxine, he'd donned a pair of bright, spangly trainers. Chloe had explained at great length, her concern for Sam and her fear for his upcoming exams. Grabbing a handful of peanuts, she sighed, shaking her head.

'I just don't know what to do next, Max. Everything I say is wrong, and he snaps back at me; he won't even let me take him out in the wheelchair after all the hassle I had trying to get one.' She grumbled.

'Maybe you're trying too hard Chlo' I mean, it's not like he's your boyfriend or anything, is it?' Max immediately regretted the badly chosen words, knowing how Chloe felt about Sam.

'No, I know that, Max, but I'm just trying to do what's best for him.' Chloe snapped back in her *mother knows best* voice.

'What about his gorgeous friend from home, they seem close; maybe he could come and see him, cheer him up, you know?'

'Hmm, I don't know Max, the last time they met, they had a huge falling out. Sam was really upset, although he was heading for the train to go home and see Rez when the accident happened.' Picking up her drink, Chloe gazed into the distance. She'd often wondered about Sam's friendship with Lorenzo; somehow, she felt resentful of his dependence on his friend. Max had even once suggested she was jealous; how absurd was that.

'So, what if you messaged Rez through Facebook and arranged for him to come, surprise him, you know?' Max persisted bravely, in full knowledge of how Chloe would react to this.

'Remember what happened the last time he turned up unannounced? I can't allow that to happen again, Max.' Chloe declared in her best *schoolmistress* voice.

'Erm, you can't *allow*? If you love him Chlo' you should want what's best for him, shouldn't you?' Max knew he was skating on thin ice, but it had to be said.

Chloe was about to object when she realised Max was right; she was being possessive and not putting Sam's best interest first. She agreed to at least think about contacting the infamous Rez.

They stayed for another drink, and Max regaled Chloe with elaborate stories about costume disasters and wigs, which refused to stay in place. Chloe let him chatter on enthusiastically, but she was lost in thought, conceding that maybe Max was right. A visit from home might be just what Sam needed. Whilst Chloe had nothing against Rez *per se*, she just didn't want him coming to see Sam. She remembered their row on the day of his accident and the look on his face when she'd suggested Rez was a bit more than a friend. She wondered, for the hundredth time, if their kiss in the garden had sparked something off…something they were both in denial of.

As they left the pub, Max and Chloe jumped out of the way as another gaggle of revellers pushed their way in the door. Max kissed her lightly on the cheek.

'Keep me posted hun; if there's anything I can do, message me. We have to get our girl back.'

Arriving back home, Chloe peered into the sitting room in trepidation; if Sam was passed out on the sofa, she was determined not to help him this time. Relieved at seeing said sofa empty, she padded down the corridor, listening carefully; she could hear the soft *tap tap* of a keyboard.

'Hiya, I'm home.' Keeping her voice light and playful, she pushed open his door.

'Nice evening, did you?' Sam growled, pounding his keys harder as he stole a glance over at Chloe. 'Did Max have any wise words to say about me? Any useful advice to help you deal with me?' He sneered.

'Yes, in fact, he did; he suggested I move out and leave you to it.' Chloe pulled his door shut with a bang.

***

Absorbed in trying to figure out how to rescue Ethan Winters's baby daughter in Resident Evil, Sam didn't hear the doorbell ring at first, but the pounding on the door soon got his attention. Glancing at his watch, he frowned, far too early for his pizza delivery; he'd only ordered it ten minutes ago.

Heaving himself off the sofa, he reached for the detestable crutches and headed slowly and painfully to the door. Lorenzo clutched a pack of beers in one hand and a huge bucket of KFC in the other, which he raised in the air by way of an entry fee.

'Wasn't sure if this was still your thing, but I am willing to eat all of it if not.' He grinned.

Struggling to regain his composure as he hung on to the door frame, Sam gawped in shock at the wonderful sight of his friend.

'You gonna invite me in, or shall we eat in the hallway?'

'Oh…erm, yeah, sure, come in.' Sam desperately tried to smooth down his wrinkled tee shirt and tidy his hair as he followed Lorenzo through to the living room.

Glancing around the messy flat whilst trying not to look too disgusted, Lorenzo headed for the kitchen, returning with two plates and a bottle of tomato ketchup. He'd been prepared to find Sam in bad shape but wasn't expecting such a big change in him. As Lorenzo watched him heave his black booted legs on to the sofa with a grunt, his eyes took in the shambolic mess that Sam had become. A grubby, stained T-shirt strained to cover his flabby stomach; his hair was long and tied back in a greasy ponytail. Various packets of pills were lying open on the table, vying for space between empty coffee cups and play-station games.

'So, you've been avoiding me, buddy, why?' Lorenzo got straight to the point, having decided tough tactics were needed after Chloe contacted him and explained her fears for Sam's mental health.

'Why the fuck do you think Rez? Look at me.' Sam snapped back, gesturing with an angry flick of a hand.

Lorenzo eyed the empty pizza boxes strewn around the room and the beer cans spewing from the bin in the kitchen.

'Well, you don't have to live like a bloody tramp, Sam. When did you last have a shower?' The words were out before Lorenzo could stop them, regretting his harsh tone as the tears welled in Sam's eyes.

'Oh Jesus, man, I'm sorry. Look, can't we just—' Sam lifted a hand.

'I know Rez, okay? I know I'm a mess; I just can't—' Sam shook his head, unable to find the words. Lorenzo waited, unsure what he should do or say. He wasn't prepared for this. Chloe had said it was bad, but he didn't think Sam would have sunk so low.

Seeming to have gained control again, Sam reached for a beer but paused in the opening of it. He stared at it for a while as if it held the answers he was seeking. Placing the beer back on the grubby table with a heavy sigh, he flopped back down on the sofa, throwing an arm over his eyes. He began to talk quietly at first before getting more and more agitated.

'You know the worst of it, Rez, I can cope with the pain, thanks to those babies.' He gestured to the various packets on the table.

'I can cope with Chloe wanting to feed me and water me like I was some sort of delicate plant; it's the boredom Rez, I sit on this sodding sofa all day watching TV and playing games. The highlight of my week is hobbling to the bathroom to have a 'Bowel Movement,' as the doctors so quaintly put it.' He glanced over at Lorenzo, who was frowning in confusion at this last activity.

'Erm, what's the deal about that then?'

'The pills, Rez, they make me constipated.'

Lorenzo nodded knowingly, unsure what to say.

'So then Chloe comes home from UNI, full of stories about her day and how everyone is missing me and wishing me well, my tutor said this, and a patient said that, and then she asks about my day, and I tell her I've had a shit.'

'Well, yeah, I guess that doesn't exactly make for good conversation, does it?' Lorenzo grinned, reaching for a beer. He passed one to Sam, who struggled up into a sitting position.

'I know I'm probably depressed; the doctors want to give me pills for that too, but I know they can be addictive, so I refused.'

Lorenzo opened his mouth to say something, but having had no experience with this kind of thing, he changed his mind and just passed Sam the bucket of KFC, the gesture seeming to break the melancholic mood.

'...and as for the shower.' Sam continued through a mouthful of chicken, 'My nursemaid constantly offers to help me. She even came home with waterproof covers for my casts so I can get wet.' Sam laughed, his mood lightening thanks to the food and the beer and the company.

'So, you don't want Chloe seeing you in all your glory then?' Lorenzo grinned, an idea forming in his head.

Half an hour later, having persuaded Sam to let him help, Lorenzo was easing the waterproof covers over Sam's casts, tightening them around the top. He balked when Lorenzo had suggested it, but he'd pointed out that he could hold Sam up where Chloe couldn't if he slipped. Seeing the logic in the plan, Sam reluctantly agreed, especially when Lorenzo reminded him he'd seen his crown jewels on many occasions in showers when they were at karate.

Except we were kids then, and things were…different.

Easing Sam gently out of his clothes wasn't as easy as Lorenzo had envisaged, terrified as he was of Sam losing his balance and crashing to the floor as he hung on to the shower rail for balance. The bruising on Sam's body had turned a vivid yellow and purple; he winced as he lifted his arms up to allow Lorenzo to remove his tee shirt. The shorts were easier, the drawstring waist allowing them to drop to his feet.

'Ah, going commando now, eh?' Lorenzo joked, trying to ease the awkward situation he'd found himself in. Looking around, he realised Sam wouldn't be able to stand in the shower unaided, so he dashed into the kitchen and came back brandishing a three-legged stool, which he placed carefully on the shower mat.

'Bloody hell, Rez, are you sure this is safe? If I go down, you won't be able to get me up.' Sam looked fearfully at the makeshift contraption.

'Let's try it and see.'

Stepping gingerly into the shower, Lorenzo plonked himself on the stool, wriggling and bouncing on it by way of demonstration. Sam shook his head fearfully but agreed to give it a try, placing his hands on his friend's shoulders for balance as Lorenzo eased him down gently on the stool before reaching over to turn on the shower.

'I'll just sit here, okay?' Lorenzo shouted over the roar of the water as he perched on the edge of the toilet seat.

Sam leaned back and closed his eyes, losing himself in the soothing effects of the warmth and steam. He washed his hair, soaped his bruised and battered body, and wondered if he could love anyone as much as he loved Lorenzo at this moment.

Leaving his uncomfortable perch on the toilet to go in search of something more suitable, Lorenzo returned with a chair from the kitchen; he glanced into the shower and smiled to himself, happy he was able to do something to help Sam. Lost in thought about work and his grandfather Lorenzo didn't hear Sam calling to him above the noise of the shower. When he finally realised Sam needed him, he leapt up and dashed over.

'Jesus, man, I've nearly dissolved in here; what were you doing?' Sam laughed as his friend reached past him and turned off the shower before handing him a towel. Lorenzo waited as Sam tried in vain to dry his hair with the towel; the activity and the heat from the shower had drained him, and he leaned forward in defeat, elbows resting on his knees.

'Here, let me.'

Taking the towel, Lorenzo began to gently dry the long, silky locks. Sam leaned back, closing his eyes, his head resting on Lorenzo's stomach. Trying hard to ignore his pounding heart, Lorenzo dropped the towel in Sam's lap and ran his fingers through his hair, carefully untangling the mass of curls.

'You need a haircut, mate.' He quipped jovially whilst desperately trying to keep his voice level.

The process of getting Sam back out of the shower wasn't quite so straightforward. Lorenzo stood looking at him, trying to figure out the best way to go about it. They decided the waterproof covering on the casts should come off first as they would be slippery. Bending down, Lorenzo began easing the covers off. Again, Sam placed his hands on his friend's shoulders for support. In this position, Lorenzo carefully backed out of the shower cubicle with Sam hanging on to him; both terrified that one little slip would be catastrophic.

'This reminds me of when we were drunk in Winchester. I had to hold you up then, too.' Lorenzo said.

'Who held *whom* up? Sam laughed, glancing up at Lorenzo, their faces inches apart as they realised this was their first physical contact since the fateful kiss in the garden. Suddenly, something changed; the laughter and the banter replaced with something deeper as their eyes met. Lorenzo's eyes moved down Sam's torso, taking in the lurid purple bruises over his ribs; he saw, reflected in the mirror, newly healed wounds on his back, the stitch marks still visible, showing white against the angry red slashes.

'Oh god, man, I'm so sorry this happened to you.' Struggling for composure, he cradled Sam's head against his shoulder, his strong arms encircling Sam's back as he held him close.

Sam's head was swimming. He was finding it hard to breathe; he wasn't sure if it was the effect of the pills and alcohol or because he was standing naked in Lorenzo's arms. Somewhere, buried deep in the fog of his brain, a voice was urging him to step back and break the contact. Lorenzo's breath, warm on his neck, was sending waves tingling down his spine. Sam felt a stirring begin to awaken deep within as Lorenzo moved his hand lower, caressing his buttock and pulling him in closer, hip to hip.

'Rez, Rez, don't.' Sam whispered.

Raising his head, Lorenzo gazed down at Sam before wiping a long strand of damp hair from his eyes. He smiled and slowly shook his head.

'I don't know what the hell's going on, Sam. I'm sorry, man, it's just, seeing you like this…you know?'

'Erm…I'm getting a bit cold here, Rez, could we—' Sam gestured to his clothes in a bid to lighten the atmosphere. The diversion worked, and Lorenzo switched back to *nurse* mode, gathering up Sam's discarded clothes from the floor. The practicalities of getting Sam dressed and into his room served to relieve the awkward moment. After easing Sam on to his bed, Lorenzo looked around the room, wondering what else he would need. Sam shifted his battered body with a groan as he tried to get comfortable.

'I suppose I'd better go, get my train home.' Lorenzo fished his phone out of his pocket, more for something to do than necessity.

'Stay for a bit longer, Rez? Please, mate.' Sam reached an arm out.

Lorenzo looked around for a chair, but Sam patted the empty space beside him on the bed.

'Okay, I promise I'll behave.' Lorenzo grinned as he gently lay back on the pillows, terrified he might hurt Sam.

'D'you remember the last time we shared a bed, well a sleeping bag actually, in that tent in—' A loud snore from Sam stopped his reminiscing, so Lorenzo lay quietly, his mind churning once again. What the hell happened in the bathroom? What sort of weird madness possessed him to behave like that, he was supposed to be here to cheer up his friend, not seduce him.

He concluded it was just the emotion of the whole thing, seeing Sam hurt and battered had affected him deeply. He wanted to hold him, caress him, mend his broken body. A small contradiction hovered at the back of his mind.

Are you sure that's all you wanted?

Sam grunted in his sleep and cried out, seemingly tormented by some dark demon. Lorenzo reached over and caressed his shoulder, careful to keep his distance this time. Sam's inner struggles ceased at the gentle touch, and he rolled over, one arm draping across Lorenzo's chest. Taking a deep breath, he allowed himself to explore how he felt at that moment. Why did he keep making the same mistake when he was with Sam? They weren't drunk, well, not very, his excuse the last time was Samantha. Turning his head, Lorenzo studied the sleeping form beside him, the soft, full lips slightly parted, long black eyelashes, and soft, silky hair that had grown far too long. This wasn't Samantha.

Deep in thought, he reached up, caressing the heavy arm across his chest. They'd never really talked about how Sam felt after the kiss in the garden. It was always Lorenzo apologising, blaming himself for his disgusting behaviour. He supposed Samantha had been too drunk to remember much of it, they were both drunk, but she more so. He chuckled to himself as he remembered the hapless guy he'd punched into the pond in the garden; he also remembered how enraged he was when he saw Samantha struggling to get away from him.

Lorenzo fell asleep then, wrapped in Sam's arms, and that's how Chloe found them when she came back from university.

Chapter 26

'Why do you always do that?' Lorenzo asked Gemma as she played with melting candle wax in the restaurant.

'Dunno really, it's just comforting, I 'spose.' Gemma smiled, her eyes glued to the flickering candle.

They'd gone out after work, and Gemma was keen to hear more about Lorenzo's visit to Sam. He'd told her as much as he could about their friendship and Sam's accident, omitting to mention the incident in the bathroom. It wasn't that he was ashamed of his close bond with Sam, more that he felt it would be a betrayal to discuss it with anyone else. At least, that's what he told himself. Gemma commented that she also had a friend whom she felt very close to, almost bordering on being in love with them. He felt a flash of irritation as he noticed her watching him for a reaction.

Lorenzo glanced out of the window at the people rushing by, huddled under umbrellas as the rain pelted down. A steady stream of water gurgled down the small, cobbled street, causing people to hop about avoiding the puddles. He turned back to Gemma, who had managed to snuff out the candle on their table.

'Ha, I knew that would happen.' He laughed.

Gemma pursed her lips in a pretend sulk whilst eyeing up a full candle on another table.

'What do you think about Malik and Jinx wanting to buy a diving club?' he asked her, by way of distraction from Sam.

'Well, it certainly has the whole office buzzing for sure.' Gemma sipped her drink before continuing.

'I mean, it would be amazing, wouldn't it, running your own business doing something you love somewhere warm and sunny, what's not to love? I think it'd be great, better than being stuck at bloody Octagon forever.'

Gemma had invited him out for a drink to celebrate his promotion at work. Richie had called him in for an interview with senior management the week before, and to his amazement, they had decided to promote him to senior administrator. Whilst Lorenzo remained unconvinced about his dazzling career in insurance, he'd welcomed the boost to his ego and the fact that he was no longer bottom of the pecking order. Even the odious Nick had managed to mumble congratulations, his face contorted with resentment.

Jinx and Malik finally arrived in the pub and settled down with their drinks, patting Lorenzo on the back as they did so.

'So, are we gonna have to call you boss now?' Jinx laughed.

'You'd better fucking not, mate.' Lorenzo grinned, secretly enjoying his newly elevated status.

'I don't get it though.' Malik took a huge swig of beer before continuing. 'I mean, you don't even like the job, do you?' He lifted his palms in confusion.

'I can't imagine anything worse than spending the next 30 years stuck in an office.' Lorenzo immediately regretted his comment as Jinx launched into his sales pitch to buy a dive club. Gemma helpfully reminded him that it would actually be 40 years stuck in an office.

'Well then, if you hate it so much, come in with us, and let's get a diving club.' Jinx warmed to his subject, and the next hour was spent plotting and planning; the more beer they drank, the more bizarre the plans got. Lorenzo pointed out that none of them were diving instructors, nor did they have any money or the capital to raise any. Jinx went very quiet and ponderous at the mention of money, and Lorenzo had a sneaky suspicion that perhaps he had a secret cache somewhere. He was about to ask him when his phone pinged. He glanced at it quickly, not intending to read the message, but it was Sam.

'Hey Rez, I'm coming home for a few days next week... crutches 'n all, you around?'

'Bloody right I'll be around Bro', I'll come over, let me know when'

Scrolling back through his messages, Lorenzo grinned to himself as he re-read Sam's account of what had happened after he left his flat the last time. It would appear that Chloe had come home whilst he and Sam were asleep on the bed; she'd jumped to conclusions immediately and had gone running off to Max to report the news. Lorenzo had messaged back to point out that they were both fully clothed, and she was being ridiculous.

Thinking back to that day at Sam's, he felt a warm, soft wave wash gently through him as he remembered helping his friend, how helpless Sam had been, and the pain he had to endure. Lorenzo had surprised himself when he'd launched into action to help Sam shower and dress. Never having to provide such personal care for anyone before, he'd felt he had to take control somehow and try to lift Sam out of the deep, dark hole he had sunk into. It had worked, he thought. It had definitely brought their friendship back to where it should be and beyond. He focused on the moment in the bathroom, a smile playing on his lips as he remembered Sam's head against his chest, his hair splayed out in a tangle. The memory of holding Sam's naked body so close was sending lightning bolts down to his groin.

'...What do you think, Rez?' He welcomed Jinx's interruption to his erotic reverie.

'Erm, sorry man, what were you saying?' Taking refuge in his beer for a moment, he tried to remember their conversation as he tried to erase the erotic images. Jinx sighed theatrically and reminded him that they were discussing diving again.

'Malik says he's gonna come into an inheritance soon, quite a bit of money apparently; we could set up the diving business, he said.'

'What? How much?' Lorenzo was suddenly very interested and allowed himself to imagine handing in his notice, giving the odious Nick the finger, and running off to the Mediterranean to spend the rest of his life scuba diving in the sunshine.

***

Trying desperately to stop his leg from tapping up and down, Lorenzo was fully aware that it was a nervous habit, and everyone around the table knew it, too. Under his newly elevated status, he'd been invited to sit in on a management meeting. Richie had introduced him as Lorenzo Murphy and laughingly told his fellow managers that he was called 'Murph' for short. An hour into the meeting, he noticed that everyone referred to him as Lorenzo. Richie, sensing disapproval from his fellow managers, also dropped the 'Murph' much to Lorenzo's amusement. As much as he tried to follow the discussion about projections and budgets, Lorenzo realised he had nothing to contribute and was struggling to think of something sensible to say. He listened carefully, hoping to seize on some small snippet on which to comment, but instead arranged his face into a thoughtful, ponderous expression with an occasional nod of the head for emphasis.

'So, what was the big boots meeting all about?' Gemma was sitting on his desk, her legs swinging as she sipped a coffee.

'I have no bloody idea Gemms, forecasts and budgets and spreadsheet after sodding spreadsheet.' Lorenzo shook his head in bewilderment as he gazed out of the large window.

'Forty years of this, you said?' His face echoing the horror.

Gemma laughed, rolling her eyes in despair. She struggled to understand Lorenzo's lack of enthusiasm for his career. Whilst she was very ambitious, never missing an opportunity to apply for senior posts, he just seemed to drift along as if in a daze. He seemed to be enthusiastic when offered the management trainee promotion, but somehow, recently, he'd gone off the boil again.

'Fancy a drink after work? Maybe you can cheer me up like.' He wiggled his eyebrows suggestively.

'Come to my place, I'll cook.' She smiled at him, amused at the lascivious expression.

***

'Can I borrow the car tonight, Dad?' Lorenzo poked his head in the kitchen door to find Angie and Jim sitting at the table looking very glum. The aroma of fresh toast wafted over him.

'Oh, erm, what's happened?' He looked from one to the other, trying to work out which one of them had been affected by the bad news. He concluded it was his mother as she kept dabbing at her eyes with a tissue. His father had his *'don't worry, I'll take care of this'* expression, which Lorenzo had seen many times.

'It's your grandfather. He's very ill in a hospital in Italy.' Jim looked up at Lorenzo whilst patting his wife's hand.

Lorenzo was torn, he knew he should stay at home and support his mother, but he really wanted to go to Gemma's for dinner and hopefully be invited to stay over.

'Oh no, how bad is it? I mean, is he—' Jim shook his head sadly, at which point Angie looked up, more tears filling her eyes.

'You off out then love?' She sniffed and smiled in a *'the show must go on'* kind of way, which always fascinated Lorenzo; why she felt the need to focus on some mundane event when clearly something very big was happening, he could never understand.

'I can stay if you want me to?' He offered, praying she'd say she didn't need him.

'Take my car, Rez, go and enjoy yourself, lad.' Jim said, taking charge.

Thanking his father, he dashed upstairs for a shower, checking his phone for the time. He messaged Gemma quickly to say he'd be late before rummaging around in his wardrobe for a clean shirt.

***

The lights were down low and there was a scented candle flickering on the coffee table. Lorenzo and Gemma were snuggled up on the sofa watching *Love Actually*, her favourite film. They'd analysed each storyline, from Emma Thompson's cheating husband to Hugh Grant's prime minister. Gemma was very keen to hear his point of view on each scenario; he felt at times as if he was being interviewed, one of those *'what would you do in this situation'* questions. The scented candle was beginning to catch in Lorenzo's throat, so Gemma leaned across him to snuff it out, sliding her body on top of his as she did so. Reaching up, he enfolded her in his arms.

'Mmm, you smell so much better than that candle,' he mumbled appreciatively.

She gazed down at him, her blonde hair falling over their faces as she lowered her lips to his. Lorenzo shifted his position slightly, his legs too long for the sofa. As the kiss deepened, she moved her hips against his. He groaned, moving his hands down to her buttocks, desperate to increase the pressure. She stopped moving and lifted her head, looking down at him through her lashes. Lorenzo panicked, instantly regretting his hand-to-buttock manoeuvre.

'Oh, jeeze, I'm sorry, Gemms, I—'

'So, are you staying tonight or what?'

Lorenzo didn't need asking twice; his intention at that moment was to scoop her up in his arms and carry her to the bedroom, romantic hero style. Unfortunately, his foot had become wedged down the back of the sofa, and they both ended up sprawled on the floor.

'Well, I s'pose here is as good as anywhere.' Gemma giggled before resuming where they'd left off before hitting the floor. Fumbling now with Lorenzo's belt, she suddenly stopped. 'Erm …do you have any—?'

Fishing around in his back pocket, Lorenzo produced the little packet with a flourish.

'Hmmm, you were hopeful then,' She laughed, one eyebrow raised.

'One can always hope.' He grinned, kissing her once more.

Chapter 27

Sam was beginning to regret his decision to come home after his mother asked him for the hundredth time if he needed anything. He'd known it was going to be difficult, always finding it hard to be back in his parent's house after living away; they could never seem to treat him as an adult, always reverting to *mother knows best* mode, although to be fair, he had somehow always reverted to childlike dependency when he was in their house.

They were sitting in the living room, Sam's crutches propped up beside him on the sofa. His big German Shepherd had insisted on squeezing his massive bulk in beside him, the huge soft head snoring gently on his lap. His mother was holding the TV remote, aimlessly flicking from channel to channel.

'What do you want to watch, Love? She asked, whilst continuing to flick.

'I don't really watch TV much, Mum, so you put on what you like.' Sam continued to scroll through Instagram on his phone. He'd hoped to have heard from Lorenzo by now, having messaged him yesterday to say he was home. He'd had several messages from Chloe, apologising for jumping to conclusions and flouncing off to see Max, who had also messaged several times in an effort to calm the troubled waters. He'd also received a message from his old flame Calum, apparently, he'd heard about the accident and wanted to catch up. An email pinged up his solicitor, updating him on how his claim for accident compensation was going. Sam's eyes widened at the figure being quoted, and he re-read the case his solicitor was putting forward. Pain and suffering, loss of earnings, loss of future career in Dentistry. This last statement hurt the most, although with the amount of cash on offer, he needn't worry too much about his finances.

'Are you hungry love?' Julia Brewer's voice broke through his concentration.

Sam managed to keep control of his face, which at that moment was transforming into a scowl; this was the third time in an hour she'd wanted to feed him.

'No thanks, Mum, I'm fine.' He managed to say the words again…for the third time in an hour. Picking up his phone again, he stared at it, willing it to display the little green circle with a phone in the middle.

For fucks sakes Rez where are you?

'What a shame Dan's not here. He could have kept you company.' Emilia turned, smiling.

'Oh yeah, where is he then?' Sam couldn't have cared less where his waste of space brother was; he was just glad it wasn't here.

'He and your father had a terrible row; it was awful, your father told him to go. I think he's staying with some friends, but I'm not sure. He hasn't been back since.' She shook her head sadly; Sam said a quick prayer of thanks whilst nodding sympathetically.

The dull ache in his left leg was building up. Sam knew that within half an hour or so, the raging fire would be intolerable. Reaching over the dog, he grabbed his pills, gulping down two with a slug of water.

'Ah love, is the pain coming back?' Emilia laid her hand softly on his leg, tears beginning to well up in her eyes. As much as it irritated Sam to have her fussing over him constantly, he knew she loved him and was devastated about his accident; it made it harder somehow, knowing the hurt he was causing her.

'Did you—' the doorbell rang, saving Sam from having to answer yet more questions. He listened carefully over the loud barking from his dog as the footsteps came down the hallway, his heart pounding as he recognised Lorenzo's voice.

'Hey Bro' how goes it?' Lorenzo grinned, holding aloft a pack of beers whilst fussing the big dog who'd jumped down to greet him.

Sam's eyes flicked over to his mother who was regarding Lorenzo with a murderous stare.

'You know he shouldn't mix alcohol with his painkillers, Rez.' She tutted, arms firmly folded against her chest. Lorenzo was reminded of a lioness protecting her cubs from the big bad wolf.

'Alcohol-free, Mrs Brewer.' He said proudly, pointing to the label.

'I'll leave you to it then.' She left the room with a suspicious look back over her shoulder.

Plonking down on the sofa opposite Sam, Lorenzo ran his eyes quickly over his friend, concluding he was in much better shape than the last time he'd seen him.

'Alcohol-free? Bloody hell, man?' Sam moaned.

'Ah well, I have the car. I thought we could go to the pub for a bit, get you out, you know?' Lorenzo lifted a shoulder, not sure if his grand plan of whisking Sam away from Emilia was a good idea.

Reaching for his crutches, Sam was on his feet in seconds, gesturing to Lorenzo to head for the front door. 'We're just popping out for a while, Mum.' He called up the stairs, ushering Lorenzo out quickly as they closed the front door.

Sam just wanted to drive out somewhere, so they ended up in a small side street that backed onto the Water- Meadows. Lorenzo fished a heavy backpack out of the boot before walking slowly and carefully down to the river, Sam's crutches crunching on the gravel path as they sat down on a park bench.

'I can't believe you'd do this to me, Rez.' Sam shook his head sadly whilst studying the rear end of a mallard whose head was under the water.

Lorenzo, who had been rooting around in the backpack, looked up, wondering what he'd done wrong this time.

'Alcohol-free, really?' Sam turned, scowling at his friend, who emerged triumphant from his bag with two cans of San Miguel.

'It's all in the planning, mate.' Lorenzo grinned, whilst cracking open a can and handing it to Sam.

'Only one, though, I don't want to be responsible for you overdosing.'

The sun was high in the sky as Sam leaned back, resting his head on the back of the seat. He closed his eyes, tilting his face up to the sun, the iridescence flickering behind his eyelids, the warmth on his face soothing away weeks of torture. Lorenzo sipped his beer quietly, sensing Sam's need to enjoy his break for freedom. He smiled as he watched some children throw stones into the river, wondering at the irresistible urge that compelled people to do it.

Sam sat up straight and looked around him, squinting from the glare of the sun. He'd almost forgotten where he was, his heart gladdened at the sight of his best friend sitting beside him.

'So where did you go then, mate?' Lorenzo grinned.

'I dunno Rez, anywhere away from me I 'spose.' Sam leaned forward, elbows on his thighs, as he, too, watched the stone-throwing contest taking place on the river.

'D'you remember when we used to come down here and do exactly that?'

'Yeah, you were always better than me, but then you cheated.' Lorenzo laughed.

They fell silent again as the children moved on, their places taken up by exuberant wet dogs chasing after balls.

'I was thinking about that day when I was going to get the train for Ali's party, the day that fucking moron ploughed into me.' Sam said out of the blue. 'That would have been the first time we'd met up after, you know.' He shrugged, embarrassed to have brought it up.

'Yeah, it's funny, I've often thought about that too, what if, you know?'

'I was going to come as Samantha.' The words were out before he could stop them. Lorenzo turned his head away, unable to trust his face at that moment. He'd often thought about that very scenario; what would he have done if Sam had made it to the party dressed as Samantha? How would his parents have reacted, or, God help him, his grandmother?

'I did wonder if you would.' He risked a sideways glance at Sam, a trace of a smile on his lips.

'I miss her.' Sam wondered at this sudden cathartic release but realised the truth behind what he'd said. This momentous change in his life had to be faced; he needed to be honest with his friend if their relationship was to continue.

'Did you ever, I mean, does it help to…erm, be her, when you're just at home like, on your own?' Lorenzo wasn't really sure what it was he was trying to say; he didn't want to cause offense with insensitive remarks, but he wanted to try and understand.

'Yeah, it helps; I know it must sound ridiculous to you, Rez, but I s'pose it's a bit like any other addiction, more like a compulsion, I guess.' Sam shrugged a shoulder before taking a big gulp from his can; he continued.

'Life gets tough and it just makes me feel like, I dunno, me I s'pose, a different me, maybe.'

'But you still don't want to, you know. Transition?' Lorenzo plucked up the courage to ask the question that had been burning in him since the fateful night in the garden.

'Nah, nothing as complicated as that Rez. I'm happy in my body. I just need Samantha, sometimes.' Sam delved into Lorenzo's backpack and emerged with two more cans, giving his friend a *'you lied to me'* look. Lorenzo put up his hands with a grin as they cracked open the cans.

'Have you told your parents about…you know?' Lorenzo grimaced as the warm beer slid down his throat.

'What? No way, man, they don't even know I'm gay.'

'I bet they do, you know, parents aren't stupid,' Lorenzo laughed and continued. 'D'you remember that time I left a load of condoms in one of my dad's cars in the showroom?'

'Oh god, yeah. Get you, *"a load of condoms."* How many was it then?' Sam chuckled.

'Mmm, at least four.' Lorenzo boasted with a grin before adding, 'The thing is, my dad wasn't half as pissed as I thought he'd be. In fact, I think he found it all very funny, so I bet your parents wouldn't care anyway…why should they?'

'I always hated her, that girl you were with. Whasername.' Sam frowned.

'Hated her, why?' Lorenzo was puzzled.

'I was jealous of her, Rez. She took you away from me.' Sam thought he might as well carry on with the big revelations, cards on the table, and all that.

Lorenzo was momentarily lost for words; his relationship with Tessa was never serious, on his part anyway. He had no idea Sam felt that way back then; he wanted to know more but wasn't sure he would like what Sam had to say. It would appear the same thought had occurred to Sam as he suddenly grabbed Lorenzo's arm.

'Oh, no, man, not like that, just like jealous of another friend, you know?' Sam sounded desperate.

Breathing a sigh of relief, Lorenzo glanced at his watch. They'd been out for a couple of hours, and he knew Emilia would be getting twitchy. As if on cue, Sam's phone pinged; he fished it out of his pocket, glanced at it, and shoved it back in.

'Mother checking up on you?' Lorenzo asked with a smile.

They sat for another hour or so, Sam asking about Lorenzo's lost and recently found Italian grandfather. Lorenzo said Sam should tell his parents about his sexuality, adding that if he met someone, he'd want to introduce him to them. It wasn't an easy conversation; the thought of Sam meeting a guy didn't sit easily with Lorenzo. He knew he had no claim on Sam's affections in that regard, but even so, he dreaded the day when it would happen. As if to compound matters even more, Sam mentioned his old boyfriend Calum from Bristol had been in touch and was coming to Winchester in a few days, which just added to Lorenzo's angst.

They laughed about Jinx and Malik wanting to buy a dive club, Lorenzo admitting that giving up his boring job at Octagon and living his life diving in the sunshine was very appealing despite their lack of money.

'Well, I have to give up dentistry, not that I ever really started; maybe I should fund your dive club with my compensation money. We could both go and live in the sun.' Sam laughed.

'Bloody hell, man, how much will you get?' Lorenzo's eyes widened at the sudden possibility.

'Dunno mate, a few hundred thousand, I think.' Sam grinned.

'We'd have to—' Sam suddenly caught his breath as a red-hot streak shot down his leg.

'Arggg Jesus, that was a bad one.' Sam reached down to massage his leg, his face contorted in agony. Feeling helpless and blaming himself for bringing Sam out and plying him with alcohol, Lorenzo decided he'd better get Sam home. They headed slowly and carefully back to the car, Lorenzo imagining all sorts of repercussions waiting for him, not least of all an angry Julia Brewer.

Lorenzo helped Sam back into his house, dashing back to the car before Emilia spotted him. On the drive home, his thoughts were racing. Calum, what did he know about this Calum guy? He cast his mind back to Sam's first few months at university, had he mentioned him then? Lorenzo didn't think there had been anyone serious, but Sam seemed very keen to meet up with him. Maybe he was just a friend, concerned about a mate? Impatient to find out, he stopped in a car park and fished his phone out, scrolling through Facebook; the need to know was overwhelming. Clicking on Sam's profile, he scrolled through the photos, and there he was, slim, blonde, with light green eyes. Lorenzo was mesmerised. He enlarged the photos, trying to get a better view of this Calum guy. Unaware he'd been holding his breath, he let it out with a sigh on realising that Calum had featured quite largely in Sam's life. He had to admit they did look good together. Sam looked so happy back then. Wondering why they had split up, he found himself hoping that it was Sam who ended it, but why? What did it matter to him? His stomach was in a knot, and he felt sick.

What the hell's wrong with you? You knew this would happen sooner or later; you'd both meet someone. Marriage, babies…all that stuff.

He thought about Gemma; he liked her, sure, but was that all? How would he feel if she went out with someone else? The answer to that was yes; he would care a lot, but Sam, his Sam, cut him to the core.

The thought police were nagging again.

You're jealous my friend, jealous, jeal—

Flinging his phone onto the back seat in an effort to erase the whispering voice, Lorenzo started up the car, ramming it into first gear before spilling out into the heavy Winchester traffic. He tried to focus on a message he'd had from Jinx earlier, something about a Diving Instructor's course in the Red Sea that would be awesome, no, that would be *essential* if they wanted to run a diving club. He wondered about the cost of such a venture; Malik had decided to use his inheritance money to buy a house, so that was no longer an option, then there was Sam. He'd mentioned funding the project with his compensation pay-out; was he serious? Could they work together to run a business?

Arriving home now and in a better frame of mind, Lorenzo pushed open the front door and headed for the stairs. The smell of hot toast wafted down the hallway from the kitchen; glancing at his watch, he frowned, three o'clock in the afternoon…something must be wrong.

'Is that you, Rez?' Angie's voice quivered. He was right, something bad had happened. Pushing open the kitchen door, he quickly glanced around; no-one was missing, thank God. Ali and his father were both there, sitting at the table, his father with an arm around his wife for comfort. He could see she had been crying but was now just sniffling into a hanky. Ali looked up at him with a *'thank god you're here'* expression. Lorenzo noted the remains of the toast fest scattered on the countertop. Heaving herself off the chair, Angie went over to her adored son, enveloping him in a bleary-eyed hug.

'Rez, your grandfather…has died love.' The saying of the words made her tears flow once more. Returning the hug, Lorenzo patted her back as she buried her head in his chest. He looked over her head to his father. Jim Murphy's face was grim.

'Does Grandma know yet?' He asked softly.

'We've only just heard ourselves.' Jim said.

Pulling out a chair, Lorenzo dropped down beside Ali, waving away his mother's offering of cold buttered toast. Angie started to tell him the story of poor grandad Lorenzo's last days, waving away her husband's attempts to take over the telling of it. Ali excused herself after half an hour, having already heard the story several times. When Angie protested, she declared that it was all too traumatic and she couldn't bear it anymore. With a sidelong glance at her brother, she escaped to her room and Ariana Grande.

Kissing his mother on the top of her head, he left them to it before slumping sadly upstairs to his room. He needed some time alone with his own grief for the lookalike grandfather he'd never met but who'd had such a big impact on his life. Staring at the once hated photo on his phone he wondered about the life of his grandparents, the love they once shared, which was cruelly snatched away because of her pregnancy, wrong time, wrong place, such a waste. He thought about Lorenzo senior, waiting in his hotel in sun-drenched Tuscany, pining for the girl he fell in love with. Did he never try to come to England? Maybe he'd be able to have that conversation with his grandmother sometime.

Looking at himself in the mirror, he held up the photo, fixing his hair and grinning just as his grandfather had; the resemblance was undeniable. He wondered how grandma would feel now whenever she looked at him…would it be even harder for her, knowing he was dead?

Chapter 28

Don't Print, Save The Planet, demanded the poster above the printer where Lorenzo was waiting for his documents to be spewed out. Sipping his coffee, he gazed out over the car park, smiling to himself as he watched Jinx fling his car into space before running into their building. He was late again and was certain to get a rollicking from Richie. Lorenzo prided himself on always being on time for work. He didn't always manage to get his work in on time, though, resulting in a summons from Richie and yet another grilling about company policy. Gathering up his papers, he shuffled them into some sort of order and headed back to his desk, passing a smirking Nick on the way.

'I see your mate's been called in to see the boss again.'

'Oh, yeah, I think he's up for promotion.' Lorenzo said nonchalantly. He knew it was a stupid thing to say, but it was worth it for the look on Nick's face. He wondered how long it would take to get around the office. Sitting down at his desk, he fished his phone out, surreptitiously checking his messages.

Jinx: *Wow that was close!*

Gemma: *What was all that about?*

Sam: *My mate from Bristol is here, want to meet up?*

Ignoring the first two, Lorenzo stared at the message from Sam, his initial reaction being one of absolute horror. Why would he want to meet *him*?

Shuffling his papers in an effort to look busy, Lorenzo struggled to control his thumping heart. When did Calum arrive? Was he staying in Sam's house? And, more importantly, had they rekindled their relationship? Lorenzo quickly messaged Sam back, ordering his fingers to type before he could change his mind.

'Yup sounds great, when?'

Immediately, he sent the message; he knew he would have to find a way to get out of it.

***

Lying back on his pillows, Lorenzo adjusted the volume on his headphones, trying to drown out the row going on downstairs between Ali and his parents. He had an idea what this one was about; his sister didn't want to go to university, her path having been made easier by Lorenzo's refusal to go. He knew they had pinned all their hopes on Ali. He'd asked his mother why she felt it so important when neither of them knew what they wanted to do with their lives. As he pondered on this, he heard the inevitable door slamming and feet stomping up the stairs.

'Rez, can I come in?' His door opened slightly, and a red-eyed Ali poked her head round.

'Sure.' Lorenzo sighed as he reluctantly removed his headphones, scooting over on the bed so she could slide in beside him.

'So…uni again?' He asked, resigned to the endless debate.

'It's just so unfair, Rez; why do they—' She stopped talking as they heard more footsteps on the stairs. Lorenzo knew this meant the row was going to continue in his room. They both lay quietly, waiting to see who was going to appear. If it was their father, there would be shouting and finger-pointing. If it was Angie, there would be tears and lots of 'disappointment' accusations. A brief knock on the door, and Jim poked his head in, glaring at the two of them, eyebrows knitted in annoyance.

'Is this you, Lorenzo?' Out came the pointy finger before he continued, 'filling her head with rubbish about not needing an education.' The finger flicked briefly towards Ali, who was building up for eruption, volcano fashion.

'I've had a bloody education, Dad, three 'A' levels worth. In fact, I've had such a good fu…friggin education that I can make up my own mind what—' Lorenzo tuned out at that point, replacing his headphones, he turned up the volume. He found it quite amusing watching Ali and his father arguing without hearing their voices. Their faces contorted with rage, arms flailing as each made their point. Picking up his phone, he scrolled through his messages, immediately focusing on the one from Sam.

'Hey Rez, me n Calum are going to the Bishops tonight, you around?

'No, I'm bloody not,' Lorenzo shouted at his phone, momentarily forgetting his father was still in the room before flinging it down on the bed.

It had the desired effect of silencing his sister as she was about to launch into another diatribe. They both glared at Lorenzo, and his father stalked from the room, waving his arm in a gesture of defeat. Ali giggled as she thanked her brother for saving her from another haranguing.

'So, what is it you're not bloody doing, oh brother of mine?' She giggled. Lorenzo shrugged, telling her that Sam wanted to meet up with his 'mate' from Bristol. Ali picked up the inference immediately, tilting her head to one side, her eyes narrowed.

'So, what's wrong with this so-called mate, don't you like him or something?'

'He was Sam's boyfriend for a while when he first went to Bristol, nothing serious; it didn't last long.' Lorenzo shrugged dismissively.

'…And you're bothered about it because?' Ali insisted.

Realising she was getting no response, she flopped back down on the bed before suddenly sitting up excitedly.

'Let's both go, Rez, I haven't seen Sam for ages, and with his accident and everything.' She pleaded, grabbing his arm.

Lorenzo dismissed the suggestion immediately, but it hovered about in his thoughts for a while before he concluded that, actually, it might be fun, and he wouldn't feel quite so much like a third wheel.

'Yeah, why not.' He laughed as Ali jumped off the bed, dashing into her room to get ready.

Sitting in the lounge with his mother, Lorenzo waited for Ali to be ready. As he glanced at his watch, Angie's eagle eye spotted the gesture.

'This is a first, isn't it, you two going out together?' She smiled.

'Yeah, we're going to meet Sam for a drink.' Lorenzo picked up his phone in a futile attempt to ward off any more questions.

'Aw, that's nice…did he—' At that moment, Ali made her grand entrance with an elaborate 'Ta Da'.

'Oh, you look nice love; just going to the pub?' Angie looked quizzically at Lorenzo, who shrugged and raised his hands in a don't ask me gesture. As they left the house, he glanced down at his sister, who was struggling to walk in impossibly high heels coupled with a very short skirt.

'Erm, you do realise these two guys are gay, don't you, sis?' He asked, bewildered.

'Doh, course I do, Rez. I'm not stupid.' She countered, pulling at the hem of her leather skirt. 'A girl likes to look her best, don't ya know.'

Lorenzo knew for a fact that his sister looked her best first thing in the morning, having breakfast in her PJ's, but declined to comment further.

Arriving at the pub, Ali hung on to Lorenzo's arm as she delved into the depths of her enormous bag, emerging triumphant with the high-heeled shoes she'd reluctantly swapped for flats half an hour earlier.

Walking into the dark interior, Lorenzo's stomach was in a knot. As his eyes adjusted to the gloom, he scanned around for Sam, hoping he wouldn't be sitting at their table. The low buzz of conversation and the occasional raucous laughter served to calm him somewhat. He'd feel better after a couple of pints.

Spotting Sam sitting at a table against the back wall, he guided Ali through the crowd, aware of admiring glances from some of the guys. Sam grinned widely when he saw Ali struggling to his feet to give her a hug.

'Oh my god, Sam, oh you poor thing, how are you feeling?' Ali returned the hug, tears filling her eyes as she watched Sam clutch a chair back for balance. Lorenzo looked around for the infamous Calum before spotting him at the bar. He'd looked at his Facebook photos so many times he knew him immediately. Slim hips, pale blonde hair with a reddish stubble. Hovering awkwardly behind Ali, Lorenzo caught Sam's eye and shot him an impatient look over Ali's shoulder. Sam grinned, extricating himself from Ali's ebullient embrace. He gestured for Lorenzo to sit next to him.

'Hey man, how are—' He broke off just as Calum returned with two drinks. Sam made the introductions with a casual wave of a hand.

'Ah, so you're the infamous Rez.' Calum's eyes lazily swept up and down Lorenzo's body.

Okay, I definitely hate you, was Lorenzo's first thought, his second was wanting to punch his lights out. Ali had resumed her interrogation of Sam, which unfortunately left Lorenzo having to make conversation with the hated Calum. After the usual 'What do you do and how long are you here for' openers, Lorenzo had run out of things to say, but aware that Sam was watching him, he resolved to at least try to be civil.

'So, how did you two meet then?' He asked half-heartedly.

'Oh, just the usual LGBGT scene, you know?' Calum sat back, his eyes constantly flicking over to Ali, who was still clutching Sam's hand enthusiastically.

'Your sister is very, um…friendly.'

Lorenzo glared at Ali willing her to shut up and stop monopolising Sam. Needing a diversion, he stood up to go to the bar.

'I'll come with you.' Sam offered, grasping the back of a chair with one hand and his crutches with the other.

'No point in you going to the bar, Sammy love. It's not like you can help now, is it.' Calum drawled patronisingly.

'*Why don't you fuck off,*' Lorenzo thought but said nothing.

Arriving at the bar after struggling through the crowd, Sam was glad to find a bar stool unoccupied. Heaving himself up on it, he grinned at the scowling Lorenzo. 'You and Calum not getting on then?'

'What the hell do you see in that guy Sam, he's a complete arse.'

'Yeah, well, that's why he's my ex isn't it.' Sam laughed, nodding his head in agreement.

'What's he doing here anyway?' Lorenzo knew he was being ridiculous but couldn't hide his jealousy.

'Heard about my accident and wanted to see me, I s'pose. I get the feeling there's more to it, though. It was me who broke it off, he was really upset when we split.'

'So, you don't, erm, want him back?' Lorenzo held his breath, dreading Sam's response

'No, Rez, I don't.' Sam sipped at his drink, looking at Lorenzo through a deep blue gaze. As their eyes locked, a fission of electricity shot between them in acknowledgement of a shared need.

'Sammy love?' Lorenzo laughed, striving to break the intimate bubble they had created at the bar.

'Yeah, well…what do you call your girlfriends Rez, eh?' Sam laughed.

Lorenzo thought about it, thinking of Gemma; he supposed she was his girlfriend. They stayed at the bar catching up for a while, Lorenzo glancing back to their table occasionally to check on Ali, who was regaling Calum with some amusing stories by the looks of it. Calum didn't seem to mind; he was laughing along with her.

'So how long's he here for?' Lorenzo asked casually, hoping his voice didn't betray him.

'Leaving tomorrow, I'm going back to Bristol with him, Rez.'

Lorenzo felt like someone had punched him in the stomach. He'd known Sam wouldn't stay at his parents' house for much longer. It was only a temporary respite. He also knew that it wouldn't have bothered him quite so much if Sam wasn't going back with him. Feeling Calum's eyes boring into the back of his head, Lorenzo turned, glancing back to their table; he was sure Calum was gloating.

'He's only giving me a lift back, Rez. I need to sort my life out, figure out what to do next.' Sam had recognised that look on his friend's face, no matter how hard he'd tried to hide it.

'Yeah, I know, you said.' Lorenzo frowned, feigning indifference.

Heading back to their table, Lorenzo knew he couldn't trust himself to carry on with this farce any longer and announced, to no one in particular, that he needed to go, checking his watch for effect. Ali, who was still deep in conversation with Calum, turned to her brother, protesting she hadn't yet finished her drink. Picking up her glass of wine, Lorenzo obligingly finished it for her.

'You have now.'

'Bloody hell Rez, what's—' Ali glanced from Lorenzo to Sam, wondering what had happened between them at the bar.

'Bye Rez.' Calum smirked, waggling his fingers for effect.

Lorenzo was about to respond, but he caught a look from Sam that told him to leave it. Forcing himself to be the bigger man, he headed for the door, closely followed by an irate Ali.

Pausing outside the pub to replace her heels with flats for walking home, Ali turned to face her brother.

'What the hell was that all about? Calum was just telling me about—' Lorenzo cut her off with a scowl.

'Oh, so you two are great mates now, are you, and what was the infamous Calum telling you about, eh?' Lorenzo knew he was being unreasonable, but he couldn't help himself. He needed to vent his frustration. Picking up the pace he walked quickly on ahead, his long legs outpacing his sister as she ran to keep up with him. Grabbing him by the arm, Ali pulled him to a halt, spinning him around to face her.

'What the hell's wrong with you, Rez? He's a really nice guy; he was telling me about his relationship with Sam and what—'

'Just leave it, okay?' He snapped, shrugging her hand off his arm.

'If I didn't know better, I'd think you were jealous, Rez, or maybe you are…'

'Oh, piss off, Ali.' This time, Lorenzo did manage to walk away. He left his sister glaring after him, her words burning in his heart.

Chapter 29

Lorenzo looked up through the shimmering blue water to the surface 12 meters above and slowly breathed out. Sitting cross-legged at the bottom of the swimming pool, a lead weight across his legs so he didn't float up, he watched as the bubbles meandered their sleepy way to the top. Knowing that Jinx, Liz, and Malik were waiting for him in the bar, he reluctantly left his underwater cocoon and headed for the surface, dragging the lead weight behind him. The diving club hired the municipal pool once a week for training. They offered 'try dives' to anyone interested in taking up the sport, but Lorenzo preferred to spend his time floating at the bottom of the deep end. Jinx and Malik had dubbed him the bottom feeder.

Heading off to the bar after a quick shower, Lorenzo dashed up the stairs, scanning the bar for his friends.

'So you made it then, I thought we'd have to go and rescue you, a bit of CPR 'n all that.' Jinx laughed.

'Yeah, sorry man, you know me when I get underwater.' Lorenzo shrugged.

'Liz has gone to pick up her friend, you remember Melissa from Malta?'

Lorenzo did indeed remember Melissa and her relationship with Liz. He also remembered his own night with Liz on the beach. His thoughts drifted back to their conversation that night, how naïve and unworldly he'd felt when he'd asked her how she could have sex with him on the beach when she was gay. The thought suddenly struck him that maybe now he knew the answer.

Liz and Melissa arrived arm in arm, laughing over a shared joke. Feeling rather awkward after his trip down a very erotic memory lane, Lorenzo busied himself with his bag on the floor.

'So, we have some sad news guys.' Liz announced with an exaggerated pout.

'The sale has fallen through; we can't buy the diving club in Malta.' Melissa looked around at them all sadly.

Lorenzo sipped his beer and listened as the girls related the story about the mortgage offer falling through and their various efforts to secure more funding. As the conversation droned on, an idea began to form, Sam and his suggestion of putting up the cash from his insurance pay-out. Was it possible? Had Sam meant it, or was it just one of their many 'what if' conversations? He tried to remember the context of the conversation, where they were at the time, and, more importantly, whether they were sober.

On the way home, Lorenzo gave his imagination full reign. He saw himself and Sam sipping cold beer on the beach after a full day of diving in the deep blue Mediterranean. Business would be good; they'd be making shed loads of money, and he even had a name for their club. He chuckled to himself, certain that Sam would love it.

Letting himself into the house he checked his watch; he was meeting Gemma later but wanted to message Sam first.

'Is that you, Rez?' Angie called from the kitchen.

Lorenzo paused, irritated in the hallway; why did she always do this, couldn't she just wait 'till he'd been home for a while before ambushing him as soon as he walked in? Glancing into the kitchen, he grumbled to himself.

'Why do you always have to ask if it's me? Who the hell else would it be when everyone else is here already?'

'Yes, Mother, it's me.' He sighed, dumping his bag of wet gear on the floor.

As he went into the kitchen, he was relieved to see that it couldn't be bad news as the toaster wasn't involved. In fact, Angie had a very odd look on her face, almost trying to control a smile whilst nervously chattering about what to have for dinner. Jim, on the other hand, was wearing his 'this is a serious matter' face. He glanced at Ali for any clue as to the reason for the family gathering. She just shrugged. Assuming this was going to be yet another row about Ali and UNI, Lorenzo headed for the fridge, returning with a plate of cold meat and tomato ketchup.

'So, wassup?' he asked through a mouthful of chicken.

His parents glanced at each other conspiratorially, Jim conceding the telling of the news to his wife with a nod of his head. As Lorenzo tucked into his chicken, Angie took a deep breath.

'Well, as you know, your grandfather's funeral was last week; his family didn't want us there, understandable, I s'pose, I would have liked to have gone, but he—'

'God rest his soul.' Jim interjected, crossing himself piously. Lorenzo grinned as Angie narrowed her eyes, glaring at her husband.

Wondering how much longer this family conference was going to take, he checked his watch, itching to message Sam. Composing several messages in his mind he wondered how to ask about the insurance money.

'Hey Sam, you know that money you're going to get ...'

'Hi buddy, erm you remember that diving club idea...'

'...so I'm giving you each £50,000.' Angie said, finally giving in to a wide beaming smile.

Lorenzo was transported at great speed back to the conversation in the kitchen, desperately trying to make sense of what his mother had just said. His father, on noticing the bewildered expression on his son's face, guffawed with laughter.

'That'll teach you not to listen to your mother, my lad.'

Looking to Ali for confirmation of what he'd just heard, Lorenzo could see that she, too, was stunned, her mouth gaping open in shock.

'Erm, could you say that again, Mum, just to be clear, you know.' Lorenzo was shaking, could this be true? Had he misheard?

By the time Angie had told the story several times whilst allowing her husband to put his own unique spin on it, Lorenzo had calmed down, his heart resuming its usual languid pace. He was stunned, lost for words as the realisation hit him. He'd just been handed £50,000. Ali was dancing around the room, chattering about getting a car and moving into a flat of her own as Jim was sagely advising on investment interest rates.

Lorenzo went back over the story in his mind; apparently, Lorenzo senior had left everything in his will to his three children, Angie being one of them. The other two back in Italy had sold the hotel and divided the assets according to their father's will. Lorenzo could only imagine how they must have felt about it.

'So, any plans for yours, Rez?' Angie asked.

'Well, if you want my advice, you'll—' his father started.

'I'm gonna buy a diving club.' Lorenzo was as stunned to say it as his parents were to hear it. But as soon as the words were out, the thought settled and took hold; maybe now he actually could.

***

As the train pulled into Bristol, Lorenzo veered between feeling extremely excited and very nervous. He'd gone over all the scenarios several times on the journey. As his father had helpfully pointed out, 50k would not buy him a business, but it allowed him to contribute. Sam would see that he was serious, willing to put his whole inheritance into the venture. It would put them on a more even footing. He'd laid the groundwork, messaging Liz to say he was interested in buying the dive club; Melissa had said the owners were desperate to sell, and she'd also offered to stay on and work for them as an instructor if they ever managed to buy it.

Walking up to Sam's flat, Lorenzo went over and over his opening line. By the time he rang the bell, he was convinced Sam would laugh and say no way.

'Hey Rez, good to see you, man.' Sam opened the door and enveloped Lorenzo in a hug. It was a man hug by definition, as in lots of fists bumping on the back, but with an added intensity they could both feel.

'Good to see you too bro; you look amazing.' Lorenzo stood back to admire this new Sam. Gone was the flabby stomach and lank, greasy hair, now replaced with a firm, muscular torso, and soft, shiny black hair, still too long for Lorenzo's liking.

'Yeah, I thought it was time.' Sam laughed, patting his stomach.

Handing his friend a beer, Sam flopped down on the sofa as they settled into their familiar camaraderie.

'Just the one crutch now, I see.' Lorenzo nodded approvingly at the solitary crutch propped up on the chair.

'It was necessary Rez, losing the weight and getting stronger, means I can hold myself better, you know?'

Sam went on to explain how a conversation with Max helped him to pull himself together. It was a choice of diet or buy bigger clothes, neither of which appealed. He'd been going for regular physio sessions after the accident and so he'd asked the guy there to design a full fitness program to get him back into shape.

'So you approve of the new me then?' Sam grinned, lifting his T-shirt to show off his newly acquired abs.

'Absolutely, man, well done, you look amazing.' Lorenzo admired said abs before adding.

'Didn't manage a haircut then?' His eyes taking in the soft black curls as they tumbled to Sam's shoulders.

Sam laughed, self-consciously sweeping back an errant strand behind his ear, a gesture so familiar to Lorenzo for many years. Feeling his mouth grow dry, Lorenzo took another few swigs of beer and tried to focus on the reason he'd come to see his friend. Realising he'd better get on with it before they'd drunk too much, he took a deep breath and told Sam the story of his grandfather's legacy.

'Jeez, Rez, that's awesome, we're both rich!' Sam tossed another can over to toast their newfound wealth. Sensing that this was the right moment to bring it up, Lorenzo seized his opportunity, leaning forward, elbows on his knees. 'Do you remember ages ago you mentioned us buying a dive club together?' He held his breath, eyes fixed on Sam's face once he'd taken it in.

'Erm yeah…could we do that? I mean, I have the money, don't I? Would you know how to run it? We'd need all sorts of advisors, experts, and all that stuff. Oh my god, Rez, that would be amazing.' Sam laughed, shaking his head in disbelief.

Lorenzo tried to stay calm; this was everything he'd hoped for, could they really do it? Sam hobbled off the sofa and limped over, his face beaming with happiness. Jumping out of his chair, Lorenzo managed to grab hold of him before he tumbled to the floor with his enthusiasm. Looking down into Sam's eyes, Lorenzo realised he was crying; pulling him in close, he held him for a while as the tears flowed.

'Oh Jeez Rez, I'm sorry, man, it's just—' He sniffed before continuing.

'It's been so hard, you know, trying to figure out what to do with my life, even with the pay-out; what was I going to do with all that money?' He looked up at Lorenzo through wet lashes.

'…And…I have a name for our club.' Lorenzo grinned, pausing for effect.

Sam watched him, his face scrutinising his friends, waiting for the dramatic announcement.

'DiverCity.' He said with a flourish.

Sam continued to stare for a while until the penny finally dropped.

'Oh my god, Rez, that's brilliant; you do realise we'll get all the LGBGT crowd.'

'Yeah, I know, that's the idea, Sam.' Lorenzo had mentioned the idea to Liz when they'd talked about him buying the Malta club; he'd been excited when she'd offered to come and work for them.

'Fancy a few at the pub, celebrate our new business?' Lorenzo was keen to get out of the hot, stuffy flat.

'Yeah, great idea, erm Rez, since we're celebrating, would you mind if I dressed up, you know?' Sam asked hesitantly.

'Dressed—? Oh, ah, I guess not, could be fun, I 'spose.' Lorenzo frowned, wondering if he could cope with being out in public with Samantha.

***

The Dancing Unicorn was heaving with people as Lorenzo and Samantha squeezed their way through the crowd. Lorenzo recognised Maxine from afar, standing as she did, head and shoulders above everyone else.

'Oh my God, look, it's our darling girl.' She squealed as soon as she spotted them. All heads turned their way as they finally reached the table. Maxine, in full drag, having been to one of Saira's shows, pulled Samantha in for a hug, fusing over her hair and make-up.

Lorenzo quickly sat down next to Chloe as Maxine made a lunge to hug him, too.

'Oh my, you look amazing, darling. Doesn't she look gorgeous?' Maxine demanded of Lorenzo.

'Erm, yeah, amazing.' Lorenzo glared at Samantha, who just grinned and fluttered her long eyelashes.

Chloe managed a brief, thin smile before turning her attention to a sequin-clad queen beside her. Lorenzo wondered what he'd done to upset her, having hardly ever spoken to her. Declaring they needed more drinks, Maxine vacated her seat next to Samantha and sashayed up to the bar, her silver lurex dress twinkling in the light.

Grabbing the opportunity, Lorenzo dived into the chair next to Samantha. 'Jesus, Sam, I thought we were supposed to be celebrating. Did you know this lot were gonna be here?' Lorenzo whispered.

'No, I'm sorry, Rez, I didn't know they'd all be here, but I feel safe here; the toilets are cool.' Lorenzo looked at her quizzically. 'The toilets are cool? What on earth does—?' Lorenzo was interrupted by Saira, who came flouncing over with two more queens in tow.

'It's so lovely to see you out and about again, darling. We were all so sorry to hear about your accident. You're looking great, by the way, did you—' Lorenzo tuned out, willing the well-wishers to move on. As he looked at Samantha, smiling and happy, so at ease with these strange and exotic people, Lorenzo began to wonder if she could leave this life behind. After all, running a diving club in the Mediterranean might be pretty mundane compared to all the glamour and the glitz.

He'd been a bit shocked when Sam had asked if he'd be okay to dress up and not a little panicky. Could he cope with seeing her again? When the bedroom door opened and Samantha came out, Lorenzo's breath caught in his throat. Her hair was longer, longer than Sam's own hair; she wore tight black jeans and a close-fitting top, a pale cream leather bomber jacket thrown around her shoulders.

'Ta Da…what do you think?' She did a twirl for Lorenzo's approval.

'Wow, I'd never have believed it, it's incredible. How do you get the ti—' Lorenzo stopped, not wanting to cause offence.

'Just padding Rez.' Samantha had laughed, lifting her top to show him the body shaper underneath.

'Do you like the hair? I thought it was time for a change.'

'I like it all, Sam, you're just beautiful.' Lorenzo shook his head, amazed he could say such a thing to his best mate. Holding up a pair of sensible trainers in one hand and very unsensible shoes with heels in the other, Samantha held them aloft for Lorenzo's approval.

'Those for sure.' He'd laughed, pointing at the trainers.

'The last thing I need is you falling in a heap at my feet.' He'd added.

'I could do that for you, Rez darling.' Samantha giggled seductively.

'Jeeze, Sam, just don't okay.' Lorenzo shoved the image from his mind as fast as he could.

As they walked to the pub, Lorenzo began to relax. It seemed the most natural thing in the world to be walking down the road with a beautiful girl on his arm, and a few envious male glances reassured him.

'You know, we'd better stay sober tonight, Sam, you know what happened the last time,' He'd laughed.

'Mmm, maybe we should Rez, could be fun.' Samantha had teased before seeing the look on his friend's face.

'Get drunk, I mean.' She'd added quickly.

Tuning back into the conversation around the table, Lorenzo realized Maxine had placed a beer in front of him. 'To Lorenzo, for bringing our girl back to us.' Maxine raised her glass, to which everyone cheered.

'To my best friend, Rez.' Samantha placed her hand on Lorenzo's thigh, giving it a gentle squeeze before kissing him on the cheek. Lorenzo was torn between recoiling in horror at the public display and grabbing Samantha into his arms, in the event he did neither and busied himself with his pint.

The gesture wasn't lost on Chloe, who had been heavily drinking all evening. She raised her glass in a toast of her own.

'To the happy couple, you're a lucky girl, Samantha. So many gorgeous guys to kiss, who was that one last week?' She slurred.

'Right, that's it, we're going.' Lorenzo stood, leaning down to help Samantha up.

'Erm, hold up there, buddy. I think Samantha can decide for herself if she stays or goes.' Kyle objected in protective bodyguard fashion.

Lorenzo waited, raising his hands in a backing-off gesture. He looked down at Samantha, willing her to leave with him. The last thing he needed was a confrontation with her friends.

'Yeah, I'm feeling a bit tired, guys. It was great seeing you all again.' Samantha looked up at Lorenzo, reaching her hand up for help. Breathing a sigh of relief, Lorenzo heaved her up, steadying her in his arms as she found her crutch.

'Have a great evening, you two.' Chloe sneered, waving her glass of wine at them.

'For fucks sake, Chloe, what's your problem?' Samantha tried to hobble over and confront Chloe, but Lorenzo steered her out of the pub, all eyes on them again as the crowd sensed a confrontation.

Walking slowly home, Samantha suddenly stopped by the river, sitting down on some stone steps. 'This is where it happened, Rez. The car came from up there.' She pointed up the hill behind them.

'Do you remember much about it?' Lorenzo sat down beside her, watching the ink-black river as it lapped at their feet.

'Not really, I was so looking forward to going home, seeing you again after, you know.' She smiled sadly.

'What the heck was wrong with Chloe tonight? She looked like she wanted to smash my face in.' Lorenzo frowned.

Samantha shrugged, feigning indifference; she knew what was bothering Chloe; she'd always known how Chloe felt about her.

'And what did she mean about you kissing other guys? Who was she talking about?'

Samantha explained about the kiss with Calum when he'd dropped her off outside; Chloe had seen it.

'So, what sort of kiss was it?' Lorenzo asked casually.

'Ooh, well, tongues and everything, you know how it is, Rez.' Samantha chuckled, enjoying Lorenzo's failing attempt at indifference.

'Jesus, Sam, just don't okay.' Lorenzo turned to look at her, deep blue eyes twinkling with laughter. Reaching up a hand, he gently swept a long strand of hair away from Samantha's face.

'Your hair always did fall in your eyes, Sam.' He left his hand resting on her cheek as he caressed it, pulling her slowly towards him. He kissed her.

It was a gentle brush; he just wanted to feel her lips, to taste her again, just once. As the surge of electricity coursed through him, he pulled back, gazing down at her, and waited for his heart to stop hammering against his ribs.

Samantha moved into his arms, clinging to him desperately, trying to close the distance between them. She kissed him back, not a gentle brush but deeply, their bodies entwined on the cold steps. A few revellers came staggering past, looking for a late-night venue, shouting obscenities as they spotted them on the steps.

'Erm, I think we'd better go.' Lorenzo whispered when he could find his voice.

The walk back home was torturous, the yearning for each other almost too much to bear. They didn't have to wait long; arriving back at Samantha's flat, she immediately came into his arms, kissing him passionately. Lorenzo clung to her, pulling her in tight to devour the kiss.

'Oh god, Rez, are you sure about this?' Samantha mumbled as her hand reached down for him, stroking and caressing.

'Mmm,' Lorenzo groaned as her hand found him.

'And you're not...' she added, feeling his hips move against hers.

'No labels, Sam, just you and me.' He fumbled with her zip, desperate to get the tight jeans off.

As they stumbled into the bedroom, Lorenzo suddenly had a thought. 'What if Chloe comes home?'

'Fuck Chloe.' Samantha laughed, kicking the door shut.

Chapter 30

Gazing out of Richie's office window, Lorenzo was trying to keep control of his face. He didn't want to lose his job just yet as there was so much he needed to organise with the diving club purchase before he could tell Richie to piss off. He'd been called in for a haranguing about his work, estimates were late going out, and clients were getting upset, none of which were of any interest to Lorenzo. He was just killing time before he could leave.

As he looked out of the window, he watched a mother bird flying in and out of her nest, feeding her babies, springtime, new beginnings.

'So you'd better watch your step, Murph, or you'll find yourself out on your ear, my lad.' Richie glared from across his desk as Lorenzo tuned back in for the final pronouncement.

'Ah, yeah, sorry, Richie, it's been a bad few weeks for me.' Lorenzo shook his head sadly for effect, his thoughts drifting off once again.

Since their night together, Lorenzo had thought about Sam constantly; what did this mean for them? Would they be together as a couple? Did Sam feel that way about him? And what did this all mean for Lorenzo's sexuality? He went over and over his chat with Liz in Malta. She seemed to find it all very easy; a person is a person, she'd said. What does it matter if they're boy or girl? It mattered for Lorenzo as he'd only slept with Samantha, not Sam. Would it be the same with Sam? What sort of screwed-up relationship would it be if he needed Sam to dress as a girl permanently? He knew Sam wasn't transgender; he'd told him once that he was happy in his skin. Lorenzo wondered what Richie would have to say if he told him why he couldn't concentrate on his work.

'Right then, you're away on holiday next week, aren't you…Malta again, isn't it? Take the time away to think about your future.' Richie waved him out of the office as if swatting an annoying fly.

Gemma came over with a coffee for him, jumping up to sit on the side of his desk.

'How did it go with Richie?' She smiled, long legs swinging under the desk as she sipped her coffee.'

'Oh, you know, the usual, work harder, sell my immortal soul to the god that is Octagon, then retire and die.' Lorenzo moaned.

'Drinks at my place later? Or I can cook for us?'

'Erm, no, I can't tonight, Gemms, some other time, maybe?' Lorenzo had been wondering if he should end his relationship with Gemma. He enjoyed their nights out and felt they could have something good together, but his newly awakened feelings for Sam were all he could think about these past few weeks. Gemma's offer was tempting, but it would feel like a betrayal of Sam, and he couldn't cope with any more heart-searching complications.

'Well, we need to have a chat, Rez, sometime soon.' She jumped down off his desk, dropping her empty coffee cup in the bin with more force than was necessary.

Chapter 31

Gatwick airport was heaving with people as Lorenzo and Sam checked in for the flight to Malta. After their initial excitement about buying the dive club, Sam had pointed out he really should see what it was he was sinking all his money into. Liz had suggested she and Melissa come too so they could all get to know each other.

'Hey Rez, how are you?' Liz kissed him on the cheek before moving on to Sam.

'Hi Sam, it's great to meet you. I've heard a lot about you.' She laughed.

Melissa hovered uncertainly in the background until Liz reached for her, pulling her into their group. A few beers later, they were drinking a toast and designing a logo for DiverCity.

Emerging from the plane to negotiate the steep stairs down to the tarmac, Sam held on tightly to the rail with one hand and even more tightly to Lorenzo with the other. The airline had offered him assistance, but he was determined to show Liz and Melissa that he wouldn't be an encumbrance. The dry Mediterranean heat shimmered as it sucked his breath away. Respite was found inside the cool of the air-conditioned terminal, where they gathered their bags and emerged once more into the dazzling sunshine.

'Liz, Rez, great to see you again.' A heavy-set guy with a beard greeted them with great enthusiasm before turning to Sam.

'Ah, so you must be our saviour.' He grinned at Sam, pumping his hand with great enthusiasm.

'Hmm, I've been called a few things but never a saviour.' Sam laughed but turned to Lorenzo; he whispered, 'Are we employing all these people?'

The drive along the rugged coastline was stunning; the road twisted and turned, every bend giving them a tantalising glimpse of the twinkling blue sea far below.

'Are you okay?' Lorenzo checked on Sam, noticing he looked pale and tired.

'Yeah, I'll be fine, my leg hurts, but nothing a bucket load of pills won't fix.' Sam managed a tired smile as he gazed out of the window.

'Jeeze Rez, this is stunning. Are we really going to live here?'

'We're gonna try Sam, that's for sure.' Lorenzo said, with confidence, he didn't feel right now. He'd been having a few wobbles about their big plan. Could they really do it? Neither of them had run a business before; maybe he'd ask his dad for advice once they were certain they could go ahead; the last thing he needed was his parents trying to talk him out of it.

The battered old minibus finally stopped in a narrow dusty lane. Josh threw open the doors and began heaving their bags out into the street. Sam gazed around, taking in the small, shabby front doors of what he assumed to be houses. A scrawny cat snoozed on one of the windowsills. The tall houses provided much-needed shade from the intense heat of the sun. Sam perched on one of the window ledges, resting his leg, which was beginning to throb.

'C'mon mate, let's get a beer.' Lorenzo could see Sam was struggling; he hoped it was just fatigue from travelling. Josh led them to one of the battered old wooden doors and wrenched it open, hauling their bags inside; he gestured for them to follow.

Sam was pleasantly surprised when they entered a large vine-covered courtyard; racks of wetsuits were hanging up to dry, and large scuba tanks were lined up along one wall along with various other equipment, which Sam hoped he'd soon become acquainted with. As they made their way round to the side of the courtyard, he was glad to see a large seating area with tables and chairs. Divers were sitting around laughing and exchanging stories about their dives.

'Après dive.' Lorenzo laughed, flopping down on a huge, comfortable-looking sofa.

Sam didn't need any encouragement to join him as Josh returned with a tray of cold beer and snacks.

'Well, first impressions?' He asked Sam as he gulped down half his pint.

Sam gazed around, recognising some of the things Lorenzo had told him about. At first, he thought people were just socialising, laughing, and chatting with friends, but he realised there was some sort of lecture taking place at each table; divers were making notes and passing logbooks to their instructors for signing. In a quiet corner, an instructor was helping a wet-suited couple with their scuba tanks. Sam could hear the air being purged through the breathing apparatus. He felt sad that he wouldn't be able to try diving for himself…maybe one day.

'Well—?' Lorenzo nudged him, impatient to know.

'I think it's great, Rez; when do we meet the owners?' Sam was keen to get the business side of things sorted out before he could relax and enjoy their new venture.

'They're coming over tomorrow, they live in Gozo.'

'What, where the hell's that?' Sam said irritably.

'I told you before, it's another smaller island, just a short ferry trip. Don't worry, it'll be fine.' Lorenzo laughed.

'After doing all the bloody legal stuff, Rez, I hope they don't change their minds.' Sam was watching a girl trying to walk in oversized flippers, or fins, as Lorenzo had helpfully pointed out.

An hour or so later, having downed some pills and more beer, Sam was sufficiently recovered to ask about their beachfrontage. Lorenzo took a deep breath. Whilst he loved the white shimmering rocks of Ghar Id Dud, he worried that Sam might have an issue with navigating himself around on the uneven surface. Even though the weather, over thousands of years, had smoothed the sandstone rocks, they almost looked like soft ice cream.

Lorenzo led the way to the front of the dive club, passing a small classroom, which he explained was for lectures, necessary to pass the various courses. They emerged from the bar area, squinting in the sunlight as it bounced off the dazzling white of the rocks.

Sam took in the scene before him. The rocks were about ten feet below them. Sunbathers stretched out on towels whilst local children flung themselves into the sea, squealing with delight before clambering back up a metal ladder to do it all again.

'Erm, we're quite high up, Rez.' Sam frowned, scanning the promenade for a way down.

'True, but look.' Lorenzo pointed to a group of divers as they emerged from somewhere below them. Sam watched with relief as several divers, hauling tanks and fins, made their way over the rocks to the sea, plopping into the water whilst holding on to their face masks.

'There's a walkway from the club, a tunnel I s'pose you'd call it, goes under the road and emerges here.' Lorenzo pointed below as he held his breath, hoping Sam wouldn't see this as a problem. He'd told him as much as he could about Malta, in particular the town of Sliema and where they'd be living, a few streets back from the dive club. Fully aware that the uneven terrain could be a problem, Lorenzo waited, placing an arm over his friend's shoulder.

'So, d'you think—?' Lorenzo was impatient, but Sam interrupted him.

'I think it's just stunning, Rez; I can't wait to get started.' Sam grinned as he gazed out over the sea.

'Ah, there you are. We wondered where you'd got to.' Liz and Melissa joined them, nervously looking to Lorenzo for confirmation that all was well.

'What do you think, Sam?' Liz asked, thrusting her hands in her pockets casually.

'I love it, Liz, it's so beautiful.'

Liz and Melissa jumped up and down, flinging their arms around Sam and yelping with delight.

'Erm, I really need to lie down, Rez, feeling a bit wobbly.' Sam whispered to Lorenzo.

'Ah, right, Liz, did you say there was a room for us on the ground floor?' Lorenzo jumped into pack leader mode, knowing that Sam had about fifteen minutes before he passed out. Liz led them all back through the bar and went off to find Josh who appeared clutching some keys and two bottles of cold drinks.

Their accommodation was a large room with a double bed and one single with an en-suite bathroom. The room was blissfully cold due to the efficient air conditioning; a ceiling fan swirled lazily above their heads. Josh placed the drinks in a small fridge, telling them it was a local speciality called Kinnie, non-alcoholic, made from oranges.

'So, you'd better have the double I s'pose?' Lorenzo announced uncertainly.

'Erm, well, if you want, we could—' Sam gestured to the double.

'Ah, no, you're alright. I'll be fine in this one.' Lorenzo flopped down on the small single bed.

'Rez, are you okay about—I mean, we haven't really talked about that night at my place.' Sam perched on the edge of his bed, massaging his leg as he waited for the pills to kick in.

'I dunno Sam, my head's just really screwed up, you know?' Lying back on the pillows, Lorenzo watched the slow, hypnotic spin of the ceiling fan as he tried to explain how he felt.

'But that night was awesome; I mean, it had been building up for so long, Sam, it just felt right, you know? When I was with Tessa or Gemma, it never crossed my mind that I would want anything different, but with you, or Samantha I should say, I really wanted that too. It's messing with my head, Sam. How can I want Samantha when she's not real? You're real, here with me now.' Lorenzo's eyes followed the fan, the long blades stirring the warm air as it wafted across his legs and continued.

'I mean, if I am gay, that's great, if we need to put a label on it, but can I only be gay with you? Not that I'd ever want to be with anyone else, but you know what I mean, don't you, Sam?'

Looking over at the other bed, Lorenzo realised that Sam was fast asleep, deep in his drug-induced slumber.

Disappointed that Sam hadn't heard his innermost thoughts on the matter of his sexuality, he headed to the shower, allowing the cool water to clear his muddled thoughts.

Changing into fresh shorts and T-shirt, he wandered down the corridor, following a tantalising aroma of garlic and onions cooking somewhere. Emerging into the small bar area, he found Liz and Josh slumped on one of the squishy sofas whilst Melissa was cooking in the small kitchen at the back of the bar.

'Hey Rez, you hungry?' Liz smiled.

'God am I…I could eat a horse.' Lorenzo rubbed his empty stomach.

'How's Sam doing?'

'He's fine; those pills he takes for pain really knock him out, you know?'

'Aw, we'll leave him some food for when he wakes up.'

Melissa came out with huge plates of spaghetti bolognaise and garlic bread for them all, Lorenzo tucked in gratefully.

'So, what happens now, Rez, with the sale, I mean?' Liz asked as she shovelled in a huge forkful of dripping spaghetti.

'Mmm, well, we're meeting the Bonichi's tomorrow, and hopefully, we'll get the thing done. Then back home to the bank and solicitors, all that sort of crap.' Lorenzo grimaced at the thought of more official documents to sign.

'So, Sam likes the place?' Liz asked, her eyes glancing over to Melissa and Josh.

Realising that the three of them were watching him carefully, Lorenzo quickly reassured them that Sam did indeed like the club and was keen to get started on their new life.

'Shall we all go for a dive tomorrow morning? Sam could come on the boat too, give him a chance to see us in action?' Josh asked tentatively.

'Erm, yeah, I s'pose he should… just to get the feel of what we do when we go out, I'll ask him when he wakes up.' Lorenzo had wondered if Sam would be able to manoeuvre himself onto a diving boat.

As Josh and Melissa cleared away their plates, Liz asked Lorenzo to go for a walk along the seafront. The sun was just sinking below the horizon for the night, leaving the sky bathed in a golden glow. Liz hooked her arm in his as they strolled along the promenade, looking very much like a young couple in love.

'Is everything okay with you two, Rez?' She asked eventually.

'Yeah, we're cool, why?' Lorenzo sensed she'd wanted to talk but wasn't too sure about what exactly.

'Have you told him about us?'

'Us? What about us?' Momentarily panicked as he thought he'd forgotten something important, Lorenzo suddenly remembered their drunken night on the beach the last time he was here.

'Oh, erm, no, I haven't.'

'Well, I'm so glad it made such a big impression on you, Rez.' Liz feigned a pout.

'Oh God, no, I meant—'

'Don't worry, just kidding, we were very drunk, weren't we.' She laughed.

Breathing a sigh of relief, Lorenzo gestured to a small stone bench overlooking the sea. They sat in companionable silence for a while; the only sound was the gentle lapping of the sea as it rippled over the stones below. Liz told him she and Melissa planned to get married back in the UK. She hoped Lorenzo and Sam would come. Having assured her they'd most definitely go, Lorenzo commented that theirs would be a very diverse diving club, also thinking of Sam, or did that include Lorenzo himself?

Am I diverse, too? he wondered.

'Oh, I nearly forgot, I'm changing the name of the club; you're gonna love it, Liz.' Lorenzo grinned.

'Go on then, hit me.' Liz had her, *I've heard it all before* face-on.

'Diver-City.' Lorenzo said with a flourish; disappointed in Liz's reaction, he tried again.

'Diversity,' He repeated slowly, accentuating the City.

Finally, Liz caught on, squealing in delight; she gave Lorenzo a big hug, insisting they go back immediately to tell the others. As they walked back into the clubhouse, Lorenzo's phone pinged: Sam.

Where is everyone? I'm starving.

Finding Sam perched at the bar with a beer, Lorenzo pulled up a stool. 'Hey Sam, how are you feeling?'

'Great, ready to hit the town, or maybe just eat?' Sam grinned.

Jumping off his high bar stool, Lorenzo headed into the kitchen in search of the spaghetti bolognaise that Melissa had saved for Sam. It felt strange poking about in someone else's kitchen, but then Lorenzo reasoned that he almost owned it now anyway.

Returning to Sam with a bowl of hot food and some garlic bread, he helped himself to a beer from behind the bar.

'I told Liz about the change of name for the club; she loves it.'

'Hmmm, wonder how many diverse divers there are out there?' Sam mumbled through a mouthful of dripping garlic bread.

'We thought we might go for a dive tomorrow, you up for coming on the boat?' Lorenzo asked casually.

'Oh, yeah, that'd be awesome if you think I can?'

Encouraged by Sam's enthusiasm, Lorenzo went on to explain, at great length, what a boat dive entailed.

The following morning saw them gathering on the marina; it promised to be another scorcher, and the sea twinkled with silent invitation. Nodding a hullo to the club instructors and feeling somewhat in the way, Sam perched on a low wall and took in the scene before him. Josh had a novice diver trying to fix his mask in place, and Liz was demonstrating how to dunk the wetsuit into the sea before putting it on. He'd ask Lorenzo about that later. Melissa was shouting something in Maltese, waving her arms by way of demonstration. He marvelled at the array of equipment lined up to be loaded onto the boat. Breathing tanks, life jackets, massive flippers, or fins, as Lorenzo called them. All sorts of things that Sam had no clue about; he watched Lorenzo as he helped load the boat with the gear, placing the air cylinders carefully in their own little brackets on the boat. As Lorenzo worked, lifting and stowing their gear, Sam felt a sense of pride in my Rez, swiftly followed by the unknown that was their future. Was Lorenzo his? Or was that night just because he'd been dressed as Samantha? Should he feel insulted if that were the case? Sam realised someone was talking to him.

'Ready to board?' Josh and Lorenzo helped Sam to navigate the small plank which had been lowered from the back of the boat.

Sam was given pride of place beside the driver.

Is he called a driver?

He was a thin, sinewy man with dark, weather-worn skin from too many years in the baking sun. Settling into his seat, Sam turned, his eyes searching for Lorenzo as he tried in vain to stop his shoulder-length hair from blowing across his face. Catching his eye, Lorenzo nodded, grinning with a thumbs up. He'd been watching Sam carefully from behind his dark glasses, terrified he'd conclude this wasn't for him and pull out. As he looked at his friend, a memory surfaced; a beautiful girl with long black hair, his arms wrapped around her in urgent need. Feeling a familiar ache down deep in his groin, Lorenzo turned his face to the wind, allowing the sea spray to wash away the distracting image.

The little boat puttered its way slowly out of the marina and picked up speed once it was out in the open sea. Twenty minutes later, they had anchored up in a small cove. Sam marvelled at the huge sandstone cliffs that towered majestically above them; the sea had changed from pale turquoise to a deep blue. Swivelling round in his seat, Sam watched with interest as the divers kitted up, strapping on various bizarre contraptions to their wet-suited bodies. Lorenzo came over to sit with Sam as he put his tank on, explaining what each piece of kit was for.

'A watch,' Sam noted confidently.

'A computer, actually, tells me how deep I am and if I need to de-compress all that jazz.' Realising for the first time how strange this must all be for his friend, Lorenzo grinned, patting Sam on the back.

'You'll soon get the hang of it; it took me a while to learn it all.' Lorenzo grabbed the back of Sam's seat for balance as a wave caused their boat to rock from side to side.

'Yeah, a bit like dentistry, I s'pose, alright when you know what it's all for, eh?' Sam shrugged a shoulder.

'Can you help me with this mate? Something's caught at the back.' Twisting awkwardly around so Sam could help him, Lorenzo balanced on his haunches; the heavy tank on his back, coupled with several breathing tubes and massive buoyancy aid, made him rather helpless, like an upside-down turtle stranded on the beach. Every movement had to be thought out carefully as falling over could cause serious injury, not to mention damage to his expensive kit.

Sam dutifully searched around the back of this alien creature in front of him and spotted a twisted strap. Several attempts to straighten it out yielded no results, so he had to shuffle around in front of Lorenzo and undo the huge buckle around his waist. A bit more shuffling, and all was resolved.

'What's this for then?' Sam patted yet another torturous contraption buckled around Lorenzo's waist.

'Ah, that's a weight belt, the wetsuit is buoyant, the sea is buoyant too so I'd just float on the surface without being weighted down.' Lorenzo grinned before continuing. 'Here endeth your first lesson.'

Helping Lorenzo up, Sam steadied himself, holding on to the gunwale as Lorenzo stood, bracing his legs wide for balance as the boat rocked once again. 'Hmm, makes a change for me to be helping you up,' Sam chuckled.

'You'll get used to that around here, Sam. Everyone has a buddy who looks out for them, checking their kit and looking out for each other when we're down there.'

'Oh right, who's your buddy then?' Sam looked down the length of the boat; the only person waiting, fully kitted up, was Melissa, hands on hips in agitation as she gestured impatiently to the computer on her wrist.

'Erm, yeah, Melissa and me, she's much more amenable underwater.'

Sam stood back, allowing Lorenzo to put on his massive fins, which now made it impossible to walk at all. Shuffling awkwardly to the side of the boat, Lorenzo placed his hand on his face mask and disappeared backwards over the side. Sam watched in fascination as Melissa did the same, meeting up with Lorenzo as she bobbed to the surface. Various grunts and hand signals followed as they both disappeared under the surface. Sam watched their bubbles disappear as they descended deeper under the ocean.

Turning back to the front of the boat, Sam was relieved to see he wasn't alone; the driver was still there, sitting in his seat, bare feet propped up and smoking a cigarette.

'So, you don't dive?' Sam asked, shaking his head at the offer of a cigarette.

'Haha, no, I leave that to you, crazy people. I never understand why they want to do this.' He gestured to the sea as only the Maltese can with an impatient flick of his wrist.

'Haha, yeah, I wondered that myself, but I s'pose I'd better try it sometime if I'm going to run the business.' Sam frowned whilst gazing down into the deep blue.

'Oh, you're the guy? I'm happy to meet you. My name is Carmello.' A wrinkled, suntanned hand reached out and grasped Sam's, shaking and patting all at once.

'What happened to you, my friend?' Carmello gestured to Sam's scarred legs.

'Oh, car accident.' Sam shrugged dismissively; he didn't really want to go over it all again, but his sun-dried companion was determined.

'Ha, you think English driving is bad, wait 'till to see the Maltese—never stop at crossroads—just toot your horn and shout.' He guffawed, resulting in a massive coughing fit as he lit up another cigarette. Despite his reluctance, Sam found himself strangely drawn to the little Maltese, telling him all about his doomed dentistry career. As with all conversations about dentistry, Carmello couldn't resist describing in great detail his latest visit to the dentist; with various lip lifting and gnashing of teeth, he eventually spat out a full set of top dentures, waving them under Sam's nose for inspection.

Recoiling in horror lest he be forced to actually touch the offending pink plastic, Sam was aware of shouting from the back of the boat; Carmello suddenly jumped to his feet and headed off down the deck before dashing back to grab his teeth. Wondering what was going on, Sam watched as Carmello lowered a ladder into the water and helped the divers back on the boat, relieving them of the heavy tanks and cumbersome fins before they clambered back on board. The returning divers were buzzing with adrenaline, chatting and laughing as they exchanged stories of what they'd seen down in the depths. Lorenzo flopped down next to Sam, grinning as he unzipped his wetsuit and checking his wrist computer.

'How was it, Rez, good dive?' Sam asked, wondering what a good dive would consist of.

'Oh yeah, man, it was amazing. Can you help me out of this?' Lorenzo indicated his wetsuit zip, which appeared to be stuck at the bottom of the jacket.

'Oh, yeah, sure, erm.' Sam grabbed the offending zipper, trying to free it where it had caught on Lorenzo's swim shorts.

'Be careful down there, man.' Lorenzo grinned nervously as Sam's hand delved deeper.

'Mmm, don't tempt me, Rez.' Sam muttered as he pulled and tugged, their bodies entwined as the battle raged against the truculent zip. He concentrated on the job at hand, but being in such proximity to Lorenzo's near-naked form was proving to be rather a distraction.

Holding on to Sam's shoulders for balance as the boat rocked from side to side, Lorenzo was very aware of Sam's head resting on his stomach as he tried to ignore the soft, silky black hair as it mingled with his own dark belly hair.

'What's going on here then, you two?' Liz chuckled before offering her services.

'Err, no, we're good, Liz, thanks.' Lorenzo quickly put her off. The last thing he needed right now was Liz grappling in his shorts.

'Aha, got you, little fucker.' Sam shouted in triumph as the zipper glided free.

Shouting something in Maltese to Mellissa, Carmello checked that everyone was seated and the equipment was all stowed safely before starting up the engine.

'So, what now?' Sam asked.

'Beer, beer and food…and maybe more beer.' Lorenzo laughed, grabbing the side for balance as the boat picked up speed.

'When we get back, we have to fill in our logbooks. I have an app on my phone. It records where we dived, how long for and at what depth…it's all on the computer.' Stretching out his legs, Lorenzo relaxed back, tilting his face up to the sun.

'So, you're gonna give notice to Octagon Rez?'

'Done it already; you should have seen his face. I'm sure he was gonna sack me anyway, so I got in there first.' Lorenzo's eyes were closed as he basked in the warmth of the sun. Turning his head in Sam's direction, he continued. 'Have you told your parents about our little plan yet?'

'Little plan? Bloody hell, Rez, this is life-changing.' Sam tutted in disgust. 'Little plan.'

Closing his eyes, Sam copied Lorenzo and lay back, soaking up the sun as the boat puttered along underneath them. Sam had been wondering how to break the news to his family. He knew his parents were concerned about him and worried about his future. He'd set the scene before coming to

Malta, telling them he might go into business with Lorenzo, but they didn't know he intended to live there; that was going to be a difficult conversation. A thought suddenly entered his head, what about his beloved dog? Sam felt his stomach clench; he couldn't leave the big German Shepherd behind.

'Rez, Rez man—' Lorenzo was snoring quietly as Sam prodded him awake.

'Jesus, what?' Sitting up in a panic, Lorenzo looked around, flopping back down on the deck when he realised where he was.

'I need to find out about Rez. Can I bring him over? What are the rules? I can't leave him, Rez.' Sam was distraught.

'I don't know, Sam, we can ask the legal guys later; I'm sure it'll be fine.'

Fishing his phone out to check the rules about dogs, Sam was frustrated at the lack of signal. Lorenzo, sensing his friend's dilemma, reached over and patted him on the shoulder.

'Don't worry, we'll make it work.' Lorenzo didn't feel as confident as he sounded; he just hoped it was possible.

Unloading the boat and helping as much as he could had taken its toll on Sam; his leg was aching, and he had a headache from the heat and sun.

'Jesus, you look terrible. Are you okay?' Lorenzo frowned in concern.

'I just need to pop a few pills and lie down for a while; I'll be fine later for the meeting with the Bonichis.' Sam attempted a tired smile before hobbling to his room.

'Is everything okay?' Liz appeared, handing Lorenzo a cold beer.

'Oh, erm yeah, he's fine, just the heat, you know, he'll be okay in a couple of hours.' Lorenzo smiled with a confidence he didn't feel. Was this a mistake? Could Sam cope with this life they both wanted?

Finding a shady spot in the courtyard, Lorenzo stretched out, listening to the soundtrack of his new life. Cicada's chattering in the trees, divers kitting up for another excursion, locals shouting at each-other in Maltese.

'Rez, Rez, wake up, the Bonichi's are here.' Lorenzo opened his eyes in confusion and groped around for his sunglasses, his shady spot now in the full glare of the sun.

'Ooh, caught a few rays there, Rez.' Sam laughed as he slapped a sunburnt shin.

'Shit, where are they?' Looking around in panic, Lorenzo realised he needed to shower before their important business meeting.

'Can you get started with them while I get ready?' He begged Sam.

'Yeah, no worries, I'll be fine.'

Several hours later, DiverCity was born, documents had been signed, deposits paid, and both legal teams satisfied all was in order.

'Well, we did it, bro, it's all ours.' Lorenzo flung an arm around Sam's shoulders as they shared a toast.

'I can't believe it Rez, it's really going to happen, and did you hear? I can bring Rez. It's a bit complicated, but it can be done; cherry on the cake for me, mate, I can tell you.' Sam grinned.

Celebrations continued long after the sun had gone down. Melissa and Josh were overjoyed to keep their jobs, and Liz decided to come and work for them, too.

'How you doing, bro?' Lorenzo glanced over at Sam, who was massaging his leg.

'I think I need to go find some pills and sleep, Rez.' Sam managed a watery smile as he struggled to his feet and carefully headed off to their room.

Lorenzo stayed up for a while, but he too was exhausted and left the others to their celebrating. Tiptoeing into their room so as not to wake Sam, he slipped into bed and was soon fast asleep. Several hours later, Sam cried out, shouting for his tormentors to go away; Lorenzo crept over, crouching down beside Sam's bed. He tried to calm him down, soothing him and stroking his arm. Sweat glistened on Sam's bare chest, the soft black hairs curling in the dampness. They both slept in just their boxers in a vain attempt to keep cool in the heavy, sultry air. Lorenzo padded over to the control for the ceiling fan, which dangled down on a wire, poking and prodding the various buttons, not really sure which was which. They'd switched it off the first night as it was too noisy, clanging loudly on every third rotation. Lorenzo managed to get it going again just as Sam resumed his torturous nightly battle with long white grasping hands, apparently a flashback to his accident by the river. Desperate for sleep himself, Lorenzo climbed in beside Sam, wrapping his arms around him and trying to soothe him back to sleep, but Sam was very agitated, thrashing around and shouting. Worried about waking everyone up, Lorenzo shook Sam awake, trying desperately to break through the sleeping pill stupor. Sam came too, wide-eyed and confused, as he struggled to push the demon Lorenzo away.

Exhausted and sweating in the heat, they lay staring up at the mesmerising swirling ceiling fan as Sam regained his faculties. As his breathing calmed, he turned on his side, reaching out and gently caressing Lorenzo's chest. His hand moved lower, hesitating as his fingertips brushed the waistband of Lorenzo's boxers. Turning his head, Lorenzo gazed into deep blue eyes fringed with long black lashes. He reached down, finding Sam's hand, and pushed it down to the hard, silky flesh that demanded release. Groaning with aching need, he pulled Sam in close, kissing him deeply.

It was then that Sam whispered, 'I love you, Rez.'

Chapter 32

As the plane descended through the dark clouds above Gatwick Airport, Lorenzo's mood hovered between overwhelming excitement for the future and fear of the unknown.

He looked over at Sam, snoring quietly next to him. They both had an awkward conversation ahead of them, explaining their plans to their families. Lorenzo had mentioned buying a dive club to Angie and Jim on several occasions over the previous few months; he was aware of the looks passing between them and the suppressed smiles of indulgent parents when faced with their offspring's latest daft idea.

The meeting with the Bonichi's had gone well; documents were signed, hands were shaken all around with beaming smiles on all faces. They'd left Melissa and Josh in charge until they returned in a few weeks' time to take over.

'So, let me know how it goes, eh?' Sam grinned as Lorenzo heaved his bag out of the taxi.

'Yeah, can't say I'm looking forward to it, Sam.' Lorenzo grimaced at the thought of telling his family what he was planning. He knew exactly how it would go; Angie would cry, the disbelief and panic at losing him would put her on the offensive, there'd be an outpouring of hurt feelings, and that most awful of parental put downs 'disappointment.'

His father, on the other hand, would be more pragmatic (he hoped), with a lot of 'Well done, lad' and 'standing on your own two feet' type comments. He would try to be the sensible businessman to Angie's hysterical mother. As the taxi dropped him home, Lorenzo tried to still his pounding heart as he heaved his bag onto his back. Regretting his choice of shorts and sliders to travel home in, he shivered in the chill of an English summer. Fishing around in his pocket for his keys, he glanced up at the kitchen window, hoping no one was home; he needed to gather his thoughts before the final confrontation.

'Rez…yay you're home.' Ali shot out of the kitchen, almost knocking him down in her enthusiasm to give him a hug.

'Erm, hi Ali…did you miss me then?' He grinned, bending down to return the effusive hug.

'Well, no, not really, but it's just that Mum said you were talking about staying there or something, so I'm glad you came home again. I can't wait to hear all about it. Did you go diving? Did you see any sharks? There's been loads on TV about shark attacks.' Ali bounced around on her toes, excited to have her brother home.

'Let me just go unpack, and I'll tell you all about it.' Kissing the top of her head, Lorenzo hugged her tightly, his guts wrenched at the thought of not having her in his life.

Flopping down on his bed, he closed his eyes, willing the sense of betrayal and guilt to pass. His phone pinged, Sam.

'Missing me yet?'

Lorenzo thought about that question, remembering back to their room in Malta and the hot, sultry nights entwined together.

'Missing you?—Needing you, wanting you.'

Lorenzo stared at his phone for a moment before adding.

'Loving you'

He pressed *'send.'*

Somewhere deep down a wave washed through him, a tide of glowing warmth flowing through his body as he recognised the truth of what he'd written. The urge to see Sam was overwhelming, to celebrate this new truth. Lorenzo had often wondered how it would feel to be loved by someone, but actually doing the loving was the most amazing feeling. Why had he not seen it before? Was it always there, and he'd just dismissed it as a close friendship? His phone rang, saving him from further self-analysis.

'Erm…Rez—' Sam mumbled, his words hesitant, choked with emotion.

'Yeah, I know. How many years has it taken me?' Lorenzo chuckled nervously.

'Rez, when you say, '*Loving me,*' Um, do you mean when we—' Lorenzo interrupted him, needing to be clear.

'Sam, listen to me, I fucking love you. I can't believe I'm saying it out loud, it's amazing, it's gonna be great, we can live in Malta and run the club together, like *together*, as a couple. We could—' Looking over to his door, Lorenzo saw his sister staring at him, her hand over her mouth in shock. She hung around excitedly while he finished his call after arranging to meet Sam in the pub. Lorenzo beckoned her over, resigned to a full inquisition.

'Oh my god, Rez, you and Sam?' she giggled, hand over her mouth in shock as she dashed over, plonking herself on his bed for the full story, which took about an hour during which he had to try and explain the when, how, what and why of his relationship with Sam. And for good measure, since they were talking about his love life, he told her about his plans for Malta, emphasising the opportunity for Ali to go and visit any time she liked.

'I'm so jealous, Rez, you know I've always loved Sam. Now you've got him.' Ali feigned an annoyed pout before bouncing up and down on the bed as a thought hit her.

'So he'll be my brother-in-law, won't he? You'll have to share him with me, Rez,' she proclaimed, pleased with this new development.

The front door banged shut, and their parent's voices drifted up the stairs, sending Lorenzo into panic mode as he realised the time had come to tell everyone his news. Grasping Ali's hands in his own, he made her promise not to say anything about Sam just yet. He needed to figure out when to tell his parents; the move to Malta would be enough to cope with. They'd find out about Sam sooner or later, just not today.

***

Julia Brewer wiped down the kitchen counter for the fourth time, pausing only to blow her nose, the tip of which was turning a brighter shade of red with every blow. She'd been crying on and off ever since Sam told them about his Malta plans.

'Mum, can you just stop the cleaning for a minute…please?' Sam begged in frustration. His mother placed her cloth carefully on the draining board, smoothing it out with trembling hands.

'There's nothing here for me, mum. Going into business with Rez gives me the chance to have a new life and a business to run. I thought my life was ruined after the accident, but this is my way out, don't you see?'

'But it's such a long way away, Sam. I mean, where is this Malta of yours anyway?' Julia sniffed and blew her nose.

'It's only a short flight, love, nice and warm there.' Sam's father paused in his rummaging through a cupboard, 'and anyway, with Dan coming home, it's probable easier if—' Mike Brewer was interrupted by his scowling wife.

'Oh, so we have to lose one son in order to gain another, is that it Mike?' Julia shouted whilst picking up her dishcloth once more.

'You know what I mean, love, Dan's so…' Sam helped him out with a few adjectives.

'Bigoted? Homophobic? Intolerant? Aggressive? Have I missed anything?' Sam made no attempt to hide his sneer.

'Hmm, true enough, he did take great delight in telling us you were gay, ruined his big moment when we told him we already knew.' Mike grinned.

'What? When? I mean, how long have you known for?' Sam looked from one to the other in astonishment.

'Oh, probably since you were about fifteen, I s'pose, we just hoped you'd trust us enough to tell us yourself.' Julia shrugged a shoulder and managed a weak smile.

'It wasn't you two, mum, it was Dan. How could I come out with a brother like him? He'd have made my life a misery. It was just easier to keep it quiet, try and sort my life out myself.' Sam flicked a wrist in dismissal.

'I'm sorry, love, I'd liked to have been able to help you. I hate to think of you going through all that on your own.' Julia patted his hand whilst Mike moved on to more important matters.

'So, the legal stuff is all done? Deposit paid and all that?' he asked, business-like.

'Yup, all done, all we need to do is finish up some stuff here, then we can go, can't wait, sunshine and warm blue sea, you'll love it, guys,' Sam said with enthusiasm.

'Hmm, well, I can't see me going out there. I hate the hot sun and heat.' Julia folded her arms defiantly.

'Ah well, in that case, it'll be cheaper if it's just me going, won't it?' Mike ducked out of the room as a clammy dishcloth was thrown at him.

Needing a break from his mother's lack of support, Sam followed his father into the living room. His big German Shepherd was blissfully snoring on the sofa, oblivious to the charged atmosphere around him. Sam squashed in beside him and glanced over at his father, who wore a resigned look of *'Well, what did you think was going to happen?'*

Sam fished his phone out but couldn't really concentrate, flicking from one random website to the next. His main concern was what Dan knew about Samantha, since he had obviously been digging around in Sam's life in Bristol, there were bound to be photos or comments about her. He thought about Maxine and Kyle, all his friends back there, in his old life as he now thought of it. He'd promised Chloe he'd go back for a few days to tie up loose ends; she'd been a good friend to him, and he didn't want to lose her.

As he fondled the big dog's ears, his thoughts drifted back to Samantha and that first night with Lorenzo in his Bristol flat; it seemed such a long time ago. So much had happened since then. He remembered Lorenzo's emotional soul-searching. *'What sort of mixed-up mess am I to only want you when you're her?'* He pictured Samantha, packaged up in a box on the top of his wardrobe, and wondered, do I still need her? Will Lorenzo need her? He shifted uncomfortably on the sofa, the ache in his groin growing deeper as he re-read Lorenzo's last message.

'I love you, Sam'.

Julia emerged from the kitchen, still sniffling and dabbing at her red nose as she slumped down opposite Sam. Rez wagged his tail lazily by way of greeting.

'What about Rez? We can't keep him, love; he's far too big for us, and the dogwalker is getting so expensive now.' Julia's eyes filled up again as yet another body blow landed.

Rez's huge head shot up with great excitement on hearing his name, ever hopeful that food would follow.

'Don't worry, Mum, he'll be coming with me.' Sam smiled as he lovingly stroked the soft head. He'd researched and discovered that he could indeed take Rez to Malta within quarantine guidelines.

'Do you have anyone, Sam? I mean, a partner, boyfriend?' Julia asked shyly.

'Actually, I do, Mum, and you know him very well.' Sam smiled, trying desperately to control his face as it teetered on the edge of a soppy, loved-up grin.

His interest peaked, Mike pulled his attention away from watching a large hairy spider, who was currently traversing the carpet towards Julia's chair. Turning towards her husband to ensure he was listening, Julia looked back at her son and waited.

'It's Rez Mum.' Sam said quietly.

'Haha…very funny. We know how much you love your dog Sam. I meant—' Realisation hit Julia, and she turned to look at her husband once again, her eyes wide in amazement.

'You mean Lorenzo? But how, I mean, he's not gay, is he?' She asked, her eyebrows knitted in confusion.

'Whatever you want to call it, Mum.' Sam shrugged dismissively, not wanting to discuss his relationship with Lorenzo.

'But didn't he have lots of girlfr-' Julia persisted but was cut short by her husband.

'Does it bloody matter?' Mike stood up, propelled by irritation, just as Rez the dog shot off Sam's lap, landing a large paw on the scurrying spider. A lot of scuffling ensued, with the unfortunate spider disappearing down the dog's throat.

'What the hell was that all about?' Sam asked, as Rez liked his lips in ecstasy.

Grateful for the interruption, Sam grabbed his crutches and headed for his room, pleading a headache.

Up in the sanctuary of his bedroom, he breathed a sigh of relief that the inquisition was over, at least for today. He knew it would drip on every day until he left for Malta, another question, another point to consider as if he hadn't thought it through himself. Flicking through his endless emails, he re-read the ones from the bank, the quarantine arrangements for Rez, and Maltese residency requirements, of which there were many. Lorenzo had been given the task of marketing their new business, posting about it on dive forums and the LGBGTQ community publications. He checked the accounts of the dive club once again and the staffing arrangements. He was particularly interested in Liz's CV, trying to get some insight into her friendship with Lorenzo. He'd come across them in deep conversation several times, her hand resting on his thigh or a hug that lasted too long. On another occasion Lorenzo had helped her carry her heavy dive gear, receiving a kiss on the cheek for his efforts. Was there something between them? Did he even have a right to ask? It was obvious, at least to Sam, that Lorenzo was bisexual, maybe even pansexual. How the hell do I compete with that? Scrolling through his phone photos of their week in Malta, Sam searched for Liz; there she was, wetsuit half undone, breasts almost unleashed but not quite out. Another picture of her and Lorenzo, laughing as they held aloft cold pints of beer, Lorenzo's arm draped over her shoulder as she grasped his hand. Sam had never considered himself a jealous person, but his guts wrenched at the thought of Liz and Lorenzo together. He resolved to ask him about it later when they met in the pub. Checking his WhatsApp, he re-read Lorenzo's message.

'I love you, Sam.'

Could it be true? Had his friend now truly come to terms with his sexuality? Did they have a future together, lovers, not just business partners?

The shower was hot as Sam shampooed his hair; he knew Lorenzo liked it long, so he allowed it to brush his shoulders. As the water cascaded over him his stomach was in knots, worried about meeting Lorenzo back in their old stomping ground for the first time since they declared their feelings to one another. Terrifying thoughts bounced around in his head. What if it was just a holiday romance type of thing; the heat, half-naked bodies glistening in the sun, all adding to the arousal they'd both given in to.

Preening in the mirror, he lamented the loss of his Mediterranean suntan, his skin returning to its pale, sallow, off-white. He smiled, thinking about Lorenzo, with his Italian complexion, which just needed topping up to glow deep and bronze lucky sod. Standing back to check his look in the mirror, he felt there was something missing; crossing the hallway into his mother's room, he went in search of make-up, finding a small tube of black eyeliner he carefully applied a line close to his lashes. Peering closely in the mirror, he remembered Maxine's advice.

'Eyeliner, my love…makes your baby blues pop.'

Although Maxine's advice on make-up was to be taken with a very large dollop of salt, Sam had to concede it did enhance the colour of his eyes.

Tempting though it was to continue in full-on Samantha mode, he satisfied himself with just the eyeliner. Running his hand over his chin he surveyed the dark stubble, which was in imminent danger of evolving into a full beard; together with his thick black hair, he worried he might be morphing into pirate territory, especially when hobbling around on a crutch. Grabbing his shaver, he tilted his chin, shaping and pruning. Stepping back once more, he checked his look; jeans, white shirt tucked in, sleeves rolled up, brown leather belt, brown boots. He ran his fingers over the braided leather necklace that Lorenzo had given him in Malta, remembering the day quite clearly.

They'd been sitting in a bar having a cold beer when Lorenzo suddenly stuffed his hand in his back pocket, fishing out a little paper bag before giving it to Sam with a casual shrug.

'I nearly forgot, I bought you a present,' He'd grinned shyly.

Sam remembered looking at the necklace and trying desperately to resist leaning over to kiss Lorenzo, unsure if public displays were acceptable at this early stage. Lorenzo had picked up his phone, casually scrolling through it as Sam put the necklace on.

'You know this doesn't mean we're engaged or anything,' He'd glanced up from his phone, laughing.

Leaving his room, Sam carefully negotiated the steep stairway. He'd been practicing using the stairs without his crutch, finding it more of a hinderance than a help lately. Grabbing it in the hallway, he gave his dog a big hug before going out to wait for his Uber.

***

It was a bright, sunny day, which meant that most pubgoers wanted to sit outside by the river. Sam spotted Lorenzo sitting with two beers as he swatted away a persistent wasp.

'Hey man, how's it going?' Lorenzo passed a beer across the table.

'Yeah, okay, I think.' Sam gazed across the table at Lorenzo, who was concealed behind very dark glasses as the sun was shining directly on him, enhancing his golden tan. He felt a stirring deep in his groin coupled with a terrifying fear that Lorenzo might have changed his mind.

'It's just so frustrating, isn't it, having to wait so long. I wish we could just go tomorrow, I'm so pissed off having to have the same conversation over and over again.' Sam said, gulping down half his pint, the cold liquid serving to soothe his jagged nerves.

'It's good to see you.' Lorenzo grinned before adding. 'I've missed you, Sam.'

'Yeah, me too. What have you missed then?' Sam teased, allowing a lock of soft black hair to fall over his eye.

Lorenzo glanced around the pub garden before telling Sam in no uncertain terms what exactly he was missing.

'Jesus Rez, you'll have me grabbing you across the table in a minute.' Sam laughed, relief pulsing through him that nothing seemed to have changed; Lorenzo still wanted him.

Declaring that more drinks were needed, Lorenzo stood up, passing behind Sam. He glanced around before planting a surreptitious kiss on his neck. As he walked to the bar, Lorenzo felt the stirring of a dilemma. Should he care if anyone saw them together? Winchester was a small town, and he hadn't yet told his parents about Sam. Ali knew, of course, and he thought he could probably trust her not to say anything. Did he need to come out? If he was out, did that mean he was out forever? Could he go back in if he wanted to? What even was *in*? Straight? He wasn't even sure if out was the right term for what he was going through.

Weaving his way back to their table with the beers, Lorenzo grinned to himself as he watched some girls glancing over at Sam. Too good-looking by far; who was it that said that about him? Lorenzo suddenly remembered; it was someone at Sam's party in Bristol on that fateful night when he'd kissed Samantha in the garden. Looking at Sam now as he squirmed under the unwanted attention, Lorenzo came to a decision. Placing the beers carefully on the table, he leaned over, kissing Sam full on the lips. Unsure what had caused this outpouring of sudden passion, Sam returned the kiss before gently pulling away with a large grin. The girls on the next table smiled and raised their glasses by way of defeat.

'Erm, what was all that about?' Sam asked, bewildered.

'I dunno Sam, I just—' Reaching for Sam's hand Lorenzo smiled.

'Maybe too much beer.' He added with a lazy grin.

'Hmm, I think like this new Rez.'

'Just like?' Lorenzo narrowed his eyes.

'Well, I—' Sam was interrupted by a pretty blond-haired girl who suddenly stopped beside their table.

'Rez, great to see you.' She exclaimed, planting a kiss on his cheek before pulling up a chair.

'Oh, erm, Hi Gemma.' Lorenzo stammered, slowly sliding his hand out of Sam's.

Lorenzo introduced Sam to Gemma, who gushed about how much she'd heard about him. Sam wondered quite how much she'd heard. Lorenzo had ended his relationship with Gemma a few weeks before he went to Malta, feeling guilty about his new feelings for Sam. She'd been upset but accepted that he wasn't ready to be exclusive with someone just yet.

Sam sipped his drink as he watched Gemma play with her hair whilst flirting with Lorenzo. An image of Liz popped into his head, her hand resting on Lorenzo's thigh. He wondered if it was always going to be like this, the jealousy, the unwanted images of Lorenzo with a girl. Was he over it with girls, or would he always be tempted, needing that which was different? Was that the thrill? Occasionally yearning for the Other? Was Sam the Other, or were Liz and Gemma?

'…enjoy diving?'

Sam snapped out of his musings as he realised Gemma had turned her attention to him, Lorenzo having escaped to get her a drink.

'Erm, sorry, what?' He stammered.

'I was just saying, do you enjoy diving too?' Gemma smiled, leaning towards him.

'Well, I haven't actually tried it yet, but from what I've seen, it looks great, can't wait to give it a go.' Sam returned her smile.

'I was so sorry to hear about your accident, Sam; it sounds horrific.' She briefly squeezed his hand.

'Yeah, thanks, Gemma, it wasn't the greatest.'

'How are you getting on with the crutches? I broke my leg a few years ago, and the worst thing was having to hobble about on those bloody things…'

Sam warmed to this happy, smiling girl who made him laugh with self-deprecating stories about her own life. By the time Lorenzo returned with her drink they were deep in conversation about his recently discovered Italian grandfather and how he thought he was adopted. Gemma confided that she was adopted, explaining to Sam how she'd tried to help Lorenzo through his predicament. Lorenzo was pleasantly surprised to see Sam and Gemma chatting animatedly, both turning to include him in their 'Lorenzo's Grandfather' chat.

'…that's where he gets his gorgeous good looks from.' Sam slurred, four pints of beer taking its toll on his tongue.

'I'd better get you home; you've had too many me old mate.' Lorenzo frowned, reaching over to caress Sam's cheek.

Gemma watched the strange interaction between her old lover and his best friend, the gentle way Lorenzo touched Sam's cheek, Sam turning his face and leaning into the touch. She frowned, eyes narrowing as the realisation hit her.

***

The bombshell was dropped in the kitchen, as always, as Lorenzo requested a family gathering. Angie giggled nervously, asking if large amounts of buttered toast would be necessary, to which Lorenzo replied by handing over a large loaf, bought especially for the occasion.

'Oh, this sounds serious; you getting married or something, Rez?' Angie quipped whilst loading the toaster.

'Mmm, no, not quite mum, but a big change anyway.' Lorenzo glanced at his father, who was patiently waiting for the cold hard facts.

'Remember I mentioned buying a diving club? Lorenzo breathed a sigh of relief; he'd said it, now would come the questions. Angie looked at her husband in stunned silence as they waited for him to continue.

'Go on.' Said Jim in his serious voice.

'Well, I'm going into business with Sam; we're pooling our money and buying a club.' He waited.

'Oh, well, that's erm, where?' Angie asked, busily buttering hot toast.

'Malta.' The bomb landed in the middle of the table, reigning silence down on them.

'What?'

The look of horror on his parents' faces was almost comical. Stealing a glance over at Ali, Lorenzo tried hard to suppress a grin. He knew Ali was on his side; long summers spent in the sun-drenched Mediterranean had done the trick as far as she was concerned and, of course, the chance to be near her beloved Sam, whom she now referred to as her new brother-in-law.

She'd finally stopped giving him knowing looks and comically winking at him behind their parents' backs. Lorenzo reasoned his sexuality was none of his parents' business; they'd find out sooner or later, preferably later.

'Malta, where the hell is that anyway? Some little dot in the middle of nowhere, Rez. What on earth are you thinking?' Angie looked to her husband for support but found none.

'Jim, say something. It's ridiculous; he can't just—' Unable to control her tears any longer, Angie abandoned the toaster and flopped down on a chair in defeat. Taking over toasting duties, Lorenzo tried to quell his own emotions. He knew it would be a difficult conversation but hadn't realised how wretched he would feel at the hurt he was causing.

Busying himself with peanut butter and bananas, Lorenzo took some deep breaths and sat down beside Angie.

'Mum, listen, it's only a four-hour flight, Sliema is a proper town with shops and restaurants; you and dad and Ali can come and stay any time. It'll be fun.'

'Hmm…I've always fancied learning to dive.' Jim mused, eliciting a scowl from his wife.

'Maybe I should go to university after all…I could do business studies and help you run the dive school; that'd be cool, wouldn't it, Rez?' Ali giggled, almost causing Angie to internally combust, so Lorenzo played it down with lots of hmm's and maybes. Jim fought with his face, finally gaining control of the large grin that threatened his marriage.

'I'm proud of you, lad. Nothing wrong with running your own business. Now, when I first started out, we didn't have—' Jim was cut off by Angie.

'Oh shut up, Jim, we don't need to hear your old rags to riches story just now.' Angie glared at her husband in frustration at his support for his son.

'But Rez love, what do you know about running a business? Especially in another country, different rules and regulations. I mean, do they even speak English?' Angie threw everything she could think of in a futile attempt to change his mind.

'Well, I can help there, lad, check contracts and stuff for you.' Jim offered, skating on thin ice once again.

'Rez think about what you're doing, all your inheritance going down the drain.' Angie buried her head in her hands.

'Down the drain? Is that what you think, Mum? Do you really think I'm that stupid that I haven't thought things through? Sam and I have gone over and over it all, and we're determined to make it work; I can't spend the rest of my life in an office, and I love diving, and I love the warm sunshine, and we're doing it okay?' Lorenzo raised his hands, palms out to discourage any further discussion for today.

The 'what if 'conversation gathered pace each day as Angie conjured up some new scenario that would devastate his plans. Immigration concerns, finances, business acumen (or lack of it), dangerous seas, strange people, and language barriers. At first, Lorenzo tried to reassure her about each and every possible obstacle, but after several days, he began to run out of steam and just refused to argue anymore.

Eventually, Angie came into his room and perched on the end of his bed. Taking a deep breath, Lorenzo prepared for yet another haranguing…or advice, as Angie preferred to call it.

'Right then.' She began, her hands twisting in her lap as she tried to retain control of her emotions. '…I know you have to go, Rez. I do. And I admire you for wanting to follow your dreams. It's just that I—' Her voice quivered as she struggled to say her piece.

'Mum, it's fine; I know how you feel. I would be the same if it was you and dad leaving.' Lorenzo didn't really believe anything of the sort, but he was rapidly running out of platitudes.

'It would be different if you were with someone, you know? But going on your own where you don't know anyone it's –' Lorenzo interrupted her.

'I'm going with Sam Mum, we're business partners.' Lorenzo felt a jolt of betrayal describing Sam as his business partner, but what could he say…my boyfriend? My lover?

'….and anyway, I know loads of people there; you'll get to know them too when you come to stay.' Lurching from one placatory comment to the next, Lorenzo thought he'd finally hit on the right track as Angie smiled a watery smile.

'How long did you say the flight was?'

Chapter 33

The printer once again regurgitated reams of paper as Lorenzo stared absently out the window. His boss Richie was off his case now that he knew he was leaving but also excited that his dopey trainee 'Murph' was emigrating to Malta, his wife's homeland. Richie had taken great delight in telling him all about his island in the sun, as he liked to call it.

'I can't believe you'll be living in Sliema.' He shook his head in disbelief as he googled a map of the island, stubby fingers spreading it for more detail.

'Look here, you walk down to the ferry here, go across Marsamxett harbour to Valetta here, up the steps, and you're in the most amazing old city, full of history, you know, knights and all that, walk over to here to the grand harbour.' Richie stabbed the map every time he said *here* for emphasis.

Lorenzo's head was filled with hidden beaches and coves, hidden from tourists apparently. The poor locals find it impossible to carry on with their normal lives during the summer influx. Lorenzo thought he'd be glad of an influx of tourists wanting to dive with him. Richie had given him several contact numbers, various relatives of his wife, and a few business owners in Sliema who might give some support. He felt a new relationship blossoming with Richie; maybe they could have been friends if they hadn't had to work together.

The printer beeped helpfully to tell him it was finished; a light also flashed just in case he didn't hear the beep. Stacking all his papers in order, Lorenzo smiled as Gemma approached, hopping up on his desk as was her custom.

'Hey Rez, how's it going?'

'Bloody assessments, I hate assessments.' He grumbled

'Well, not for much longer, eh? When do you leave?'

'In a months' time, hopefully all the paperwork will be done by then, then it's off to the sun for me.' He punched the air, almost scattering his precious assessments.

'Erm, could we go for a drink Rez?' Gemma looked worried, her voice tentative.

'Yeah, sure, that'd be great, maybe next week sometime, I've got to—' Gemma interrupted him.

'Are you free tonight, Rez? I really need to speak to you.' Her smile didn't quite reach her eyes.

'Oh, um, sure after work then?' Lorenzo watched her walk back to her desk as he pondered what could be so urgent that it needed to be tonight.

The bar was busy as usual, with Octagon people chatting about work and a few builders from a nearby site slaking their thirst after a hard, dusty day. Lorenzo went in and waited for his eyes to adjust to the gloom of the interior. Spotting Gemma at their usual table, he headed towards her, his progress impeded by Octagon colleagues slapping him on the back by way of congratulations on his leaving the company.

'What can I get you, Gemms? He hovered uncertainly at the table, unnerved by the look on her face.

'Just a coke, Rez, thanks.'

Sitting down opposite her, he sipped his beer, wondering what tonight was all about.

'So—'

'Rez I don't—'

They both laughed and sat in silence for another moment. Gemma played with the melting wax on the candle as Lorenzo sought refuge in his beer.

'Rez, this is really ha—' Jinx came bouncing over to their table, pulling up a chair. He chatted enthusiastically about Lorenzo's dive club plans.

'I can't believe you're actually gonna do it, man, that's just amazing. I'll expect a discount, of course, as it was my idea after all.' He laughed.

Glancing over at Gemma, she gave Lorenzo a 'get rid of him' look, her eyes wide as she conveyed her silent message. Turning to Jinx, Lorenzo glanced at his watch for effect.

'Erm, I can't stay long, Jinx, and I just need a quick word with Gemma first, if that's okay.' It wasn't a question.

Jinx got the message loud and clear, apologising as he returned to his mates at the bar.

'So what—?'

'I'm pregnant, Rez.'

Lorenzo heard the words, but they refused to stay in his head, floating around as he refused them entry to his brain. He stared at Gemma in stunned silence, his body refusing to breathe as he waited for her to giggle and say she was only kidding. Lorenzo had watched plenty of movies where the girl tells the guy she's pregnant. He'd often scoffed at the hapless guy who got his girl pregnant then refused to accept his own part in the creating of the dilemma.

Gemma watched him carefully; she'd long abandoned her candle wax sculpture and was clutching her hands under the table. If she was trying to appear calm and pragmatic, it wasn't working. She waited, eyes glued to Lorenzo as she clamped her lips together in an effort to stop them trembling.

Leaning across the table, she grasped his hand, trying to keep him connected somehow, as his blank gaze roamed around the pub, looking at everyone and everything as long as it wasn't her.

'Rez.' Her thumb caressed his as she tried to bring him back.

He looked down at her hand holding his, focusing on a small scar on her wrist; he remembered when she burnt it cooking for them one night before passionately tumbling into her bed. He looked up, searching her face for answers.

'But we used condoms, how come?' As soon as the words fell out of his mouth, he realised it was a juvenile comment and hardly relevant now.

'I don't know Rez, maybe that time in my car, we weren't planning to, well, you know.' She wiped a tear away with a delicate finger, looking as distraught as he did. He squeezed her hand, running his thumb over hers as he remembered the time in her car.

It was early on in their relationship, and they'd driven back from a friend's house with the intention of her dropping him home; instead, she'd diverted to a local beauty spot and parked under the trees. Lorenzo was no stranger to sex in the back of a car, his father's prized showroom SUVs providing teenage opportunities. Gemma's mini, on the other hand, necessitated a rather more inventive approach, Lorenzo being over six feet tall. He smiled at the memory in spite of the dire situation he now found himself in.

'How far along are you?' He asked reasonably, fighting the urge to shout, '*What the actual fuck?*'

'Twelve weeks.' She sniffed again. 'I'm keeping it Rez.' She tilted her chin defiantly.

Lorenzo automatically looked down in wonder at her abdomen, expecting to see proof of the life growing within.

'Oh, right, well that's good…isn't it?' The thought of her getting rid of his child was unthinkable, but the thinkable alternative was even more scary.

'I don't expect anything from you, Rez, but if you want to be involved, that's great.' She smiled sadly.

As they talked, a new bond seemed to form between them, this life they had accidentally created, bringing them closer. It wasn't quite what Lorenzo had expected when told he was going to be a father, but then he'd never given it much thought, assuming that phase of his life was in the far distant future, but now the future had come to him, demanding he step up.

'Erm, Jesus, Gemms, this is so hard.' Running his hand through his hair, Lorenzo realised he owed Gemma the truth about Sam.

'I'm in love with someone, he, erm—'

'Is it your friend Sam, Rez?' Gemma smiled at the look of confusion on Lorenzo's face.

'What? I mean, how did you know? I haven't told anyone. It's all been so confusing.'

'It was that day in the pub garden, the way you two were with each other, it was so obvious, Rez. Have you been together this whole time? Even when you were with me?' She asked tentatively.

'No! No, Gemms, I wouldn't do that to you, to either of you. My feelings for Sam came out of nowhere. I've known him all my life and never once thought about him like that.' Lorenzo could see she was hurt and needed her to understand.

'I turned up one night unannounced to a party at his house. He was dressed as a girl Gemms, a beautiful sexy girl called Samantha, I had no idea that was a thing for him, but we were both very drunk, and I was pissed off that he hadn't told me, we had a big falling out about it, the next time I saw him was in the hospital with metal rods in his legs, it made me realise I'd almost lost him.' Lorenzo shrugged a shoulder, smiling at the memory.

'I can imagine how Samantha would look; Sam is a very beautiful guy.' She nodded, concurring with Lorenzo's description of her.

'I broke up with you as soon as things with Sam, erm…when I realised how I felt about him.'

'So, you must be bisexual? I mean, you like girls,' she mused before adding smugly: 'I should know after all.'

Lorenzo smiled, nodding in acknowledgement of their passionate encounters. He sighed, running his hands through his hair in frustration at his confused sexuality.

'I dunno Gemms, all I know is I love Sam, that simple really, why does it have to be rubber-stamped and labelled by everyone, I'm this, or I'm that…I'm just me, and I love Sam…end of.' He shrugged, palms up, questioning.

'So where does that leave us, Rez, you, me, and our baby.' Gemma looked at him sadly, tears glistening again on her lashes.

'I have to go to Malta Gemms; that's my life, my future. I can't back out now; it's all signed up and ready to go.' Lorenzo pleaded with his eyes, needing her understanding.

Gemma left her seat, coming round to sit beside him before gathering him into her arms. Burying his head in the warmth of her neck, he gave vent to the tears he'd been holding back.

'Oi, you two, get a room.' Jinx shouted from across the bar.

'Does he know?' Gemma asked quietly.

'No, no one knows Gem, only you.' He mumbled.

'Did you ever feel that I was different, somehow?' Unfolding his head from Gemma's embrace, he sat up, picking up his beer in an effort to control his emotions.

She giggled, a pink flush rising up from her chest to her neck. 'No, not at all. In fact, I always thought you were…erm…very enthusiastic. I thought you liked me, I —' Lorenzo cut her off, alarmed that she would think he hadn't cared for her.

'Oh god, Gemms, I did…I do, but with Sam, I don't know it just suddenly hit us. It's weird, you know? I've known him all my life; I'd never felt like this about him, ever, until that night in the garden. Samantha was just so, sexy, beautiful; I felt she was mine and had been forever.' He smiled shyly, embarrassed at sharing his deepest secrets.

'So you can honestly say you've never fancied other guys, just Sam?' Gemma frowned, trying to make sense of it all.

'Nope, not in a million years, Gem. I always liked girls, still do, I guess.' He shrugged a shoulder, baffled by his own admission.

'So, me and you…?' She asked hesitantly.

'Oh god, Gemms, don't do this, I'm with Sam now.' Lorenzo had always considered himself to be a faithful partner; the idea of cheating on Sam was abhorrent to him. Gemma smiled sadly, acknowledging defeat.

'I liked Sam, Rez; I think we could be friends, that is, if he could bear it.'

The knot in Lorenzo's stomach, which had begun to ease, suddenly gripped tight once more. Sam, I have to tell Sam, Jesus, what a sodding nightmare.

Chapter 34

'Brings back memories, eh?' Lorenzo glanced around the small flat as Sam gathered up the remains of his life in Bristol, stuffing it into bags brought for the purpose. Opening and closing various drawers and cupboards, he stood back, allowing the memories to flood back: Chloe and him cooking in the small kitchen, Chloe insisting on waxing his legs, the laughter and the pain that ensued. Chloe caring for him when he was too drunk to stand up.

'You know, I just don't get it, Rez…Chloe, of all people, she was my best friend here, and she couldn't even be bothered to meet me for a goodbye drink.' Sam turned to Lorenzo, who was lounging on the sofa, long legs dangling over the end, looking at his phone.

'Dunno Sam, she was always a bit spiky with me. I think she's just jealous coz I got you, and she lost.' Lorenzo looked up from his phone and grinned.

'Jealous? Well, maybe a bit. But we were just friends, Rez, or so I thought.' Sam shrugged sadly as he gazed critically around the room.

Raising his eyes to the top of the wardrobe, he asked Lorenzo to lift down the precious box.

'Oh right, what's in here then?' Lorenzo plopped the bag on the bed, wiping a layer of dust off the top.

'That, my love, is Samantha.' Gesturing to the bag with a theatrical sweep of his hand, Sam opened it tenderly.

Kissing Sam lightly on the forehead, Lorenzo left the room, feeling that Sam needed a moment alone. As he sat back on the old, battered sofa with the dodgy spring, he thought about the last time he'd been here. He and Samantha had slept together for the first time. It seemed like years ago; so much had happened since then. He remembered his confusion, looking for answers all the time…what was he? Who was he?

Picking up his phone again, he immediately wished he hadn't; a message from Gemma awaited his attention.

'Have you told him yet?'

Lorenzo ignored the message, irritably stuffing the phone back in his pocket as Sam emerged from his room, seemingly none the worse for his reconciliation with Samantha.

'So…all good to go?' Lorenzo asked, noting that Sam hadn't brought his holdall out with him.

'Yup, all done.' Sam picked up a black bin liner and held it aloft.

'Say goodbye to Samantha Rez.'

'Erm, what? Are you sure about this? I mean, you might want to, you know?' Lorenzo shrugged, unsure of his words.

'Nah, Samantha can come out to play any time, Rez…maybe you'd like to see her again?' he teased, hand on hip as he flicked his hair back.

'Hmm, maybe I would.' Lorenzo grinned as he pulled Sam in for a kiss, pinning him tightly against his hips. As the kiss deepened, Lorenzo's hand reached down, urgently fumbling with Sam's belt.

'Not here, Rez. Chloe could come home any minute.' Sam mumbled through kisses.

'Oh Jesus, Sam, where then?' Lorenzo groaned.

'Bathroom.' Sam shouted with some urgency.

***

Looking around for his hastily discarded clothes sometime later, Lorenzo chuckled as a memory surfaced.

'D'you remember that time I helped you shower in here?'

'Ha…yeah, we nearly did it then, didn't we?' Sam laughed, fishing his shirt out of the bath. 'But you were still fighting it. It wouldn't have worked back then.'

'Sam, there's…something I need to tell you.' Lorenzo hadn't planned on having this conversation right now, but his tongue thought otherwise, the words tumbling out before he could stop them.

'Mmm, sounds serious.' Sam sat on the sofa, making an elaborate gesture for Lorenzo to sit opposite.

'Do you remember Gemma, the blonde girl in the pub that day?' Lorenzo sat down, remembering all the dramas they'd sorted out sitting in these same chairs; this one would be the one to top the lot.

Sam nodded.

'Well, you know we had a thing for a while before you and I got together?'

'Oh yeah, nice girl, does she want you back then, is that it?' Sam asked casually.

'She's pregnant, Sam.' Lorenzo wanted to snatch the dreaded words back, bury them deep so they couldn't hurt anyone.

Sam said nothing for several long agonising minutes. Lorenzo knew better than to speak; he, too, sat in silence, terrified for their future together.

Sam's eyes were focused somewhere across the room, anywhere other than at Lorenzo; he leaned forward, massaging his leg before glaring over at Lorenzo.

'How far gone is she?' Sam couldn't quite hide the tremor in his voice, knowing the absolute importance of the date.

'Twelve weeks, well actually fourteen now, I s'pose.' Lorenzo watched Sam's face as he mentally calculated the dates, safe in the knowledge that he hadn't cheated.

'She doesn't want anything from me, Sam—'

'Oh right, well, that's okay then, isn't it?' Sam cut him off before continuing.

'I didn't realise you were sleeping with her; quite the player, aren't you, Rez?' Sam's mouth twisted as he spat out the accusation.

'Come on, Sam we weren't together then; it's not as if I cheated on you.' Lorenzo snapped back, flinging his arms up in frustration.

Sam gazed around the room, his eyes drifting over all his belongings, ready to leave to start a new life. His old fears flooded back about Lorenzo and Liz; now it was Lorenzo and Gemma…and their child.

'So where does this leave us, Rez?' Sam said quietly.

'Nothing's changed, Sam. I've told her I'm with you, and we'll be living in Malta, running a business.' Lorenzo was relieved to have something positive to say.

'And what about when you and her become 'us', where does that leave me, Rez? Running a diving club on my own whilst you play happy families when I don't even dive.'

'You're my family now, Sam. I love you, only you.' Lorenzo pleaded as he fought back the tears, wondering why he seemed to hurt everyone he loved.

'And your baby? You can't just ignore the fact that you're a father, Rez. Surely you'll need to see your child *sometimes*?'

'Yeah, I know, maybe I can come back a few times a year, or she could come out to visit us?' Lorenzo hadn't thought that far ahead, and the look on Sam's face gave him his answer.

Sam stood up and headed for the bathroom, closing the door slowly behind him, needing to put a distance between them. Sitting down heavily on the toilet seat, he tried to make sense of the tidal wave that threatened to wash away their lives. He knew Lorenzo hadn't cheated on him with Gemma, but somehow it didn't help; he still felt betrayed, not in the physical sense but in the sense of a bond being broken. Lorenzo would always need to share his life with Gemma, and their child, Sam, would be an outsider, not part of their cosy little threesome. Various 'what ifs' tore at his heart; Lorenzo deciding he wanted to have a family life with Gemma, leaving their dive club for good and going back home to her; Lorenzo realising he'd made a mistake and just got caught up in the thrall of his newly discovered sexuality? Maybe it was just an infatuation, and he'd suddenly wake up and decide he wasn't bisexual after all.

'Sam, are you okay?' Lorenzo tapped gently on the door.

'Yeah, just give me a minute Rez.'

Emerging eventually from his refuge, Sam realised he wasn't alone in his suffering. Lorenzo was standing stiff backed, looking out the window, when he suddenly dropped his head into his hands, shoulders shaking.

'Rez, we can—' Lorenzo turned, grabbing Sam as he sobbed into his shoulder.

'I'm so sorry, Sam. The last thing I want to do is hurt you.' He stood back, gazing down at Sam as he fought for control.

'Well, it's not like you planned it, is it?' Sam mumbled.

***

Stowing the last of Sam's stuff in the boot Lorenzo helped him into the car, leaning in to kiss him lightly.

'It'll be fine Sam; we'll get through this.' His hand dropped to Sam's shoulder, squeezing it reassuringly.

Sam was anything but reassured, his stomach was still in knots as he tried to come to terms with what he considered to be their wrecked plans. Lorenzo's 'It'll be fine' mantra had been his coping mechanism all their lives, more often than not it was 'all fine' as Lorenzo just adapted to whatever circumstances he found himself in. Accepting that he too would have to adapt or lose Lorenzo, Sam popped some pills, closed his eyes and waited for oblivion.

'Wake me up when we get home.' He reached over, resting a hand on Lorenzo's thigh.

Weaving in and out of the traffic on the journey home Lorenzo was aware he was driving too fast, his black mood causing him a few close calls as he lost concentration. Following a terrifying squeal of brakes and loud hooting from irate drivers, he pulled into a service station, parked up and switched off the engine. Glancing over at Sam who was still snoring quietly, he closed his eyes and tried but failed, to sleep.

His brain was like a tumble dryer, churning over and over, he couldn't figure out if Sam had accepted the news with whatever complications it was sure to bring or was so devastated that, that what? What would happen then? He couldn't bear to think about the 'what if.'

He'd been hurt by Sam's '*player*' comment, feeling this to be an unfair personal attack. He'd never cheated on anyone, always finishing a relationship before starting another one, what did Sam mean by the accusation? Is that what he really thought of him? Longing to poke Sam awake and demand he account for his accusations, Lorenzo got out of the car, slamming the door in the hope of waking him up; realising he didn't have a hope once the pills had kicked in, he made his way to Costa.

Sipping a Green Tea, he gazed across the car park, eyes fixed on the car just in case Sam woke up in a stupor and came looking for him. His thoughts flickered briefly on impending fatherhood but he quickly moved on, focusing instead on how to rescue their Malta plans and reassure Sam, if he was willing to be reassured. Checking his messages, he smiled at the one from Richie, more useful contacts in Malta, this one was a local florist, very useful when running a diving club, he thought. Feeling calmer now, he headed back to the car and its comatose occupant, setting off down the M4 at a steadier pace.

As he waited patiently at a red traffic light, he stole a glance over at Sam, still snoozing quietly, his soft black hair curling over his eyes; Lorenzo's breath caught as a wave of emotion overtook him.

'God, I love you so much.'

He longed to nudge Sam awake, needing to tell him how much he wanted and needed him. A young family crossed at the lights, the father carrying a crying toddler whilst the mother tried to soothe the wailing child. As Lorenzo watched the domestic scene unfold, he waited for the pull towards parenthood to hit; it didn't; with relief, he realised he felt nothing.

'Sam, Sam, wake up, we're home.' Lorenzo had parked up and unloaded Sam's belongings into his parents' house. He wasn't entirely convinced that Sam was still asleep, thinking that maybe he just didn't want to talk. Looking around in bleary-eyed confusion, Sam eased himself out of the car, reluctantly accepting Lorenzo's arm.

'Erm, okay…ah, message me, yeah?' Hovering uncertainly, Lorenzo was at a loss as to what to say, inexplicably expecting that when Sam woke up, everything would be okay between them, he realised he was very wrong when Sam waved a dismissive hand as he disappeared into his house.

Driving home, Lorenzo's mood veered between annoyance at Sam for not understanding his predicament and guilt for putting them through yet another emotional rollercoaster. The accusation of '*player*' still stung, did Sam think he was some sort of fuck boy, jumping into bed with anyone who asked him? What sort of future could they have if Sam didn't trust him? He'd ended his relationship with Gemma as soon as he'd realised how he felt about Sam…what more could he have done? They'd always used protection. It wasn't as if they'd been reckless, apart from the one time were.

Turning into his drive, he switched off the engine and sat in the car. Anger, guilt, fear of losing Sam…a spiralling cocktail of pent-up rage exploded in an anguished bark of frustration as he banged his hand hard on the steering wheel.

Feeling somewhat better, he headed into the house, straight for the kitchen, hoping to find it empty as he was gasping for a coffee. Flicking through his phone, he read a message from Gemma.

'*How'd it go then?*'

'*Great, wonderful, he was really happy Gemms*'

'*Did he take it badly?*'

'*Well, of course he did…what d'you think he'd say?*'

'I'm sorry, Rez. Is there anything I can do?'

'No thanks, you've done quite enough already.' Lorenzo scrapped this last one, conceding it wasn't any more her fault than his.

'Nah…we just need to figure it out; he's hurting Gem. I need to convince him he can trust me.'

'We really hit it off, you know…me and Sam, maybe if we all got together, I could reassure him?'

Lorenzo was about to respond with a resounding *'No way,'* but the suggestion was growing on him. Would it be a good idea? Could the three of them be friends? Would Gemma accept he was with Sam now? And more to the point, could Sam bear to have Lorenzo's Ex in his life? His head was beginning to pound as he sipped his coffee; maybe caffeine wasn't such a good idea. Resting his head down on his arms on the kitchen counter, he began to doze off to sleep, only to be rudely awakened by his parents coming back from a shopping trip. Happy laughing voices echoed down the hallway as they bustled in, shopping bags bashing against the doorway as they came into the kitchen.

'Oh hi love, you're home.' Angie planted a kiss on her son's head before unloading her bags.

'Everything okay? Did you get all Sam's stuff back from Bristol?' She chatted as she opened and closed various cupboards.

Lorenzo longed to reply.

'Actually, mum, it's not okay. In fact, it's all totally fucked. I'm in love with Sam, who sometimes dresses up as Samantha, and my ex-girlfriend is pregnant.'

He laughed quietly to himself, thinking of her reaction if he only had the nerve to spit it out.

'Yeah…all good.' He smiled reassuringly.

'Oh, I've bought you a few things you might need for Malta.' Angie delved deep into one of her bags and retrieved two pairs of smart shorts, a pack of short-sleeved shirts, and several sets of underwear. Holding the shorts up for inspection, she chattered on about the possible lack of suitable shops on 'a little island in the middle of nowhere' and the fact that, as a business owner, he should always look smart. Lorenzo decided to allow her the illusion of a smartly dressed diver and gave her a hug, thanking her for the gifts. He filed the 'Little Island' comment away for further discussion; he wasn't going to let her off that one quite so easily.

His father popped his head around the door, enquiring how the car had performed on the journey from Bristol.

'Erm, yeah, it was fine, Dad, no problems.' Lorenzo wondered, not for the first time, why his father had to check on the status of the car every time he drove it. Was the car upset? Did it cry when he said they had to leave?

Did it sulk when left outside all by itself? Lorenzo chuckled to himself as his father asked for the keys, just to go and check.

Enjoying the mundane domesticity that was his parents' life, Lorenzo suddenly had a pang of emotion.

He would miss this.

Chapter 35

The big dog lifted his head and galloped across the fields in his dreams, his large paws scraping at the bedclothes as he chased an imaginary rabbit. Sam soothed him, scratching his ears and murmuring endearments. They were curled up on Sam's bed, entwined like lovers in an embrace. Sam was ever grateful for the emotional support his dog unwittingly gave him, never so much as today. He knew he had two choices, neither of which filled him with confidence for his future. Accepting that choice number two was a non-starter, he focused on number one, how to swallow his pride and move forward with Lorenzo.

After recovering from the shock of Lorenzo's devastating news, Sam tried to be pragmatic, not usually his strong point, being more of a follow-your-heart type of person, but on this occasion, it was necessary. He loved Lorenzo, always had he supposed and the thought of that now being snatched away just when they had newly discovered it was unbearable. Having come to this conclusion, Sam knew he had only one course open to him; he had to accept this new twist in their complicated life and place his trust in Lorenzo. His heart pounding, he made a decision; he had to see Lorenzo.

Searching around for his phone, he finally located it underneath Rez's soft, furry tummy; the dog lifted his head and stared at Sam in protest at the disturbance before flopping back to his rabbits. Sam scrolled through his messages; several emails from solicitors and a couple from the dog relocation people about Rez's travel arrangements and quarantine for Malta. A lump began to form in his throat as he thought about the trauma he was planning to put his beloved dog through.

'Am I being selfish in wanting to bring him with me?' He quickly shelved that thought, unable to even consider the idea of living without Rez, either of them!

Several WhatsApp's from Lorenzo helped to ease his anguish as he read each one, his smile widening with each message.

'Hey Sam, erm, can we meet?

'Please Sam ...we need to talk ...I love you'

'Hey buddy, look, just put me out of my misery, okay.'

'We can do this, Sam, it doesn't change anything, I love you ...want YOU'

Sam's leg was throbbing as he reached for his pills, but changing his mind before taking them; he needed a clear head today and couldn't afford the luxury of zoning out for several hours.

'Hey Rez, yeah, we need to talk asap, you're at work today?

'Yeah, but I'll come out, shall I come over to yours or meet in the Bishops?

'Meet you in the pub, 12 ish?'

As Sam hit send, his head was spinning; this was it then, decision time.

He hit the shower and shaved, leaving a bit of stubble. Lorenzo liked the stubble. Peering in the mirror, he applied a line of black liner next to his lashes, remembering Max's advice. He fluffed out his hair, then smoothed it down again with a heavy sigh, unsure what he was trying to achieve. Did he want to look like Samantha? Would that help? Or would it just confuse matters even more? Maybe Samantha in jeans and a T-shirt? A sort of hybrid look. Rummaging through his wardrobe, he fished out some tight jeans and paired these with a black T, Lorenzo's leather necklace finished the look. Glancing in the mirror once more, he mumbled to himself.

'What the hell does it matter now anyway?'

***

The Uber dropped him at the pub and he limped in, unsure if he wanted to be first there or if he preferred Lorenzo to be waiting. As it was midday, midweek, it was fairly empty, with just a few people sitting quietly supping their pints. Sam glanced around as he headed to the bar, concluding he was the first to arrive. He ordered a San Miguel and a Peroni, the barman offering to bring the drinks to his table, when he noticed Sam leaning heavily on his crutch. As he waited, eyes nervously fixed on the door, it suddenly opened, and several girls came in, dressed for the office, so obviously on their lunch break. He girls headed for the bar, chatting excitedly, when one of them suddenly stopped and stared at Sam, smiling as the recognition kicked in.

'Sam, is that you?' Tessa came over, embracing him as she pulled out a chair.

'Oh, erm, Tessa, hi.' Sam shifted uncomfortably, praying that Lorenzo would arrive soon, which he did at that very moment.

'I was so sorry to hear about your—' The look on Sam's face caused her to pause and look around as Lorenzo stood frozen to the spot, eyes boring into Sam's in confusion.

'Rez! Oh my god, this is so cool. How are you?' Tessa abandoned Sam and dashed over to give Lorenzo an effusive hug. Sam watched with amusement as the scene played out between Lorenzo and yet another Ex-girlfriend.

'Any more women you want to tell me about Rez?'

He decided he was being unfair. After all, Tessa was a teenage romance a long time ago. A flash of pale pink caught his eye as Tessa's skirt swirled around her legs, reminding him of Samantha's pink silk dress tucked away in a drawer in his room. Unable to bring himself to part with it, he'd fished it out of the black plastic bag he was planning to dump. A sadness crept over him that Lorenzo had never seen her in the dress, maybe one day. As he watched Lorenzo with his Ex, he suddenly remembered she was the girl with the condoms in Lorenzo's father's car all those years ago. Grinning at Lorenzo's efforts to extricate himself from Tessa, he buried his head in his pint and waited.

'Jesus, man, what bad luck, of all the people to meet.' Lorenzo sat down opposite Sam, keeping his back to Tessa and her friends.

'How did you get rid of her?' Sam laughed.

'What, just now or back then?' Lorenzo chuckled, picking up his drink and downing half of it in one gulp.

The inopportune arrival of Tessa served to ease the atmosphere somewhat, and they talked for a while about Lorenzo's work and how the promotion of the dive club was coming along. Having run out of mundane conversation, they sipped their drinks in silence, both aware that whatever was decided now would seal their future.

'So, erm—'

'Look, Rez, I didn't—'

'Okay, you go first.' Lorenzo picked up his drink again, his hand shaking as he waited, terrified he was about to lose Sam.

'Right, so, I need to know, Rez, are you absolutely sure this is what you want, you and me, Malta and everything?' Sam couldn't breathe. He could feel his palms damp with perspiration as he awaited his fate. Opening himself up for rejection, he knew there were no compromises here; it had to be all or nothing.

'Absolutely sure, Sam, no doubts whatsoever. I want us to be together. I love you so much, and I'm so sorry I've hurt you.' Reaching for Sam's hand, Lorenzo squeezed so hard that Sam feared for the bones in his fingers. Luckily, at that moment, Tessa and her girls started waving and making 'phone me signs' as they left the pub. Releasing Sam's crushed hand, Lorenzo returned the wave, looking decidedly sheepish.

'Any more ex-girlfriends popping out of the woodwork, Rez?' Sam immediately regretted the spiteful comment, but it was out before he could stop it.

'Jesus man, how many times, and anyway, what was that 'player' gibe all about?'

'What gibe, when?' Sam frowned in confusion.

'Never mind, it doesn't matter.' Lorenzo decided to leave it there, not wanting to get into another row just as they were beginning to see a way through their dilemma. He nodded at Sam's empty glass as he stood up to go to the bar.

'Yeah, and some dry roast peanuts.' Sam's eyes followed as Lorenzo went to the bar.

'Can I trust you with the rest of my life Rez?'

Returning with their drinks and snacks, Lorenzo gulped down a few more mouthfuls, tossing Sam's peanuts over to him.

'So, erm, I don't know how you feel about this, but Gemma was thinking maybe it would be good if we all met up, like, just for a chat, so we can prove to you that there's nothing between us, she knows I'm with you Sam, and she's accepted that but obviously, I'd like to be part of the child's life, if I can, that's if you—'

'Yeah, why not, looks like we're all gonna be in it together, doesn't it, Rez, one big happy family.' Sam's mouth turned down in a grimace, the sarcasm thick and heavy as it spewed out. He shook his head sadly before adding.

'So let me get this right, just so I understand it, Rez. You and Gemma have had a cosy little chat about *me*, and decided that if we can all be friends, it would be so much easier all around…right?'

Lorenzo ignored heavy sarcasm, which was very unlike Sam. He understood what he must be going through and what he was asking of him.

'Yeah, that's about the gist of it, I s'pose. We don't have to be friends with her, just keep in touch so I can see the kid now and again. I don't want to be a father, Sam. Not yet anyway, and if I do in the future, I want it with you.' Lorenzo was shocked as heard his own words spoken out loud. Was it true? Did he really want a family with Sam? He laughed out loud as the truth hit him; yes, he really did. Sam gazed at him open-mouthed as he grappled with his bag of peanuts.

'What? You're joking, right? Kids, you and me?' Sam scoffed, mainly because they'd never discussed it. Most of their time was taken up with trying to understand their relationship; adding a child to the mix was never on the agenda.

'Well, maybe not in the next ten years or so, but it would be nice, wouldn't it?' Lorenzo grabbed Sam's peanuts, deftly opening the bag before handing them back to him.

'Why can you never open these?' He laughed and reached for Sam's hand again, tracing the faint scarring where the needles had gone in. He brushed his lips gently over the bruised flesh.

'Why are we fighting Sam? After everything we've been through, can't we just—'

Sam leaned in, caressing Lorenzo's cheek as the tears threatened to embarrass them both. He kissed Lorenzo, nodding his head in silent agreement. Glancing around the pub in case they were seen, Lorenzo pulled Sam in closer, desperately needing to hold him, touch him.

'Not here, Rez, it's too risky; that was just a little taster.' He smiled seductively, Samantha style.

'I see you're still wearing my necklace.' Lorenzo's voice was husky as he fingered the soft brown leather, his fingertips brushing Sam's neck.

'Yeah, well, I wasn't sure if I'd be giving it back to you or not.'

'What? Would you really have broken up with me?' Lorenzo sat back, his eyes wide in astonishment.

'Mmm, maybe.' Sam teased, provocatively running the leather necklace through his lips.

'Right then, what about this meeting with Gemma? Are you going to set it up?' Sam thought they'd better get back to the business at hand. His leg was beginning to throb, having not taken any meds that morning, and he didn't know how much time he had left before it became unbearable.

'Really, are you sure?'

Lorenzo helped Sam up from the table after he'd ordered his Uber.

'Yeah, seems like a good idea, I s'pose, mummy, daddy and uncle Sam.'

'Come on Sam, it's not gonna be like that, we'll be—'

'Rez, chill, man. It'll be good, you're right. Gemma and I need to get to know each other if this is going to work, for your sake.' Sam smiled, congratulating himself on his pragmatic approach.

His car arrived, and he sank into the back seat, grateful to be sitting down once more as his leg was gearing up for full-on inferno mode. The car weaved its way slowly through the traffic jam that was Winchester town centre. Sam urged the driver to go as fast as he could, but the guy just shrugged, protesting he didn't have a lot of say in the matter.

As he opened the front door, his eyes fell on a large holdall and a pair of battered trainers lying in the hallway. Manoeuvring carefully around the obstructions, Sam replaced his scowl with what he hoped was a more genial expression as he followed the voices into the sitting room. The first thing he saw as he entered the room was his older brother Dan sitting on the sofa with Rez, the traitorous dog, curled up beside him. Dan looked up with a cocky grin as Sam came in.

'Hey, little brother, German Shepherds. One-man dog, eh?' He sneered as he stroked Rez's head.

'Hey Dan,' he sighed. 'Come Rez.'

The dog immediately abandoned Dan, coming to sit obediently beside Sam before following him upstairs. Sitting down at his desk, Sam wondered at his brother's innate ability to piss him off in a few short words. As he pondered on this for the hundredth time, he suddenly remembered his mother's words. Dan was here to stay, the bags in the hallway confirming his worst nightmare.

'So, how's your arrangements for Malta going, love? Not long to go now, is it?' Julia Brewer valiantly tried to keep the conversation flowing at the dinner table as her two sons glared at each other over a huge dish of lasagne. She'd made it, especially for Dan, as it was his favourite, hoping it might play to his ego and take the edge off his spiteful attitude towards his brother.

'Yeah, going well, mum, just a few things to sort out for Rez's quarantine, then we're good to go.' The last thing Sam wanted right now was a cosy family chat about his plans in front of his odious brother, but he knew his mother's nervous chatter was covering up the angst she felt when her two boys were in the same room.

'So, effing big balls business owner now, eh?' Dan scoffed through a mouthful of garlic bread.

'Watch your mouth, boy.' Mike Brewer growled menacingly, his infrequent interjections of authority intended to shut down Dan's opening salvo.

'Yup, thought it would be nice to spend the rest of my life living in the sun, earning a living being my own boss, not beholden to anyone, you know?' Sam glared at Dan, gratified to see his barb had hit home.

'Yeah, sounds great, little bro, and is Samantha going too?'

Struggling for composure, Sam busied himself with another helping of lasagne as his brother waited, gloating across the table. Sam could almost see the drool dribbling down his chin as his prey struggled and squirmed. A thousand thoughts rushed through his head as he struggled for mastery over his face. How much did he know? Was this sodding Maxine and her Facebook posts? And worst of all, did his parents know?

'Oh, who's Samantha, Love, a friend from Bristol?' His mother asked genially.

'Sam's life's his own, Emelia. We don't need to go pocking around in other people's private business, do we?' Sam was ever grateful once again for his father's interjection.

'Shame, I'd liked to have heard a bit more about her.' Dan persisted, his lizard tongue licking his lips in anticipation.

'Really, why's that Dan? What is it you'd like to know?' Sam was ready.

C'mon then, bring it on you piece of shit…

He didn't care anymore what they thought; he was leaving, moving on with his life to a better place. Dan shrugged and attended to his food; seemingly, he didn't want to drop his bombshell just yet, but he would, sooner or later. He'd gleefully told their parents he'd found out Sam was gay, but they'd shrugged with a casual, '*So what we knew already,*' but Samantha was different. He didn't want to discuss her with anyone; she belonged to him and Lorenzo.

The torture that passed for a family dinner was finally over, and Sam retreated to his room, having made up his mind to leave tonight. After booking an Uber and a hotel, he began to pack.

Chapter 36

'Have you arranged anything yet, Rez?' Gemma asked, glancing around the office to make sure they weren't overheard. They'd been discussing Lorenzo's meeting with Sam, and she was heartened by his positive response. 'Was he okay about it? I mean, has he accepted you want to be involved?'

'Well, yeah, Gemms, but it's hard for him, you know?' Lorenzo was reminded of Sam's 'Uncle Sam' comment, and he didn't want to give Gemma the wrong impression; he and Sam were the couple here, not he and Gemma.

'Yeah, I know Rez, but when the baby comes, we—' Lorenzo stopped her there to read a message from Sam on his phone.

'Moved out of the house last night, staying in a hotel for a couple of nights.'

Lorenzo started to tap his phone but needed the reassurance of Sam's voice. Leaving Gemma rolling her eyes in exasperation, he dashed out to the corridor to phone Sam.

'Sam, hey, what's going on?' Lorenzo paced up and down, impatient to hear what could have happened.

'Fucking Dan's home Rez, he knows about Samantha; the bastard asked me about it in front of my parents at the dinner table. I had to get out before I thumped him one.'

'Jesus, Sam, the sooner we get away from here, the better; where are you staying? I'll come straight over after work.' Lorenzo glanced at his watch, half an hour to go. Having made their arrangements, Lorenzo returned to his desk to find Gemma leaning back against her desk, arms folded, awaiting an explanation.

'So what was all that about? We really need to get this meeting sorted out, Rez.' She said, schoolteacher fashion.

'Sam's had to move out, Gemms; it's a long story.' Lorenzo flicked a wrist, dismissing any further questions, which, in any event, he wasn't prepared to answer.

Heading home to get showered and changed, he sent Sam a quick message.

'Hey, I could stay over, couldn't I?'

As Lorenzo warmed to this idea, a frisson of electricity shot down to his groin, reminding him that he and Sam hadn't spent the night together since Malta. A few grubby snatched moments couldn't make up for a soft bed and the possibility of several repeat performances.

'Haha, yeah, the bed here is huge, bring a bottle'

The tantalizing aroma of roast chicken wafted down the corridor as Lorenzo opened his front door; he hoped he'd have time to have a quick bite before heading off to meet Sam.

'Rez, is that you love? Roast dinner ready if you want some?' Angie's voice echoed from the kitchen. Lorenzo pondered, not for the first time, why his mother had to ask who he was when everyone else was sitting around the table. As to the second question, he was fairly sure he'd have time to gulp down one of Angie's famous roast dinners.

'Yeah, sure do, mum, thanks, I'll just go and wash up.' Chuckling to himself as he took the stairs two at a time, Lorenzo wondered what Sam would think about coming second only to his mother's roast dinner.

Ali was reaching for crispy roast potatoes as he sat down, chattering on about her friends online.

'Saw a load of stuff on Facebook about your dive club Rez, LGBGTQ, and all that. I think it's really great that people can go there for a holiday, learn to dive, and just be themselves, and the name DiverCity is just so cool, especially as you and—'Lorenzo shot her a lightning-bolt death stare across the table, which served its intended purpose.

'Ooh, I like that Rez, Diver City; what do you mean about the LGBGTQ community, Ali? I mean, just because Sam's gay, it doesn't mean all your customers will be, does it?' Angie paused mid-mouthful, looking from her daughter to her son in confusion.

'Oh, well no, of course not, but erm –' Ali was interrupted by her father, itching to have his say in the debate.

'Ha, he'll need all the custom he can get, love, whatever weird and wonderful persuasion they are, they can be as queer as they like as long as they hand over the cash, eh Rez?' Jim stated, guffawing into his chicken.

Ali eyed her brother across the table, her eyes wide with amusement as she tried to control a grin. The silent question dripping from her twitching lips

'When are you going to tell them?'

'Ah, yeah, that's right, Dad, I don't care who they are as long as they book a dive course.' Lorenzo glanced at his watch, quickly mopping up a pool of gravy with his last potato.

'You going out love?' Angie asked, observant as ever.

'Yeah, sorry mum, I'm in a bit of a rush, meeting up with Sam.' Lorenzo waited, knowing full well what was coming next.

'You treat this house like a bloody hotel boy, your poor mother cooking for you, the least you can do is—' Angie interrupted as the scene played out.

'Oh, leave him be, Jim; he has a lot to do.' Angie smiled indulgently as she cleared the plates away, brushing her son's hair with a loving caress. Feeling he needed to make a bit of an effort, Lorenzo gathered up a few dishes and helpfully deposited them beside the dishwasher, eliciting an eyebrow twitch from his father. Making his escape, he headed for the door, picking up an overnight bag on the way. Sam's hotel was just round the back of the high street, so Lorenzo stopped in at a local shop to buy a bottle of Jack Daniels, tucking the bottle in amongst his overnight stuff.

***

'Welcome to my humble abode; I hope you've brought an entry fee.' Sam laughed as he opened the door, a towel draped loosely around his hips.

'Don't I always?' Lorenzo grinned, holding aloft the bottle as his eyes travelled hungrily down Sam's torso. Producing two glasses from the bathroom, Sam poured them a hefty slug.

'To getting away from here.' He coughed as the burning amber liquid trickled down his throat.

'Yeah, the sooner, the better; it's getting a bit awks for sure at home.' Lorenzo poured them another as he kicked off his shoes and sat on the huge bed, swinging his legs up with a sigh. Sam swung up beside him where they sat, sipping their drinks in companionable silence, each lost in their own thoughts as the strong liquor seeped through their veins, warming, arousing.

Lorenzo turned his head, eyes devouring Sam's bare torso, still damp and glistening from his shower. He indulged himself for a moment, remembering their nights together in Malta and the sweltering heat as their bodies entwined, wet with perspiration. Concluding he'd done enough remembering and desperate to get on with doing.

'Nice shower?' he asked, slowly easing Sam's towel off.

'I think you're a bit overdressed, Rez.' Sam smiled, reaching for Lorenzo's belt.

'Hmm, I might need a bit of help with that, Sam…I've had a hard day.' Lorenzo grinned lazily, lifting his hips as Sam eased him out of his jeans and boxers.

'Oh, so you have; maybe I can help you out with that.' Sam bent his head, his hair cascading in soft black waves over Lorenzo's stomach.

'Jesus Sam, that's…arghhh.' Lorenzo clutched Sam's head, unsure if he wanted him to stop or carry on.

'You know, I never noticed before.' Sam looked up, deep blue eyes glistening through black lashes.

'Eh, what? For god's sake, Sam.' Lorenzo peered down, brows knitted in frustration.

'Some of your hair is red down here, Rez.'

'Well, that'll be the Irish side.' Lorenzo muttered. 'Will you stop poking around like a bloody monkey looking for fleas and get up here.'

'Hmm, well, since you ask so nicely, darling.' Sam slithered up the bed into Lorenzo's waiting arms.

'D'you want to talk about what happened at home?' Lorenzo fervently hoped he didn't, as his body was crying out for release.

'No, we can talk in the morning; I had other stuff in mind.'

***

They ordered breakfast to the room, neither of them wanting to shower and dress just yet.

'Why is it that hotels always do breakfast so bloody early? I mean, who wants to flog down to a room full of people when you're half asleep and unshaven.' Sam grumbled through a mouthful of scrambled eggs.

'You look great unshaved.'

'You look great naked; you finished eating yet?'

The king-size bed, having been put to excellent use once more, stood empty and rumpled as both occupants headed out, feeling the need for a walk and some fresh air. As they walked through the town, Sam described the scene at home the previous night.

'I wonder if stuff about Samantha was posted on Facebook.' Lorenzo said as they went into a pharmacy. Sam had decided to wean himself off the prescription drugs and went in search of paracetamol.

'You know what, Rez? I really don't care anymore.'

Lorenzo didn't believe for one moment that he didn't care, and he knew Sam was hurt when Chloe refused to meet up and say goodbye.

'Could Chloe have posted something about Samantha?' he asked tentatively.

'What? No, she wouldn't do that. She knows what Dan's like.' Lorenzo thought this proved his point exactly but decided to stay quiet.

Sam paid for his tablets, and they emerged once more into the busy high street. Lorenzo's head was thumping from too much Jack Daniels, and his stomach was growling from lack of breakfast. He conceded the events which replaced his breakfast were far more enjoyable but he was paying the price now. The aroma of egg McMuffin was wafting out of McDonald's, and Lorenzo dragged a protesting Sam in.

'Bloody hell, Rez, we've just had breakfast.'

'I didn't finish mine, if you remember.' Lorenzo smirked.

They concluded that in the bigger scheme of things, it didn't really matter about Samantha's outing on Facebook. They were leaving, and the odious Dan could gloat as much as he liked.

'So, what about this meeting with Gemma? Is it gonna happen, or does it even matter?' Sam asked, gulping down two pills with a coke.

'Shall I message her now, see if she's free?' Lorenzo fished his phone out, tapping out a quick message before lathering more ketchup on his muffin.

Sam had been secretly hoping he wouldn't be subjected to a meeting with Gemma and Lorenzo, feeling, not without good reason, that she had wrecked their hopes and plans. He felt awkward watching Lorenzo with girls; was it jealousy? Or fear he would suddenly declare a desire for women again? What did it matter anyway? Male or female, it would still be a betrayal. After last night, Sam found it hard to imagine Lorenzo wanting to go back, but a small doubt nibbled away at him if he lost Lorenzo now…

He wondered about Gemma; would she try to come between them? Use their child as an excuse to spend time alone with Lorenzo? He reluctantly accepted she was going to be a permanent fixture in their lives, their futures bound together from one night of carelessness. He couldn't shake the feeling that she thought of him as a passenger, a hanger-on in her and Lorenzo's relationship, an irritant she had to put up with for Lorenzo's sake.

Gemma arrived just as Lorenzo finished his second burger; having grumbled, one was not enough.

'Hmm, hungry, were you?' She giggled as she surveyed the remains of Lorenzo's meal.

'Yeah, well, I got distracted at breakfast, didn't I?' Lorenzo grinned at Sam, his left eyebrow raised, teasing him with the memory.

Gemma looked from one to the other like a haughty schoolteacher admonishing two naughty boys.

'Shall we go somewhere less…messy?' She suggested.

'Yup, pub?' Lorenzo jumped up, fortified at last, and with his headache gone, he felt fit and ready for their next challenge, Gemma.

'Erm, I just need—' Pointing towards the toilets, Lorenzo hurried off, leaving Sam and Gemma to make their way out of the restaurant. Remembering how they'd hit it off when they first met, he hung back for a while, hoping it would give them a chance to get to know each other a bit without him.

***

'So you don't need the crutches at all anymore, Sam?' Gemma asked as they weaved their way slowly through the high street shoppers.

'No, the stick works fine, took me a while to get used to it, but I prefer it.' Sam smiled genially, wondering when the heavy stuff would begin. He didn't have long to wait.

'Erm, look, Sam, I know how difficult this must be for you. We both love our Rez, don't we.' Gemma turned to face him as Sam bristled at our Rez.

'You still love him then?' Sam asked guardedly, panic surging through him.

They wandered into the Cathedral grounds and, luckily, found an empty seat. Sam's heart was making a bid for escape from his ribcage as he sat down in abject misery.

'I think I probably always will, Sam, in a way, but it's not the same when you know that person doesn't want you, that they're totally in love with someone else. Maybe over time, if I meet someone, who knows?' She shrugged a shoulder and smiled before reaching for his hand.

'He wants you, Sam, ever since, I dunno, whatever happened between you—he never told me, but it was clear to me that it was over between us; I had no idea I was pregnant.' She waited, watching his face carefully as the gamut of emotions washed over him. Feeling now that she really wanted him to understand, she continued.

'There was never any doubt Sam. He never once considered staying with me, told me in no uncertain terms that his plans with you would go ahead regardless of the baby, he told me he loves you and that nothing could change that.' Gemma's mouth tightened as her lips trembled. 'I'll never forget what he said, *'Sam is a part of me, always has been, I just never realised it before.'* She attempted a watery smile, but her face refused to comply.

'I know something happened between you, apart from the obvious.' She flicked a wrist, batting away her banal words, and continued. '…something that upset him for a long time. I tried to get it out of him, but he wouldn't tell me.' Her eyes bored into Sam's, the question dropping like a boulder in his lap.

'Ah, yeah, we had a bit of a falling out when he came to see me one time in Bristol; I guess it was then that he realised how he felt.' Sam scratched the back of his head, a comforting gesture that failed to give the desired effect. He was pleased that Lorenzo obviously hadn't told her about the kiss in the garden in Bristol and hoped that she wouldn't ask any more about it. As he thought about that night, the images surged up from the depths, captivating him once more; The heady smell of jasmine, Lorenzo bursting in to save his honour like some medieval knight, and their first-ever kiss.

'…so he's all yours, Sam.' Pulled out of his reminiscing, he realised Gemma had been talking to him.

'Oh, erm right, well, as long as you're okay with it.' Unsure what he should say at that point, having missed the gist of it, Sam just smiled and nodded agreeably.

'Look over there; that could be us in a few years' time.' Nudging his arm, Gemma pointed to the river where two guys, a woman, and a small child, were looking at the fish.

'You really think so? I mean, if you're still in love with him, would you—' Gemma interrupted, shaking her head as she grasped his hand.

'I just want him to be happy Sam; you make him happy, so—' She squeezed his hand and kissed him on the cheek.

Elated at these revelations but also feeling sad for Gemma as the tears started to overwhelm her, Sam suggested he give her some space and get them an ice cream; giving him a watery smile, she nodded her head.

Lorenzo wandered slowly through the crowds, stopping to look in shop windows in the hope that Sam and Gemma had a chance to talk. His phone beeped, Sam.

'Sitting in the Cat grounds'

Lorenzo couldn't decide if that was good or bad. Had they fallen out on the way to the pub? Scanning through the inevitable hordes of tourists, he spotted them sitting on a bench eating ice cream. Gemma was laughing, leaning into Sam with her hand on his leg.

'Ah, didn't make it to the pub then?' Lorenzo flopped down on the grass opposite them since there was no room on the bench.

'It's a lovely day, Rez; seemed a shame to sit inside.' Gemma smiled, much to Lorenzo's relief.

'So, erm, everything okay?' He asked nervously.

'Yeah, we're good.' Sam put his arm around Gemma, demonstrating their newfound alliance.

They continued to chat amiably about their combined future plans, Gemma even going so far as to suggest she come and stay with them in Malta when the baby was born. Sam's initial thoughts were *'No bloody way,'* but he reasoned Lorenzo would need to see his child, and he'd rather have them meeting up where he could keep an eye on them, still not quite convinced about Gemma's innocent intentions.

Lorenzo tuned out, thinking about the next big drama facing him; What should he say to his family?

'Hey mum, you're going to be a grandma. And since we're discussing my decadent lifestyle, I'm in love with Sam and we're together.'

As he ruminated on his family's reaction, he watched some children running around the old statues, screeching and laughing as they played. Suddenly, one of them tripped, heading straight into their bench. Lorenzo made a grab for the fallen child just as she was about to bang her head. Standing the hysterical toddler up and checking for obvious injuries, he looked around, hopefully for a parent. Sam and Gemma paused their chat and were looking at Lorenzo in bemusement.

'Where the hell's her mother?' Lorenzo looked frantically around the grounds at several clutches of potential patents, all too busy chatting to observe their child's mishap. Eventually, someone noticed their offspring screaming in hysterics and ran over, grabbing the child and thanking Lorenzo for saving her.

'Well caught there, Rez.' Sam laughed.

'Not all heroes wear capes.' Lorenzo quipped proudly.

Gemma laughed, commenting on Lorenzo's parenting potential as Sam agreed, telling him they could both do with some lessons for future reference. Lorenzo was heartened by his comment, feeling that maybe Sam didn't feel so threatened anymore.

'Right then, I'm off, lots to do.' Gemma checked her phone and kissed them both on the cheek with promises to meet again soon.

Heading back to Sam's hotel, Lorenzo was keen to hear all the details; he was fairly confident things had gone well between Sam and Gemma.

'She still loves you, you know.' Sam said quietly as they kicked off their shoes in his room. Lorenzo frowned before reaching for their bottle of Jack Daniels.

'What do you mean *still loves* me? She never *loved* me. We never loved each other, Sam. It was just an office romance sort of thing.' Lorenzo was puzzled; where did this come from? He'd never told anyone he loved them before Sam.

'I dunno, she seems to think it was more serious than you do, evidently.' Sam raised his eyebrows by way of admonishment.

'So, you're okay with it now? I mean, you're happy for me to see the baby and all that?' Lorenzo ignored Sam's veiled disapproval.

'I think we owe it to Gemma Rez; she's gonna need our support.'

'Oh, like that is it? Our support.' Lorenzo laughed, wondering what on earth Gemma had said to convince him.

'Hmm, I think I like the idea of being an uncle, maybe a dad one day too.' Sam smiled and reached for Lorenzo, pulling him in for a kiss.

'Oh yeah? Well, at least I won't get you pregnant.' Lorenzo returned the kiss with enthusiasm.

'You never told her about that time in the garden in Bristol?' Sam asked quietly.

'Nope, Samantha belongs to me. I'm not sharing her with anyone, talking of which, I like your hair like this.' Lorenzo twirled a long strand through his fingers, pushing it back over Sam's ear.

'Maybe you'll get to see her again in Malta, DiverCity 'n all that.' Sam chuckled, pulling away from Lorenzo's embrace, he picked up his drink and sat in a large, comfy armchair, feet propped up on the bed.

'You should have heard the comments in our kitchen about DiverCity and gay divers, Sam; it was hilarious; bloody Ali almost let the cat out of the bag, then my mum said, *'Just because Sam's gay, it doesn't mean all your guests will be.'* Lorenzo reclined on the bed with his drink whilst giving a good impression of his mother.

'What have you told them?' Sam sipped his drink and realised he had no idea how things were going in Lorenzo's household.

'Erm, nothing yet, to be honest, I really don't know what to tell them; it's just so—'

'Diverse?' Sam interrupted, guffawing with laughter.

'It's not funny, Sam, you're used to all this stuff, I haven't even—'

'Come out yet?' Sam finished for him.

'Ali knows about you and me; she keeps giving me these big questioning eyes which shout from the rooftops, *'Tell them'*. I'll have to tell them about the baby, though, hard to keep that one a secret.' Shoulders slumped under the massive burden, Lorenzo looked at Sam, hoping for some support.

'So, you're happy to tell them about Gemma and the baby, but I'm your dirty little secret? Nice.' Sam stood up, stony-faced, and headed for the bathroom, leaving Lorenzo wondering how he could have come to that conclusion.

In the privacy of the bathroom, Sam slumped on the toilet seat; he was surprised at the sudden surge of emotion at Lorenzo's words. Having been elated at the meeting with Gemma, he was now suffused with doubts once more. Did Lorenzo still think of their relationship as something to be ashamed of? To be hidden from respectable family members so as not to upset them? He imagined Lorenzo's parents, happy and excited to be grandparents, then the bombshell bad news, that was him.

'Sam, come on, please, it's not like that, it's just, it'll be such a shock for them, you know?' Lorenzo stood outside the bathroom door, berating himself for his crass comments. He sighed and tried again to find the right words.

'Look, Sam, you know this is all very new to me. I wasn't expecting this to happen, I'd just about got my head around it when Gemma—' The bathroom door opened, and Sam emerged, looking slightly less murderous than when he'd gone in.

'I'm sorry Sam, I get how you feel, it's all so fucked up I—'

'So if Gemma wasn't on the scene and the pregnancy hadn't happened, would you have told them about us?' Sam sat down again and reached for his shoes as he waited for an answer.

'Erm, I don't know, I guess I wouldn't have had to tell them, would I? They'd soon find out when they came to visit, wouldn't they?' Lorenzo hadn't given it much thought up until then; he'd just assumed they'd find out sooner or later.

'Don't forget Sam, my parents think I'm straight; they have no reason to think I might be, whatever I am.' Feeling irritated by Sam's attitude, Lorenzo gave vent to his own feelings on the matter as he paced around the room, arms flailing as he made his point. 'I mean, the whole big reveal is going to be a lot to take in. They have to be told about the baby; they might want to be in contact with Gemma. After all, it's their grandchild, and I'll be out of the country. I think it's unreasonable to dump two loads of shit on them at the same time—we're together, and that's never gonna change, so why can't we just wait ''til things settle down a bit? Then I'll tell them. You know how hard this has been for me, Sam. Don't start judging me now after all we've been through.' Grabbing his drink, he gulped down a good few glugs, the heat of the liquor serving to dampen his rising temper.

'Okay, I didn't realise how you were feeling. I'm sorry, Rez, just do what you need to, and it'll be fine by me.' Pulling a still-prickly Lorenzo in for a hug, Sam gazed up at him, kissing him tenderly.

'I'm sorry, Sam, I didn't mean to—' Sam placed a finger over his lover's lips.

'Shh, it's all good, Rez, we're fine. Go talk to your family.'

Chapter 37

Several days passed, with Lorenzo still rehearsing his story. He told himself he had a lot to do organising last-minute things for Malta. Octagon had organised a leaving do for him, but Jinx and Malik demanded they go for a curry as Jinx was itching to arrange a diving trip.

'So, how long d'you think it'll take you to get everything sorted?' Jinx didn't try to curtail his excitement as he munched his way through a chicken madras. Lorenzo grinned, pleased that his diving buddies were keen to support him. He'd reluctantly offered them both a discount, feeling he owed them since it was their idea in the first place, although wasn't too sure how Sam would feel about it.

'The media posts for your club look great, Rez, nice touch to put it on the LGBGTQ platforms.' Malik said.

'Oh, I didn't realise you followed those.' Lorenzo was surprised. How come Malik was checking out those groups?

'Yeah mate, need all the help I can get, don't I?' Malik laughed, mopping up his curry with naan bread.

'Erm, what? You mean you're gay?' Lorenzo was aware his mouth was hanging open like some sort of comic book character, a chunk of lamb rogan hovering on his fork.

'Yeah, I thought you knew?' Malik said with a frown before continuing.

'Brown, Catholic and gay, I've got it all going on mate.' He opened his arms wide in a gesture of *'who cares?'*

'I didn't take you for homophobic Rez.' Jinx frowned as he gave Lorenzo a quizzical look. Momentarily stunned by the accusation Lorenzo stared at Jinx, what the hell was happening? Him, homophobic? How the hell did that happen? He shook his head and guffawed with laughter at the irony of it, much to the amusement of his friends who stared at him in bewilderment.

'Erm guys, you know how we've called the club DiverCity?' He waited to gain their full attention. Jinx shrugged, impatiently urging him on with the story.

'Well, the diverse bit of it is me. Me and Sam, we're together.' On the saying of the dreaded words, he felt suddenly free, as if some sort of confessional had taken place, cleansing him of all his fears. He waited, a wide grin traversing his face. It was now their turn to stare open mouthed as his words took time to register.

'What? How? I mean, bloody hell Rez why didn't—' Malik was interrupted by Jinx.

'But you were seeing Gemma from work, weren't you? When did—?' Jinx paused then continued. 'You know what mate, it doesn't bloody matter.' He flipped a wrist in dismissal and added. '…DiverCity…that's so cool. Hey Mal, maybe you'll get lucky in Malta, eh?' Jinx chuckled before launching into another round of questions about holiday discounts.

On his way home Lorenzo pondered on the conversation with his friends. He hadn't intended to blurt it out like that but maybe that was the best way. He realised that actually, no one really cared about his sexuality, no one who cared about him anyway. He thought Sam would be proud of him, what was it he'd said '*Rez's dirty little secret*?' Feeling bad about their argument he messaged Sam, adding a googly eyed emoji for good measure.

'Hey Buddy, I've just come out to some diving mates'

'Great, still in one piece, are you?'

'Bastard'

Sam responded with a kissing heart emoji, to which Lorenzo retorted a middle finger. Chuckling to himself as he read his messages, he resolved to tell his parents about Sam and maybe if it all went well, he'd mention the baby. As he approached the house, he could see his parents' car on the drive, feeling emboldened by his great reveal to Malik and Jinx he took some deep breaths and went in.

'Is that you Rez.' The inevitable greeting from his mother.

Lorenzo went into the sitting room where his parents and sister were gathered around a flickering TV. He was glad Ali was there for moral support if things went pear shaped.

'Hey guys, erm, can we have a chat?' he asked tentatively, his courage failing by the minute.

'Oh, can it wait love, we were just going to watch something.' Angie smiled, gesticulating to the TV.

'Erm, yeah sure it can wait.' Lorenzo was relieved and turned to scurry out the door.

'Oh no you don't— get back in here,' said Ali. 'Mum turn off the TV, Rez has something to tell us, don't you Rez.' Ali sat grinning at her brother.

Both parents turned towards Lorenzo, eyebrows raised, giving him their undivided attention. 'Ooh, do I need to get the toaster on?' Angie giggled nervously, sensing something big was about to happen.

'Haha, I don't think any amount of toast is going to help what I'm going to tell you mum.' Reluctantly Lorenzo went back in and perched on the edge of a big comfy armchair opposite his parents, Ali scooted on to the floor, all the better to observe her parents' reaction. Angie looked quizzically at Jim, checking to see if he was privy to the big mystery.

'Right then...' Lorenzo took a deep breath, his voice quivering as he tried to find the right words. '...you know that me and Sam are business partners for the dive club?' He waited as their heads nodded in unison. 'Well, erm, we're more than just business partners, we're together, like, you know?' He waited again, it was almost comical watching their faces; first the acknowledgement that they were partners, then the processing of the word '*together*', he hoped they would get the idea without having to spell it out.

Lorenzo watched his sister, watching her parents. She too was waiting for that moment when realisation dawned, when all the words had time to rattle around for a while before they made any sense. Jim was the first to react, with a clearing of his throat and a large sniff.

'I need a drink.' Jim headed for the drink's cabinet, returning with two glasses of whiskey; he handed one to his son and sniffed again.

'Together? You mean—' Angie said, eyebrows knitted in confusion as her husband impatiently interjected.

'Well, of course that's what he bloody means, Ang. What did you think he meant? Am I right, lad?' Jim had his *I'm in control here* face on as he sipped his drink.

'Yeah, Dad, I realised I wanted to be with Sam a few months ago. We, ah, we love each other.' Shrugging a shoulder, Lorenzo swirled his drink around his glass and waited for the inevitable inquisition.

'But, you're not gay, love, are you?' Angie's look of loving concern almost made Lorenzo chuckle when he thought of the number of times someone had said that to him. What he really wanted to say was, '*Does it fucking matter what I am it's who I am and who I love that matters.*' But he just shrugged and smiled.

'I s'pose I must be if you have to put a label on it, Mum.' He said quietly.

'I think it's great; people should be whatever they want to be. If Rez loves a guy, so what? He—' Ali piped up in defence of her brother but was cut off by her mother.

'Oh, do shut up with your preaching, Ali. I'm just trying to understand.' Angie rounded on her daughter, flicking a dismissive hand in her direction.

'But I thought you were seeing a girl from work, Gemma?' Angie turned to her son, confusion etched on her face.

'Erm, yeah, since we're all here, that's something else I need to tell you about.' As the roof hadn't caved in with his first big reveal, he took a huge swig of whiskey and decided he might as well drop part two of his good news.

It was Ali's turn to frown now, the smug expression replaced with eager curiosity. His parents just looked generally stunned but seemed to have accepted his news without too much fuss. He knew this next part of the story would probably tip them over the edge, but he felt relieved at their acceptance of part one.

'So, you mentioned Gemma, the girl at work I was seeing for a while?' He waited, allowing them all to digest what he'd just said, especially *'for a while.'*

'It was never really serious, and we broke up once I knew how I felt about Sam.' Lorenzo directed most of this towards his mother and sister as Jim seemed to have tuned out, his thoughts immersed in his whiskey glass.

'Well, erm, she's pregnant.' Jim sputtered into his drink, and Ali and Angie stared at Lorenzo, their mouths comically hanging open. An ominous silence fell over the room as the word pregnant permeated through everyone's pores.

'Jesus Christ boy, what the hell are you playing at—' Jim finally found his voice but was cut short by his wife, who thought it more important to get the details rather than listen to her husband's unhelpful expletives.

'Oh my god Rez, how did? Well, never mind—is she keeping it? I mean, when's it due? And what about Malta?' Angie wanted every detail, so it all came tumbling out together. The realisation that she was going to be a grandmother suddenly dawned, and her face moved from shock to delight as she tried to hide a wide smile behind her hands, but her ever-watchful husband missed nothing.

'Why the hell are you smiling Ang? This is just bloody irresponsible, Rez. Didn't we teach you anything? You get this girl pregnant, then just throw her aside and have a seedy little affair with your boyfriend. I thought I brought you up better than this.' Jim was up and out of his chair, his voice rising as he gave vent to his rage.

'It wasn't a seedy little affair, Dad, Sam, and I —'

Ali tried to butt in at this point, wanting to defend her brother.

'And you can just keep out of this, my girl. It has nothing to do with you.' Jim rounded on his daughter. Lorenzo shot Ali a wry smile, grateful for the support.

'I didn't throw her aside, Dad. I had no idea she was pregnant; she only told me a couple of weeks ago, Sam knows about it and–' Jim cut him off.

'Oh well, that's all right then, isn't it? As long as Sam knows, everything will be fine and dandy, will it?' Jim paced around, a pit stop at the drinks cabinet helping to keep a lid on his rage.

'Jim, Love, we need to stay calm and talk about this. Rez needs our—' Angie started, but Lorenzo interrupted her, raising his hand.

'Actually, Mum, I don't need anything from you—if you'll just let me talk.' He glared at his father, his tone serving to bring them to attention. 'I'll tell you what we've decided to do.' Feeling in control now and not a little annoyed at his mother's assumption he'd need help, Lorenzo told them about Gemma's meeting with Sam and how they'd agreed to all be part of the child's life. His father continued to sniff and slowly shake his head, his face veering from disappointment to disgust at his son's irresponsible behaviour. Ali looked ecstatic, her hands over her mouth as she exclaimed between '*Oh my god*' and '*I'm going to be an aunty.*'

Unable to trust himself to remain civil, Jim eventually left the room, but not before issuing one final proclamation. 'You'd better sort this mess out, boy, d'you hear me?' A warning finger pointed in Lorenzo's direction as he slammed the door.

After taking a deep breath and deciding he would let his father have the final say without further comment, Lorenzo looked at his mother and sister and knew it would be a long night.

Chapter 38

The sun was high, and the glare off the white rocks was dazzling. Angie shielded her eyes as she watched her beloved grandson Alfie cavorting in rock pools with the large German Shepherd. She'd been assured the dog was no threat, but she wasn't about to take any chances; scooping the giggling toddler up under her arm, she headed into a covered courtyard in search of shade and a drink.

The diving club was busy as she made her way past the classrooms. Lorenzo was giving a talk to a small group, demonstrating the use of some strange-looking apparatus with long, dangling black tubes. Angie spotted her husband, listening attentively to his son as he prepared for his third dive. The squirming child under her arm demanded to get down, so she lowered him carefully to the ground, keeping hold of one tiny hand as she wandered around, mindful of various bits of scary-looking equipment scattered about. Angie searched around for the child's mother, needing a break from her childminding duties before she remembered that Gemma had gone out to get party supplies.

It was Lorenzo's birthday, his second one since they'd moved to Malta, but Angie and Jim hadn't been able to visit the first time as Angie's mother had been ill, subsequently dying a few months later. Wandering into the kitchen in search of cold drinks, she spotted Sam, perched on a high stool at the counter, tapping away on his laptop as he sipped a cold beer.

'Hey Sam, how's it going?' She sighed as she opened her drink, sitting the wriggling toddler up on the counter.

'Oh hi Angie, too hot outside, eh?' Sam closed his computer, swinging the child down onto his lap.

'Hey you, what've you been up to, hmm? Playing with Rez, have you?' He kissed the blonde curls, damp and sweaty in the heat.

'He feels very hot Ang', d'you think he's okay?' Sam laid a gentle hand on Alfie's forehead.

'I think he's tired, Sam; he's due for his afternoon sleep.' Angie looked fondly at her grandson, who was rubbing his eyes as he resisted the urge to sleep.

'I'll take him, you relax, finish your drink. You look exhausted.' Sam grabbed his stick with one hand, the sleepy infant with the other, and headed for the bedrooms.

Angie, much relieved of her burden, sat back and relaxed, turning her face up to the fan swirling lazily overhead.

'Ah, there you are. I've been looking for you everywhere.' Ali bounded in, closely followed by Josh to announce they were going kayaking.

'Hmm, all the tanks filled up? Wetsuits washed?' Sam had returned from toddler duty and was looking quizzically at Josh through narrow eyes.

'Yeah, boss, all done.' Josh grinned.

'Lifejacket.' Sam ordered, pointing at Ali.

Angie smiled, pleased that Sam had cared for her daughters' safety, much to Ali's annoyance. Taking her drink, she wandered out to the vine covered courtyard and found a comfy sofa to lounge in as she watched the busy goings on of the dive club. Lorenzo waved over as he continued his instruction. Angie smiled as she sipped her drink, reminiscing over the last eighteen months.

She had been devastated when Lorenzo moved away. WhatsApp and video calls were all very well, but nothing could fill the void left by the physical presence of her beloved son. Gemma's pregnancy had kept them busy, Lorenzo having introduced them before he left. Unfortunately for Angie, Gemma decided to spend her maternity leave in Malta with her boys, as she fondly referred to Lorenzo and Sam.

'Alright, love?' Jim slumped down beside her, clutching a cold beer.

'Yeah, I s'pose so.' Angie sighed.

'What's wrong?'

'It's just weird, isn't it? I mean, how can they all live together like this?' Angie waved a hand.

'Don't ask me, love; seems to work okay though, doesn't it.' Jim wasn't up for any more meaningful conversations about his son's colourful lifestyle. He and Angie had talked the subject to death; she constantly trying to understand the intertwined relationship between her son, Sam and Gemma. Jim didn't admit to being relieved it was all sorted and feeling somewhat proud of his son for finding a solution to what could have been a disaster.

'Have you seen Ali this evening? She seems to have disappeared.' Angie looked around, expecting her daughter to appear as if summoned.

'Hmm, she went off with that Josh guy, haven't seen her since.' Jim said, pleased at the change of subject.

'That's it, all done for today, god it's hot.' Lorenzo joined them, still wet from a cool shower, as he kicked off his sliders.

'You guys okay? Where's Alfie?' He looked around for his son.

'Having a nap, he was shattered, poor lamb.' Angie smiled but added with veiled criticism. 'This heat is no good for little kids, Rez; he'd be much happier back home, you know.' Her husband shot her a look for appearance's sake, but secretly, he longed to have his grandson back home, too.

'He's grown up here, Mum. How do you think the locals do it?' Irritated at his mother's comment, Lorenzo went off in search of Sam.

'Jesus, man, how long are they staying? She's driving me potty with her constant jibes.' Finding Sam hanging up some wetsuits, Lorenzo busied himself with stacking away the scuba tanks.

'Well, not long to go now; they're leaving in a few days, aren't they?' Sam finished his chores and went to help Lorenzo with the tanks.

'At least your lot want to come to Rez, mine would—' Sam was interrupted by Gemma, who'd come back loaded with party food.

'Hey guys, I have food and cake. Lots of cake.' Gemma grinned, heading off to the kitchen after enquiring about the whereabouts of her son.

'Hmm, looks great, Gemms. What time is everyone coming?' Sam surveyed the tasty treats spread out on the countertop.

'Any peanuts?' He asked hopefully.

'Peanuts? Bloody hell, Sam, this is party *food,* not party snacks. Seven o'clock.' She slapped his hand away as he tried to pinch a sandwich.

Lorenzo appeared carrying his son, who had just woken up, closely followed by Rez, the dog who had taken up guard duty beside the sleeping child. His services no longer required, the big dog wandered around the kitchen, tail wagging expectantly, in the hope of a spare morsel.

'Guys, could you all just bugger off somewhere else, please? I'm trying to get things ready here.' Gemma shooed them all out, but not before she dropped the dog a sausage roll.

Grabbing some suitable food for Alfie, Lorenzo, and Sam went back out to the courtyard. It was still hot and sultry outside, but the sun had helpfully dropped lower, leaving a gentle, warm breeze in its wake.

'I love our life.' Sam said dreamily as he spooned mashed-up banana into Alfie's demanding open mouth.

'I love you.' Lorenzo dropped a kiss on Sam's bare shoulder.

'She's gonna go back home sooner or later, you know.' Sam said sadly.

'Who? Oh Gemma, yeah, I know, I'm dreading it, to be honest, mate.'

'Maybe she could stay? Get residency and all that?'

'We'll ask her when my parents have gone, can't cope with any more helpful observations from granny.'

Gemma came over, wiping her hands on the back of her shorts, kitchen duties completed she brandished a cold bottle of wine and poured them all a glass. 'You guys look so cute feeding him.' She smiled lovingly as she watched Lorenzo wearing the yoghurt he was trying to spoon into the squirming toddler.

'Happy birthday Rez.' She raised her glass, savouring the ice-cold wine.

'Oh, erm yeah, I s'pose it is, isn't it?' Lorenzo grinned, thinking inexplicably that he had to wait until the party to share a toast.

'Yes, my love, all day.' Sam laughed as he wiped a dollop of yoghurt from Lorenzo's hair.

***

Lights twinkled all around the dive club as people arrived for Lorenzo's party. They'd tidied away as much of the equipment as they could, covering what they couldn't move with brightly coloured sheets and beach towels. Gemma had declared she was going for a Moroccan Souk theme, all dark reds, and glowing lights. She'd even found an old rug and covered the stone floor of the courtyard with it. Extra-large pillows and beanbags were scattered around as extra seating, and candles flickered down on the white rocks below them, reflecting in the rock pools.

Angie and Jim had gone off to their hotel to get ready for the big night, taking Alfie with them, having engaged a babysitter. Lorenzo and Sam had retired to their rooms to get ready.

'What do you think? Ali says If I don't wear it, she will.' Samantha held up the pink silk dress for inspection.

'Love it.' Lorenzo took the dress from her, tossing it on the bed as he pulled her in for a kiss.

'You'll mess up my make up, Rez.' Samantha giggled but returned the kiss, making a note to re-apply her lipstick.

'Are you sure you're up for this Rez? I mean, your parents don't–'

Lorenzo put a gentle finger to Samantha's lips, silencing her protest.

'I'm done caring what everyone else thinks. I just care about you and me and our little family.' Lorenzo slid his hands down, cupping Samantha's buttocks; his need to feel her body in contact with his was overwhelming.

'Actually, about the dress, I like white jeans and black T better, you know, the one you bought when you went shopping with Gemms.' He mumbled into her neck before adding. 'In fact, I prefer you with no clothes on at all, but hey, we have to conform, don't we.' He chuckled at his own feeble joke as Samantha turned to her wardrobe, rummaging around for white jeans.

***

The entrance to the club was lit up with dozens of twinkling lights, the doors were open wide, and loud music drifted out onto the street. Angie and Jim could hear the chatter of happy partygoers as they approached the door, nervously hoping they wouldn't be the oldest people there. Ali had disappeared a couple of hours earlier, mysteriously saying she had to help Sam with something. Much to Angie's annoyance, she could have done with the moral support.

'Let's go and find Rez's love.' Angie said, hanging on to Jim's arm.

'I think I saw him over by the bar chatting to some girl.' Jim was more than happy to head for the bar and an ice-cold beer. As they approached, Angie was about to call out to Lorenzo, but she stopped dead, pulling back on her husband's arm.

'Oh my god, Jim, look.' Jim followed his wife's line of sight and was astonished to see his son kissing a pretty girl, her hand resting on his thigh.

'What the fu-' Jim frowned in confusion.

'But where's Sam? This is going to be—'

Angie was interrupted by Lorenzo, who appeared hand in hand with the dark-haired girl.

'Hey mum, dad, I think you already know Samantha?' Lorenzo grinned as Samantha smiled awkwardly.

'Hey guys, we wanted to tell you, but it just seemed easier this way.' Samantha shrugged a shoulder.

There was a pause.

'Get me a drink, son,' Jim sighed, slowly shaking his head.

Samantha led Angie over to one of the soft squishy sofas, feeling she should try and explain.

'So you're not, erm, transit—' Angie stumbled over her words, unsure about the correct terminology and worried about getting it wrong.

'No, Angie, I just like dressing up sometimes, just like you do. You look amazing, by the way. I love your hair like that.' Samantha smiled as Angie demurred, patting her hair.

Back at the bar, Jim was still shaking his head in confusion. 'Did you know about this, erm, thing before you came out here, Rez?' he asked with a frown.

'Yeah, Dad, it's just something Sam likes to do sometimes.' Lorenzo said, before adding in a menacing tone, 'and I like it too.'

Jim turned his head, watching his wife and daughter chatting amiably with the beautiful dark-haired girl. 'I must say he, *she* is pretty stunning, Rez. It must be a bit…um, confusing…sometimes?'

'Yeah, adds to the excitement, Dad.' Lorenzo chuckled as his father tried to suppress a smile.

'Oh, there you are, love, we're just having a girls chat.' Angie giggled as Lorenzo and Jim joined them. Lorenzo sat on the floor, one arm draped protectively across Samantha's lap.

'Anyone seen Gemma?' Samantha asked, looking around for her.

'Over there, on the beanbags with a guy.' Ali piped up.

Lorenzo and Samantha simultaneously looked over to where Gemma was locked in a passionate embrace with a man they recognised from a local restaurant.

'Haha, didn't think about that one did you guys.' Jim guffawed when he saw the look of consternation on his son's face.

The rest of the evening passed quickly, with Angie declaring she was tired and needed to go.

'I love that sign, don't you?' Angie said, gazing up over the door as they left.

The DiverCity sign was an arc, following the curve of a rainbow tonight, it was lit up in a blaze of twinkling lights.

'What's that little squiggle thing underneath Jim? I can't quite make it out.' Angie squinted up into the dazzling lights in the vain hope of deciphering the small words in italics underneath.

'No idea, Ang,' Jim grumbled impatiently.

The little squiggle thing glinted down at them.

No Labels, it said.

The End

www.ingramcontent.com/pod-product-compliance
Lightning Source LLC
Chambersburg PA
CBHW072043110526
44590CB00018B/3023